# Touch in Sports Coaching and Physical Education

In our increasingly risk-averse society, touch and touching behaviours between professionals and children have become a fraught issue. In sports coaching and physical education, touching young sports performers and participants has, in some contexts, come to be redefined as dubious and dangerous. Coaches find themselves operating in a framework of regulations and guidelines that create anxiety, for them and others, and for many volunteer (and sometimes professional) coaches, this fearful context has led them to question the risks and benefits of their continuing involvement in sport.

*Touch in Sports Coaching and Physical Education* is the first book to explore this difficult topic in detail. Drawing on a series of international studies from the US, UK, Australia, Canada, Sweden and elsewhere, it presents important new research evidence and examines theories of risk and moral panic that frame the discussion. By challenging prevailing orthodoxies the book makes a significant contribution to critical discussion around practice, pedagogy, politics and policy in sport and physical education, and also informs current debates around the nature and quality of all *in loco parentis* relationships.

**Heather Piper** is a Professorial Research Fellow in the Education and Social Research Institute, Manchester Metropolitan University, UK, and is a qualitative researcher whose interests and research experiences span a broad range of educational and social issues. She has co-authored and edited a number of special issues and books (including *Don't Touch!* and *Researching Sex and Lies in the Classroom*, both published by Routledge).

# Routledge Research in Sport, Culture and Society

# Touch in Sports Coaching and Physical Education

Fear, risk, and moral panic

## Edited by Heather Piper

Routledge
Taylor & Francis Group

LONDON AND NEW YORK

First published 2015 by Routledge

2 Park Square, Milton Park, Abingdon, Oxon OX14 4RN
711 Third Avenue, New York, NY 10017, USA

*Routledge is an imprint of the Taylor & Francis Group, an informa business*

First issued in paperback 2016

*British Library Cataloguing-in-Publication Data*
A catalogue record for this book is available from the British Library

*Library of Congress Cataloging-in-Publication Data*
Touch in sports coaching and physical education : fear, risk, and moral
    panic / edited by Heather Piper.
      pages cm. — (Routledge research in sport, culture and society)
    Includes bibliographical references and index.
  1. Coach-athlete relationships—Moral and ethical aspects.
2. Touch—Moral and ethical aspects.    3. Child sexual abuse—
Prevention.    I. Piper, Heather.
  GV711.T68    2015
  796.07'7—dc23
  2014009889

ISBN 978-0-415-82976-2 (hbk)
ISBN 978-1-138-69541-2 (pbk)

Typeset in Times
by Apex CoVantage, LLC

# Contents

# Notes on contributors

**Jake Bailey** is a Senior Lecturer in Sports Coaching in the Cardiff School of Sport at Cardiff Metropolitan University, UK. His research interests lie in the sociology of sports coaching, and he is currently undertaking a PhD that explores the way coaching discourses can both constrain and evolve coaching identity. Alongside his academic role, he runs a trampoline club, has been Welsh National Coach for Trampoline-Gymnastics, and works as a coach educator for British Gymnastics.
Email JBailey@cardiffmet.ac.uk

**Dean Garratt** is Professor of Education in the Faculty of Education and Children's Services, University of Chester, UK. His research interests are eclectic, including the critique of education and sports policy and practice, citizenship theory and education, and the applied sociology of sport. Recent work has focused on the professionalization of sports coaching, politics of touch, risk and identity in sports coaching and physical education, and theorising the niche sport of natural bodybuilding, using gendered and auto-ethnographic perspectives. He has a long-standing interest in qualitative research methodologies, utilising phenomenological-hermeneutic, post-structural, psychoanalytic, and transgendered perspectives.
Email d.garratt@chester.ac.uk

**Carin Grundberg-Sandell** is the Project Manager of *Safe from Harm* for The Guides and Scouts of Sweden, leading the work and development of the project. *Safe from Harm* is a training programme on child protection aspects and prevention of abuse, run for scout and guide leaders since 2005. The programme aims to provide leaders with relevant knowledge and the confidence to act early against bullying and assault. Since 2013, the project has been extended to spread the approach to other organisations in Sweden.
Email carin.grundberg-sandell@scouterna.se

**Alun Hardman** is Senior Lecturer in Applied Ethics of Sport, in the Cardiff School of Sport at Cardiff Metropolitan University. He is published in *The Journal of the Philosophy of Sport* and *Sport, Ethics, Philosophy*. With Carwyn Jones, he is co-editor of *The ethics of sports coaching* (London: Routledge, 2011). He is a practising cricket coach and father to two sporting teenagers, one of whom is a national-level trampoline gymnast.

Email ahardman@cardiffmet.ac.uk

**Richard T. Johnson** is a Professor at the University of Hawaii at Manoa, USA, and a member of faculty in Curriculum Studies. His recent research and field-based work includes no-touch policies in education, risk, trauma and education, childhood subjectivity, and visual culture. He has taught and served extensively in various field-based pre-service early childhood/elementary teacher-education programs for over twenty years. He earned his EdD at Vanderbilt University.

Email rich@hawaii.edu

**Rhiannon Lord** is currently completing a PhD at Cardiff School of Sport, Cardiff Metropolitan University. Through applying ethnographic research she is exploring the experiences and storied narratives of trampoline gymnasts. Her wider research interests include the sociological study of embodiment, identity (re)construction, child populations, and narrative inquiry within sporting contexts. Alongside her academic role, she also runs and is head coach of a trampoline club. As part of her position at the club she is influential in the writing and implementation of child protection policies, and in mentoring junior coaches in their professional and sport-specific practices.

Email rhlord@cardiffmet.ac.uk

**Keith Lyons** has been involved in physical education teaching and sport coaching for forty years. He has a particular interest in the open sharing of inclusive teaching and coaching practice. After a career in teaching and teacher training, Keith developed a keen interest in the systematic observation and analysis of performance. He moved to Australia from the United Kingdom in 2002 to work in high performance sport at the Australian Institute of Sport. He is an Adjunct Professor in the University of Canberra Research Institute for Sport and Exercise.

Email Keith.Lyons@canberra.edu.au

**Marie Öhman** has a PhD in sociology, and is an Associate Professor in Sport Science in the School of Health and Medical Sciences at Örebro University, Sweden. A teacher educator in physical education since 1993, in recent years she has completed various projects funded by the Swedish Research Council. Her main area of research is observational studies in physical education. Drawing on Michel Foucault's work, she has focused several publications on questions of health, body, socialisation, power relations, and governing processes. In a recent project, *No Touching*, she considers how public discourses concerning 'child protection' influence pedagogical work in physical education.

Email Marie.ohman@oru.se

**Maria Papaefstathiou** is completing her PhD in the School of Education and Lifelong Learning at the University of East Anglia. Her ethnographic case study research explores the experiences of competitive-level track and field child athletes in Cyprus, and the related meanings of child protection and welfare. Before PhD studies, she completed an MA on 'Child welfare and protection in sport' at Brunel University, publishing her research outcomes as *Child protection in ballet: Experiences and views of teachers, administrators and ballet students.* She has taught Greek language, physical education, and dance at primary level in Cyprus and in England.

Email: m.papaefstathiou@uea.ac.uk

**Simona Petracovschi** is an Associate Professor in the Faculty of Physical Education and Sport at West University Timisoara, Romania, where she teaches the sociology of sport. She completed her PhD at Henri Poincare University, Nancy, France in 2005, and postdoctoral studies during 2013, at West University Timisoara. In 2007 she received a postgraduate scholarship for Olympic studies from the International Olympic Committee.

Email: ionescusimo@yahoo.com

**Heather Piper** spent fifteen years in social work, mainly in child protection, before becoming a researcher at Manchester Metropolitan University, where she is a Professorial Research Fellow in the Education and Social Research Institute (ESRI). Joint author or editor of a number of books, and responsible for over forty refereed journal articles, she has led two UK ESRC-funded research projects. Her work focuses on policy and practice on the borders between education and social work. A consistent theme has been the problematic consequences of risk-averse policy and practice, particularly in relation to adults acting *in loco parentis,* in schools, childcare and sports coaching.

Email h.j.piper@mmu.ac.uk

**Clive C. Pope** is an Associate Professor of Sport Pedagogy at the University of Waikato in New Zealand. His research has mainly addressed the areas of youth sport and youth sport settings, in particular the cultures that interplay within such settings, and has predominantly adopted an ethnographic approach. More recently, he has developed and employed visual research methods to explore sport cultures and meaning making. His teaching and supervision also focuses on youth sport and effective instruction in coaching and teaching settings.

Email: cpope@waikato.ac.nz

**Bill Taylor** holds an EdD, and is a Senior Lecturer in Coaching Studies in the Department of Exercise and Sport Science at Manchester Metropolitan University, UK, where he leads postgraduate taught provision. His research interests are varied, and include the conceptualisation and critical deconstruction of professionalism in sports coaching, coaching in the 'risk society', and the use of critical sociology to examine coaching practice. He has undertaken funded research projects for the UK National Sport Centres, Sports Coach UK, England Hockey, the British Canoe Union, the Football Association, and a number of other sport organisations.

Email w.taylor@mmu.ac.uk

**Jan Toftegaard Støckel** is an Associate Professor in the *Active Living* research unit at the University of Southern Denmark. He received his PhD from the University of Copenhagen, having completed a thesis on sexual abuse in sport. He contributes regularly to articles on youth sport issues, including sexual abuse in sport and related welfare issues. He teaches sport pedagogics and is strongly interested in the pedagogical, organizational, and political dimensions of youth sport. He has contributed with expert knowledge to a number of international peer assemblies on sexual abuse in sport.

Email JToftegaard@health.sdu.dk

# Preface

All contributors to this book have devoted their careers to coaching, teaching, researching, or caring for children and young people in sporting or other contexts; all believe that children should be able to develop and achieve in safe environments, where they will not be abused. Yet these contributors share a common, if variably nuanced, concern that some mainstream approaches to child protection in sport (and elsewhere) are in reality more about calming adult fears than protecting children, and cause significant collateral damage.

The book and its arguments are likely to offend many who have invested heavily in imposing pre- or proscriptive policy and practice on sports coaching, particularly those whose investment has been rewarded with welcome funding streams. In response, they may suggest that those associated with the book care little for children, and that even if the mainstream regulatory approach saves only one child from abuse then the dramatic change visited on coaching and teaching in recent decades is justified. The counterargument is that such a 'cost (and collateral damage) no object' approach to social policy is unusual to say the least, and that interventions based on simplistic understandings of risk are likely to produce disproportionate and even counterproductive responses. While every case of significant abuse by a coach is appalling, a sensible solution cannot be to, in effect, require all coaches to treat themselves and their colleagues as active risks to children in their care, and to make them perform a theatre of safeguarding. Such practice damages trust and humanity, and diminishes the moral and social values on which intergenerational encounters like coaching should be based, without delivering apparent benefits in terms of child protection. There must be a better way.

These are the issues with which the expert contributors from eight national contexts grapple. Many are conscious of being overmatched in this argument, because the proponents of fear-based discourse and practice in sports coaching carry a mighty big stick. Yet they still recognise an imperative to object, resist, and to speak truth to power. The pendulum has swung so far towards risk-aversion and dehumanised practice that it will not be pushed back easily, but this book may at least provide a nudge in the right direction.

Heather Piper

# Editor's acknowledgements

I am grateful to all the contributors to this book, for making my role easy through their expertise, enthusiasm, and prompt responses. It was Hannah Smith who first alerted me to the strange way that adult fears around touch and abuse had paradoxically fostered a less human and nurturing environment for children, and I thank her and all my many colleagues who have contributed to relevant research and writing over the last decade. Appreciation is also due to John Piper for his contribution in helping produce the final text, and to Bill Taylor for his early reviewing and inputs on a number of the chapters.

# 1 Child protection in sports coaching and physical education

*Heather Piper*

## The book

This is the first international collection which addresses how the imperative of protecting children and young people from abuse has impacted on sports coaching and physical education (PE). The contributors, from countries with diverse histories and cultural characteristics, range from highly experienced and well-published researchers to younger colleagues, at an earlier stage in their careers. They also vary in terms of their chosen research focus and methodological preferences; their chapters are characterised by a welcome diversity of research approaches and methodologies, including documentary analysis, a composite vignette, visual analysis, and varieties of discourse analysis, all supported by the application of mainstream qualitative research techniques. All the authors bring academic and research expertise, combined with rich and varied experience in sport, coaching, and PE, and their passionate commitment to such activity is evident. They demonstrate and explore concern at the way that, in their particular contexts, the imperative of keeping children and young people safe from abuse has been interpreted in sporting environments in ways that are variably problematic, with the result of reducing the effectiveness of teaching and coaching, and of diminishing fundamental ideals of humanity, personhood, and trust.

Nobody involved in the production of this book would dissent from the idea that children should be kept safe, but this commitment does not entail blindness in relation to the serious collateral damage caused by blinkered, simplistic, and misguided approaches to 'safeguarding'. While detailed understandings vary in distinct national and cultural contexts (a subtle reality which is too easily ignored by purveyors of the dominant safeguarding discourse), what is evident from the rich and varied contributions which follow is that although this book was prompted by research in the UK, the issues are recognised internationally and the concern felt by many who care deeply about both children and sport.

It has been a pleasure to work with the authors of the chapters which follow, and to access their interest and enthusiasm for the subject. What follows is a brief introduction to each of the nationally focused chapters, to alert the reader to the diversity and scope of the issues and problems which the international contributors identify and discuss. Subsequently, to complete this opening chapter, editorial prerogative is briefly exercised through an attempt to highlight and explore at least some of the common and overarching themes and insights illuminated within and across the different chapters. Obviously, a reader may choose to save reading that section until they have read the chapters for themselves. At the end of the book the concluding chapter offers a more synoptic and argumentative account of the topic area, featuring some significant and complex questions: where are we, how did we get here, and what can we do about it?

## The chapters

The nationally based chapters have been ordered so as to start with countries in which the dominant prescriptive and proscriptive approach to regulating inter-generational contacts in sport has been most evident and documented. Indeed, these countries may be considered responsible for encouraging the export of such regulation overseas. They have also been characterised by the effect of generally neoliberal politics and policy over an extended period. Then follow contributions from and about countries which are experiencing the impact of these develop-ments, and are seeking to deal with issues around abuse and protection in their particular national and cultural context. As is demonstrated, cultural diversity in this sense is highly significant: understandings of both the problems around touch and of the balance of cost and benefit attached to possible externally defined solu-tions are extremely varied. Finally, there are chapters which demonstrate both the potential for principled decisions at national and sporting levels to reject the dominant international model of child protection in sport, and also the level of subtle analysis which is required to help make sense of these sensitive and com-plex issues. Sadly, this has usually been notable for its absence.

Drawing on research funded by the UK Economic and Social Research Coun-cil, **Heather Piper**, **Bill Taylor**, and **Dean Garratt** explore particular themes from their data, focusing on issues around the individual and collective identity of sports coaches and PE teachers, and the impact of high degrees of anxiety and oversight arising from extreme concern in relation to child protection. The pro-ject, conducted mainly in the North West of England, but also involving national organisations and spokespeople, featured three exemplar sports (swimming, foot-ball, and paddlesport), and included over 100 individual and group interviews, observations, and documentary analysis. Touching behaviours and related prac-tices were understood and analysed as discursive activities, in relation to compet-ing discourses around effective teaching and coaching, and also child abuse and protection. This work built on earlier research on touch and relationships, policy and practice in varied educational and childcare environments.

While variations between experiences in particular sports contexts and organi-sational environments are recognised, a number of common themes are illustrated and explored. Feelings of self-doubt, prompted by the idea that adults working with children and young people in sport are obviously dangerous, are linked to anxieties around other people's perceptions of behaviour and intention, and a notable fear of accusations. This lack of confidence in self and others leads to a range of self-protective practices, including planning to ensure the presence of witnesses (a strategy which in this context brings its own problems, as perceptions will remain varied and unpredictable). While these circumstances are shown to be variably acute, depending on structural position and local variation, the research indicates how a particularly crude understanding of risk and protection is propagated through child protection in sport training, from which fear and extreme caution appear to be the likely outcome. Generally, the current circumstances in sports coaching are characterised here as more about adult protection than real safeguarding for children, and harmful to valued ideals of humanity and care. Given their negative effects, they are properly subject to contrarian responses and principled professional critique.

In his chapter focusing on the United States, **Richard Johnson** is able to draw on substantial, even seminal, experience of research, writing, and practice on the front line of arguments around touch and care in intergenerational contexts. Having previously focused on issues in early years education, he has more recently drawn and reflected on his regular and longstanding commitment as a volunteer youth soccer coach. Here he uses this ongoing experience to inform a critical discussion of how the panic around child safety and the abusive non-parental adult has impacted on the self and collective concept of the coach, coaching practice, and the experience of the children and young people they work with. Crucially, the discussion is set in the context of a broader social phenomenon, the habitual orientation to life's events and uncertainties through the lens of risk, and the corollary entailed response of implementing comforting programmes of risk management. The power and pervasiveness of this discourse in the United States in particular (not that other societies are immune) made the self-protective and risk-averse approach adopted by governing organisations in sport virtually inevitable.

Through interrogating his changing experience of being an adult male, caring for other people's children in various contexts, and also of adapting to the safeguarding and coach training programmes of the American Youth Soccer Organization, Richard Johnson develops a heartfelt critique of an approach characterised by greater loss than benefit. The *in loco parentis* teacher or soccer coach has been rendered (and has come to think of themselves as) abject; energy and resources are squandered on unproductive activity and window dressing, and children and young people lose out, by receiving both less effective technical instruction and experiencing less emotional warmth and nurturing touch. This situation is sustained by the continuing application of a simplistic and unnuanced notion of the child, as always vulnerable and needing adult protection and regulation, and also by the apparently general willingness to collude with dominant ideas about policy and practice which are simply based on untruths. In the absence of case-sensitive, reliable, and authoritative data on child abuse generally, and with no good reason to think that children are more at risk in organised sport or educational settings than anywhere else (indeed, the opposite is more likely), coaches and teachers have been too passive in accepting a counterproductive disciplining of their bodies, selves, and practices. While it may be possible to take the line of least resistance and adopt and adapt to this approach in an ironic or humorous way, and rationalise it as ensuring that young people can still access the best available coaching opportunities in spite of the foolishness of 'no touch', in fact there is a moral imperative to do more than that. As coaches, teachers, researchers, human beings, and citizens, we should be deliberately contesting the dehumanising discourses and practices which diminish the quality of the coaching experience for all those involved.

In Aotearoa New Zealand, levels of participation in sport (and school sport in particular) and the proportion of secondary school teachers engaged in sports coaching beyond the formal requirements of their role have historically been remarkably high by international comparisons. **Clive Pope** provides a rich personal account of a thirty-year career in secondary school PE and teacher training, an experience allowing him to chart and reflect on the changed environment and culture emanating from the implementation of neoliberal education policies and a heightened managerialism from the late 1980s. It has an elegiac quality, charting the world that has been lost. This is matched by data showing incontrovertible changes, including the flight of males from the teaching profession, and the reduced willingness of teachers to commit long extra-curricular hours to supporting school sports teams. Exploring the growth of panic around child safety, and risk-averse practice, he demonstrates the wide and lasting impact of heavily reported investigations and prosecutions, and the way in which the individual dangerous teacher has been transformed into an archetype. Further, he effectively punctures the logic of the policies and practices which have been introduced that purport to protect children by controlling what all teachers may do, in order to restrict the minority intent on abuse.

From his long experience of pedagogy, professional preparation, and coaching, Clive Pope makes a passionate argument that coaching is best experienced and understood as a deeply human, emotional activity. To constrain it by imposing artificial and performative definitions of what is 'good' or 'bad' practice, imposing mechanistic injunctions on touch, is inevitably to subvert and diminish its chemistry and effectiveness. This account is consolidated through the deployment of visual data gathered during sustained research at diverse school sports events. Visual images are presented as an illustration of the fundamentally intangible quality of coaching interactions, their 'greyness', where binary ideas are unhelpful and meanings are imported by the viewer. Thus, to ascribe motives involving such categories as 'abuse' or 'grooming' to particular images, is just that – judgemental ascription – and, particularly in the context of disproportionate panic, may be wrong and perverse.

The chapter by **Marie Öhman** and **Carin Grundberg-Sandell**, drawing on their experience in Sweden, is focused on the context of PE and the professional ideals and responsibility of the PE teacher, while implicitly demonstrating the important point that issues and dilemmas around touch, abuse, and protection do not recognise sectoral boundaries. Employing a Foucauldian lens in considering a rich selection of Swedish documentation, they demonstrate the pervasive effect of a particular discourse across a range of contexts. The discursive pressures affecting perception and practice in classrooms (and school gymnasiums and sports fields in particular) cannot be understood in isolation from experience in sports clubs and organisations like the scouts and guides, where high quality intergenerational relationships are essential to making ambitious holistic goals a reality. Thus, even if Swedish schools have not laid down draconian guidance regarding touch in PE or more generally, instead relying on more general statements of intent, PE teachers are still affected by more generalised and proscriptive discourses and their translation into other contexts where they may operate, including sports coaching outside school.

Referring to recordings and transcripts of PE teaching sessions drawn from a wider Swedish study, Marie Öhman and Carin Grundberg-Sandell explore the tensions between teachers' practice in different PE activities and the explicit general expectations of what should be happening in, and achieved by, all Swedish schools and teachers. While recognising the importance of child protection in stopping bad things from happening, they argue that there is an equally significant imperative to ensure that good things happen in teaching contexts. Acts which are nothing of the sort now risk being interpreted as obviously sexual. They stress the importance of caring and that, if it is to be appropriately understood, respected, and protected, then a more sophisticated and holistic understanding of intergenerational and pedagogic interactions than that employed in current discourses on child protection is essential. In its absence, not only is teaching impoverished, but so too is the pupils' experience. The loss, virtually by default, of key ideals of Swedish education is obviously significant, but so too is the transgression against fundamental elements of children's rights, all in the name of a limited conception of protection.

Reporting and reflecting on recent fieldwork contributing to her doctorate, **Maria Papaefstathiou** focuses on track and field athletics in the Republic of Cyprus, a national context characterised by powerful and pervasive interactions of religion, family, and community, as well as high levels of tactile behaviour and interpersonal trust; few people are unknown quantities. She draws a number of themes from data comprising lengthy discursive interviews with individuals with varied, often very substantial, experience of Cypriot athletics and coaching, and sets the discussion in both wider critical frameworks and a clearly described situation of what might be termed neoliberal imperialism. While traditional Cypriot culture has been based around imperatives of community, neoliberal discourses associated with the European Union (of which Cyprus as a small nation wishes to be seen as a 'good' member), and also international frameworks around child protection, emphasise the primacy of the individual. This disjuncture prompts a number of obvious tensions around the practice and experience of coaching, and a varied and penetrating set of responses from the sports people who were interviewed. While the goal of child protection is warmly accepted, this response is not extended to the normally proffered means of achieving it.

Maria Papaefstathiou argues that the import and imposition of internationalised definitions and solutions can in practice be insensitive to local cultures and traditions, and thus provoke unhelpful tensions and possibly counterproductive responses. The distinction is made between mere *protection* of the athlete and real *caring* for the person; the latter entails the acceptance of emotion and spontaneity, both of which are rendered problematic by prescriptive approaches to protection, with significant diminution of the coaching process for all involved. Similarly, the simplistic and contextually blind application of universal children's rights discourse can damage effective established practices and relationships. Unwilling to lose the benefits of a tactile and demonstrative culture, which incorporates *in loco parentis* contexts like coaching, respondents stress that with contextual sensitivity the difference between good and bad touch is evident. The tensions and difficulties in the current situation are understood and recognised, and while clarification and educative assistance for coaches is suggested, it is argued it must not be of the type which promotes individual anxiety and guilt, or wider moral panic.

While social, cultural, political and economic change is characteristic of all societies, the chapter from Romania demonstrates that, while people everywhere may comment or complain that things are not as they used to be, for some the speed and extent of change is particularly intense. **Simona Petracovschi** provides a valuable reminder that issues and tensions around touch in PE are far from constant or consistent; understanding the sociopolitical context and the meanings which it generates is centrally important. In pedagogy generally, and PE in particular, issues in Romania around the body, touch, and perceptions of abuse are shown to be just as sensitive and potent as in other national contexts; the priorities evident in the relevant discourses are different, but suggestive and significant. The Romanian experience since the late 1940s, with forty years of a communist regime with variably tight connections to Soviet models and assumptions, followed by its seismic collapse and overthrow in 1989, provides an example of the changing politics of touch which is in many ways far removed from that featured in relevant literature. When society, education, and particularly PE, are predicated on notions of domination and command, in the interests of achieving the greater good (formerly defined in this case by the tenets of Marxism–Leninism), then ownership of the body, and ideas concerning rights, touch, punishment, and abuse, take on distinctive meanings.

Drawing on broad social and historical data, and also field interviews with twenty-four PE teachers with varied experience of training and practice before and after the upheaval of 1989, Simona Petracovschi shows how significant tensions arising from changed ideas about education, the role of the teacher, the rights of the child, and the appropriateness of touch in PE, are having a profound effect on both teachers and pupils. The change to a market-based society, in which individual rights are given greater prominence, has been fundamental and rapid, but characterised by variable speeds in different sectors and contexts. The previous dominant role enjoyed by sport, PE, and PE teachers, has made transition in this area particularly difficult, and has impacted strongly on some teachers, depending on their age and biography. Contradictions and tensions abound; taboos tend not to be addressed and the situation is unsatisfactory for many, with the potential benefits of PE being lost. While a moral panic around abuse and touch is not apparent, faced with newly assertive pupils and parents (emboldened by market choice), many PE teachers have decided that touch of any type is obviously unwise, leaving PE impoverished, and open discussion of such issues and tensions difficult to achieve.

In his chapter discussing the ideas and practices associated with child abuse and protection in Danish sport, **Jan Toftegaard Støckel** is able to deploy the experience acquired through having worked as a researcher for the governmental commission of inquiry into the perceived problem, which began work in 2002. From this vantage point he is able to chart the development of sensitivity to the issue of abuse in Denmark generally, particularly in sport, and the way in which government and sporting organisations have responded. While noting that the incidence rate for abuse in sport reported by the commission was, at 1 per cent, lower than international comparators, he recognises the extent to which such figures are dependent on the stringency with which categories are defined and deployed. He also illuminates the way that the (frequently incorrect) use of the word paedophile to describe predatory sports coaches and other adults has the effect of constructing an 'othered' category and a pathological discourse, even though many offenders cannot accurately be classified as paedophiles. In this light, he considers particular heavily reported cases of abuse, which had a major impact on the Danish experience, and on debates around the problem and the appropriate policy response.

The singular element of that experience is that, having researched and discussed the issue of risk and abuse in sport, and in full awareness of bureaucratic approaches to safeguarding endorsed by international organisations and implemented in many societies, Danish sports organisations and governmental agencies have stood by a light-touch response. Substantial reliance is placed on criminal record checks on employees and volunteers working with children and young people (interestingly, 446,576 checks identified 59 applicants with relevant previous offences, a strike rate of less than 0.02 per cent), but after that there is no intrusive regulatory regime. Coaches are told not to exploit their power or to be abusive, but their coaching practice is not constrained by performative guidelines around touch and so on. This approach means that sports organisations must be willing to defend themselves when things go wrong, but clearly they see the benefits of their chosen approach as outweighing the costs of such exposure. Jan Toftegaard Støckel traces this situation decisions back to *de facto* decisions at high levels of sport politics, but also to key characteristics of Danish society, including a commitment to trust as a vital aspect of being human in a healthy and effective society.

Sport has long been a central feature of Australian national identity, with high levels of participation and public engagement. Drawing on a long career in teaching and coaching, which began in the UK, **Keith Lyons** describes and reflects on the particular ways in which concern around intergenerational abuse and touch in sport have been dealt with, in a context where both competitive and recreational sport is frequently closely intertwined with family and community life. While recognising the imperative of care, he insists that real caring in coaching and teaching should be understood as requiring more than defensive practice; some approaches to eradicating the risk of inappropriate touch carry the risk and reality of other types of damage. These issues are explored through a brief survey of statutory responses (which are complex in a federated system of government), an account of a major national initiative (though locally managed) to deliver high quality and safe sport and exercise provision at thousands of sites after school hours, and a personal reflection on a specific self-initiated coaching experience and how touch and relationships were managed within it.

While teachers and schools in Australia have been subject to significant pressure in terms of having to be seen to take child protection (and in practice adult protection) very seriously, in part as a result of well documented scandals around the past treatment of children from indigenous communities and also abuse in residential institutions, the response in sport has been more careful. While criminal record checks are made, principles and duties of care are made explicit, and supervisory and monitoring systems are applied, there has been less specific prescription and proscription of coaching behaviours and practice than has been observed elsewhere. With mass participation and high level community engagement, this approach has retained public confidence; sports participation and interpersonal trust are positively correlated. From his experience in coaching canoe slalom, Keith Lyons illustrates how coaches can consider and negotiate issues around relationships and touch without diminishing either their effectiveness or humanity. He argues that concern and pressure in this area can be converted into a positive influence, encouraging the coach to adopt an activist stance, considering and planning their interactions with those in their care, and being ready to respond to scrutiny. While challenging, this optimistic approach is preferable to the retreat from professionalism implicit in the heavily regulated alternative.

Focusing on the particular context of trampoline gymnastics in the UK, **Alun Hardman**, **Jake Bailey**, and **Rhiannon Lord** are able to draw on long experience of coaching at club and elite levels, doctoral research applying social science–based analysis to coaching, and professional expertise in moral philosophy and ethics. Trampoline gymnastics is a sport in which pressures around touch may be expected to be pronounced: it is popular with many young children, clothing is skimpy, and in coaching the judicious use of touch is essential in preventing potentially serious injury. Noting the prevalent orthodox discourse around coaching, touch, and child protection, which has the effect of sterilising and depersonalising the nurturing and educative process, they argue powerfully for an understanding of coaching founded in the notion of praxis, stressing its characteristic as a moral and social encounter in which the imperative of care is paramount. They identify the advantages of caring being practiced by coaches as a natural, individual activity, rather than being behaviours which are reliant on and imposed by the views and frameworks of others.

In order to explore these issues and tensions further, a vignette is provided, based on composite experiences and insights from the authors; this serves as a prompt for a dialogue in which the complexities and contradictions in the current experience of coaching trampoline gymnastics are exemplified and analysed, with a level of insight and detail which is usually sadly lacking. It is argued that decontextualized policymaking and regulatory approaches both miss the proper target and actually harm coaching by stifling essential innovation. Such approaches have less to do with protecting children than protecting coaches and their employers; and caring coaches do not need predetermined care frameworks anyway – they actually reduce effectiveness and diminish the whole process. While female coaches may appear to have an easier ride, paradoxically they are placed under extra pressure by the constrained experience of their male colleagues. The dialogue, and the subsequent reflective conclusion, indicates the gulf between the simplistic way in which the mainstream discourse conceives and presents these issues, and the nuanced subtlety and open discussion required to facilitate clarity and help coaching escape from its current unhappy situation. Given the pattern of sports governance currently operative, simplistic and self-protective responses to sensitive issues may be inevitable, but the analysis offered in this chapter indicates the type of intellectual and practice-informed inputs that can redress the balance in favour of real care and humanity in coaching.

## Some themes

It was a pleasurable challenge to work with the authors who drew on their local knowledge and broader awareness to produce the chapters which constitute the bulk of this book. Each provided context-specific information and analysis, and also rich and generally relevant insights. While each chapter considers issues around touch and abuse in sports coaching and PE through a lens formed by personal and national experience, producing accounts which are redolent of cultural and contextual particularity, together (and through the way they are imbricated) they demonstrate that the contested assumptions, policy debates, and practical arguments which prompted the book have broad international salience. They may be understood in diverse ways, but the perception of a widely acknowledged problem remains. What has been presented as unarguable common sense, the idea that the risk of bad things happening to children in sports contexts will be countered by approaches and interventions which make good things less likely too, has caused doubt and confusion in all the countries discussed here, and this book may encourage more people to recognise this reality and seek to challenge it. Later, in the concluding chapter, I attempt to develop a more overarching account and critique of the situation on which each of these nationally focused contributions is focused, but now want to identify some broad and overlapping themes arising from the chapters, which seem worth further exploration.

The baleful significance of the generic misuse of the term 'paedophile' is identified by Jan Toftegaard Støckel, and its implications resonate in many other chapters. The lazy reference to a misunderstood portmanteau concept of paedophilia, particularly when a very substantial proportion of offenders against children cannot be thus classified, serves to define a distinct category of sick Other, while unhelpfully obscuring the ordinariness of many offenders. It also facilitates a panic-friendly language which has found a comfortable home in mass media and public consciousness. The attention-grabbing *sixty-fold* increase in the use of the terms paedophile and paedophilia in Danish media between 1995 and 2009 reflects a rise in anxious sensitivity rather than any rise in actual incidents of abuse, and may be understood as creating a form of self-fulfilling prophecy. This telling observation, of a phenomenon for which it is hard to imagine a rational explanation, provides the backdrop to the significance (also identified here in Aotearoa New Zealand, the United States, the United Kingdom, Sweden, and Romania) of relatively few, but very heavily reported, cases of abuse by sports coaches and PE teachers in fostering a generalised climate of fear and suspicion across the sector.

The dubious application of medical, pathological terminology, particularly in the context of the pervasive public discourse of risk (referred to by Richard Johnson) has encouraged the interpretation of issues of abuse and protection in terms of individual failure and responsibility, and discouraged more nuanced social and cultural analysis. This tension was highlighted by Maria Papaefstathiou in comparing the disjuncture between the traditional Cypriot emphasis on community with the individualist assumptions and discourse promulgated by the European Union and other agencies. In such a context, the definition of child protection as an individual imperative rather than a societal and community issue and responsibility is uncomfortable and arguably counterproductive. In some societies the imposition of such an internationalised discourse can reasonably be characterised as a form of cultural imperialism. In Cyprus and elsewhere (including Aotearoa New Zealand, the United States, the United Kingdom, Sweden), the interconnection of overarching discourses of fear and risk management, proscription- and prescription-rich intervention in coaching policy and practice, and the general imposition of neoliberal frameworks over recent decades, can be identified as a common theme. This insight explains the quite frequent reference by contributors to Foucault, whose ideas help in understanding how an essentially individualist discourse underlies the situation identified in a number of the chapters; a situation has been created in which coaches and teachers can only doubt themselves, subject themselves to endless scrutiny, and all must doubt and scrutinise all others too.

The pervasive presence of neoliberalism and new-right discourse across a range of national policy contexts, with variable degrees of recognition and fit, is a significant element in another issue identified, implicitly or explicitly, by a number of contributors. It is interesting that in Denmark, where senior figures in government worked directly with sports organisations (rather than choosing to govern at a distance), greater account was paid to authoritative evidence, and a relatively unprescriptive policy response was arrived at. Considering the different cultural and historical backdrops, particularly as they impinge on sport and coaching, of the nationally focused chapters from for instance Cyprus, Denmark, Romania, and Aotearoa New Zealand, it is very difficult to believe that all could be well served by any single way of understanding, or responding to, the possibility of abuse and the need for protection. The authoritarian Stalinist legacy carried by Romanian society and schooling, and its clash with the dash towards free-market individualism, described by Simona Petracovschi; the very high levels of community based participation in Aotearoa New Zealand sport described by Clive Pope; the tactile and emotional Cypriot context outlined by Maria Papaefstathiou; and the particular cultural context of Scandinavian sport discussed by Marie Öhman and Carin Grundberg-Sandell, and also Jan Toftegaard Støckel, appear intrinsically unlikely to prove equally amenable to a common, internationalised, one-size-fits-all approach to child protection in sport. In response to its attempted imposition, it is unsurprising that many are confused and anxious. Some sports coaches and administrators have decided that they warmly support the goal of child protection, but cannot accept or support the dominant prescription of how to achieve it. Their preferred responses vary, as discussed by Jan Toftegaard Støckel, and also in the Australian context by Keith Lyons.

In determining particular non-mainstream responses, different national constituencies have in effect informally evaluated the costs and benefits of adopting particular policies and come to different conclusions. This diversity would be considered normal in most policy areas, but appears difficult and challenging in the context of child abuse and protection, where a particularly big stick is always available to punish dissenting voices. What becomes apparent from the chapters here is that in most cases the policy and practice response to issues of child abuse and protection in sport has tended to be dominated by broader social discourses of risk and panic. Even when sports coaches or PE teachers are formally able to work within a well-judged framework, they inevitably bring with them into the sports context ideas, fears, and self-defensive practices which they have picked up elsewhere. The implementation of risk-averse practice appears to match the highest common denominator; fear and self-protection are powerful instincts, and in a risky environment a 'better safe than sorry' approach, doubting both oneself and one's colleagues, is an understandable and attractive option. Yet many of the contributors here note the wide recognition that the dominant risk-averse approach is irrational and ineffective, both in terms of child protection and the goals of sports coaching and PE. Richard Johnson argues that the environment in which teachers, coaches, and other adults *in loco parentis* operate has been changed for the worse on the basis of untruths. As a result, as Marie Öhman and Carin Grundberg-Sandell observe, pedagogic practice in sports contexts has been weakened, both in professional terms and in relation to the humanity of its practitioners.

For a professional or a committed volunteer, working in a manner understood to be less effective than known alternatives, feeling under scrutiny and pressure, and following the party line while doubting its wisdom, are behaviours unconducive to well-being. In most of the national cases discussed here there has been a failure of systematic evaluation to balance the costs and benefits of policies presented as being about child protection and safeguarding and, characteristic of single-issue moral crusaders, the proponents of strict regulatory regimes are unwilling to recognise the collateral damage caused. Thus, rather than supporting real security and developmental support, the reified notion of the pure child, vulnerable to victimhood, always in need of protection and governing, actually does children and young people a disservice. The quote from a tutor at a UK sports coaching and child protection workshop, 'if I'm their coach I can't be their friend', reported by Heather Piper, Bill Taylor, and Dean Garratt, has a chilling quality. In previous decades, such a curtailed understanding of *in loco parentis* responsibility could have been considered as an outrageous dereliction of duty. This evidence from a nationally sanctioned and credit-bearing training event exemplifies the way that, even though the mainstream discourse of risk and protection may aspire to sophistication and subtlety, it is transmitted in a wholly different way: as crude and prescriptive injunction. The highest common denominator of fear leads to the lowest common denominator of practice, and it may be that this is a result of the way that high level sports organisations in the UK have responded to issues of abuse and protection. As Keith Lyons shows, in Australia developments in relevant policy and practice were driven from the Sports Ethics Unit within the Australian Sports Commission, as part of a broadly conceived initiative. In contrast, in the UK the initiative was in effect contracted out to the Child Protection in Sport Unit of the National Society for the Prevention of Cruelty to Children. The different organisational dynamic and conception of problems and priorities which resulted (i.e. a broad approach, internally driven, as opposed to a narrow or single-issue approach, externally driven), appears significant.

In a number of chapters there is a palpable feeling of regret and loss regarding the damage over recent decades to the culture and experience of coaching and being coached, exemplified by Clive Pope's reflection on what being a teacher and coach in a sport-rich community used to be like. Such reflective nostalgia is based on a determination to understand coaching as human, social, and moral encounter, as discussed by Keith Lyons, rather than merely as a performative and logical practice. The significance of this distinction is highlighted by Alun Hardman, Jake Bailey, and Rhiannon Lord, whose forensic examination of the choices and thought processes inherent in coaching practice demonstrates the poverty of the dominant risk-averse approach. Their discussion of natural care as the fundamental element of effective coaching, and their critique of decontextualized policy which diminishes both real care and technical effectiveness, illuminates and serves to sharpen points made by other contributors. Thus in Sweden an official rhetoric stressing the primacy of care in teaching and coaching could be thwarted by self-protective approaches, and Cypriot voices assert the intrinsic role of emotion in holistic coaching practice, in which the difference between good touch and bad touch in a given context *can* be accurately assessed. Also from Cyprus came a recognition of the need for a much more sophisticated discussion and understanding around 'rights', echoed by a Romanian coach's identification of problems being caused by too much poorly understood freedom, and also in Marie Öhman and Carin Grundberg-Sandell's observation that taking children's rights seriously should mean more than focusing on their protection.

The recognition of the impoverished and dehumanised character of self-protective practice, rich in fear but poor in trust and care, spans national contexts and cultures which are often assumed to be very different. A veteran Cypriot sportsperson is quoted as worrying that:

> If we begin to think of all the potential risks then everything will be 'framed' . . . the personal appropriate communication, which includes emotion will disappear . . . you . . . cannot . . . think about everything so to avoid being misunderstood . . . you will not be able to perform to your maximum . . . there will be no result . . . I speak as a human . . . I mean as a human being you will not be able to function and achieve your objectives as a coach.

These words from the 'emotional' and 'tactile' Mediterranean were probably spoken without the benefit of having read the work of the Danish moral philosopher Løgstrup, quoted by Jan Toftegaard Støckel:

> In advance, we believe each other's words, in advance, we trust each other. It may be strange enough, but it is part of being human. It would be hostile to life to carry on differently. We simply could not live, our lives would wither, life would be crippled if we met each other with distrust.

The Australian data reported by Keith Lyons, showing a suggestive positive correlation between individual engagement in sport and a propensity to trust others, indicates again the potential social significance of sport, and these quotes illuminate the weight and scope of the issues considered in this book. Once the human and professional community of sports coaches and teachers concede that, individually and collectively, they constitute a particular risk to children and young people, and act accordingly, then something fundamental has been lost, which will be hard to recover. A number of contributors note the downward spiral of suspicion and regulation which threatens to be the consequence of mainstream approaches to safeguarding. Richard Johnson suggests that, consciously or otherwise, this damaging encroachment on coaches' and teachers' humanity, professionalism, and effectiveness has in effect been colluded with. He argues that there is a powerful moral imperative to resist, which I think would be understood by all contributors to this book.

Obviously, a fuller discussion of themes, shared or otherwise, emanating from the chapters which follow could be developed. On balance however, the particularity of each of the distinct contributions, based as they are in diverse national contexts, personal experiences, disciplinary strengths, and methodologies, seems to render too much meta-consideration at risk of being redundant, artificial, or even disrespectful. The chapters which follow can all stand on their own, with their own data, methods, and arguments; thus I am delighted to recommend them to the reader's attention.

# 2 Hands-off PE teaching and sports coaching in the UK

*Heather Piper, Bill Taylor and Dean Garratt*

## Introduction

In 2008, the authors attended the 4th International Congress of Qualitative Inquiry Conference, and the time spent travelling between Manchester in the UK and Urbana-Champaign (Illinois) in the US included opportunities for sharing experiences and ideas. Although we contributed to the conference on apparently quite different topics, the 'Professionalization of sports coaching' (Taylor and Garratt) and 'Ungrounded theory' (Piper), it became apparent in discussion that our current research interests offered potential areas of synergy. The prevalence of disproportionately risk-averse policy and practice in relation to touch and related behaviours between adults and children in nurseries and schools, prompted by an overarching moral panic about child abuse and protection, had been well established in Heather Piper's previous work (Piper *et al.* 2006). What became clear in our conversation was that the same pressures, and possibly even more problematic consequences, had become evident in the context of sports coaching and physical education and, beyond our academic backgrounds and theoretical preferences, our varied non-academic expertise and prior experience made us particularly sensitive to the issue. Heather Piper had been a child protection social worker before becoming a researcher and working on issues of touch and abuse; Bill Taylor had been a high level performer in paddlesport before progressing to senior coaching roles; and Dean Garratt had committed the long hours in training and coaching contexts required to achieve significant competitive success in natural bodybuilding. Thus the team was greater than the sum of its parts, and we resolved to seek funding for a substantial research initiative, to explore how sports coaching and physical education (PE) had been affected by the high level of anxiety around intergenerational touch, abuse and protection, as mediated through the layers of regulation and governance which characterise organised sport. Given the difficulty of winning research funding, we were delighted when our project proposal to the UK Economic and Social Research Council (ESRC) was successful (Piper *et al.* 2011a),[1] facilitating fieldwork over a twelve month period, the production of substantial original data, and the potential for subsequent publication and dissemination.

A core aspect of the successful research proposal realised in the planning and execution of fieldwork was to identify and explore the thoughts and feelings of adults, acting *in loco parentis* during sports coaching and physical education con-texts. We were keen to focus particularly on the nature and consequences of child protection regulation and policy in the field, through interviews and observations, and also to consider this data in relation to previous findings from research with teachers and carers. We wanted to understand the broader context of assump-tions and imperatives which had contributed to such developments, and widened the focus to incorporate interviewing senior policymakers and administrators in sport and child protection. Since the available funding and time was strictly lim-ited, we selected three sports (association football, swimming, canoeing/kayaking [paddlesports]), characterised by strong childhood and youth participation rates as well as varied characteristics regarding facility usage and team or individual involvement. Some of these sports have also come to public attention, sometimes regarded as problematic, with high profile cases of abuse and/or a perception of being dangerous in relation to coaches' engagement and touch with young people. In response, policy-makers and administrators had invested heavily in working with child protection organisations to develop substantial (and often frequently revised) policy and practice designed to avoid the risk of such cases in the future.

## Research approach and design

The theoretical framework that underpinned the research was informed by dis-course analysis and post-structuralist theory, and was necessarily wide-ranging. Approaches drawing on discourse analysis regard subjectivity as being produced in the discursive practices that make up the social world:

> Discourses authorize what can and cannot be said: they produce relations of power and communities of consent and dissent, and thus discursive bounda-ries are always being redrawn around what constitutes the desirable and the undesirable and around what it is that makes possible structures of intelligi-bility and unintelligibility.
>
> (Britzman 2000:36)

Developing this argument, Foucault (1980) would regard such discursive arrange-ments as themselves constitutive of knowledge and power, which through the productive capacity and micropolitics of practice, serve to construct 'truth', thus influencing the community or 'régime' about which it speaks. Our interest throughout the research has been how 'communities of consent' have allowed and contributed to adults' fear of touching children and young people (and of other practices discussed throughout) when acting *in loco parentis,* particularly as sports coaches and PE teachers. This is double-edged; sports coaches and others create a surface appearance of individually consenting to examples of defensive practice, as evidenced in this and previous research data, but 'consent' is actually also 'communal', shaped by the many social and institutional discourses impact-ing on what makes a 'good' practitioner and what counts as 'proper' safeguarding.

Following Foucault (1988) we recognise these processes as simultaneous (see later in this chapter). This notion of a conjoined self and Other is also reflected in Butler's (1997) work, where she argues that subjects maintain their status as good and proper by the threat of being bad and improper, such statuses being continually in tension. Subjects achieve their subjectivity by repeated acts of vigilance, where they are 'continuously in the process of acquitting [them]sel[ves] of the accusation of guilt' (119). Our research confirms this account, documenting coaches and others describing their vigilant attempts to avoid accusations of guilt for acts previously considered innocent.

Like MacLure *et al.* (2012), we found the ideas drawn from 'membership categorisation analysis' (a strand within conversational analysis) to be useful in our thinking. The assumptions behind such an analysis treat a subject's identity as not just a matter of them belonging to a particular category or group, but as an identity developed through discourse itself. In Jean-Luc Nancy's account of community, for example, the concept 'individual' is a logical impossibility, as we cannot be alone by ourselves but are rather always constituted through our relations with others: 'there is no singular being without another singular being' (Nancy 1991: 28). Therefore, aloneness exists only in death; in life, the self is inescapably conjoined with Others, and community always *is* where discourses (again drawing on Foucault) speak into existence the practices to which they refer relationally. As such membership categories are organised by 'category bound activities' where practice is formed via the 'common/communal sense' and tacit assumptions and discourses of the category members, and where the categorisation becomes a moral order (Jayyusi 1984). Failure to comply with a category's 'common sense' is likely to lead to pathologising by others and/or self-censure. This account supported our attempt to understand the ways in which those acting *in loco parentis* are inducted into particular ways of thinking and behaving, even when these seem at odds with their previously held beliefs. Professional identity is always in flux; practitioners, including sports coaches, see themselves through the eyes of others and modify their behaviour through comparisons with other sports coaches who they consider must be following the 'common sense' assumptions of the profession.

In our thinking and writing (e.g. Piper *et al.* 2011b, 2013b) we also drew from and discussed the theorising of risk society and its commitment to calculating and exterminating ambivalence in the attempt to avoid all risk (Beck 1992; Bauman 1991; Giddens 1999), a wide range of work around moral panic and moral regulation (e.g. Hier 2011), and also conceptual frameworks around biopolitics and governmentality, derived from Foucault (1991).

These briefly introduced understandings enabled our research methodology to be situated in the ethnographic tradition, where we applied established qualitative methods (Lather 2007) and utilised a case study approach (Stake 1978, 1995). Crucially, this research project was able to benefit from the previous project (Piper *et al.* 2006), and some data from that project is included here to show how the consequences of living in a 'risk society' go way beyond sport.

The three sport case studies selected were significant. Football (soccer) in the UK is commonly considered the national game, with approximately two million people playing each week (Football Association [FA] 2013). Alongside the wide and pervasive culture of performativity, the FA has embraced the move to enhance 'professionalism' and standards within the game and has recently launched a number of new coaching awards, including courses particular to coaching young people (FA 2013). With 125,000 full or part-time coaches, including professionals, volunteers, and willing parents, it incorporates activity in elite high profile contexts as well as in the mass participation environment where community and local clubs are run for diverse age groups. Swimming is taught in the majority of secondary schools in the UK as part of the National Curriculum, and PE teachers normally staff this educational delivery. Beyond schools, swimming clubs often utilise local authority–owned facilities and have to conduct swimming sessions, not only under the guise of regulations imposed by the governing body Amateur Swimming Association (ASA), but also under local government guidelines. Coaches working outside the direct employment of the sport may also deliver these sessions (e.g. PE teachers). Paddlesport activities are provided and experienced in a wide range of environments including local beaches, rivers, lakes, and swimming pools. Changing in and out of canoeing clothing is often done in the back of a car or behind a hedge next to the river or other venue. The activity is delivered through clubs, Outdoor Education Centres, commercial providers, youth organisations including the scouts, guides, and Sea Cadets, and through school-based PE.

Between September 2010 and September 2011, in fieldwork approved through the research ethics procedures of Manchester Metropolitan University, data collection in each of the three sports utilised interviews with a convenience sample of ten coaches, a number of observations of coaching practice, and a focus group. In addition, we conducted ten expert interviews with respondents including relevant academics, local government officers, central government officers, representatives from the British Olympic Association, the national Sports Councils, sports coach UK, the Association of Physical Education, the Sport and Recreation Alliance, and specialist officers from the Child Protection in Sport Unit (CPSU) of the National Society for the Prevention of Cruelty to Children (NSPCC), which provides guidance and training on safeguarding to sporting organisations. To gather data from the school context, we interviewed ten physical education teachers with experience of both school-based delivery and teacher training in higher education institutions. To gain insights and opinion from a wider range of interested people, beyond the three case study sports, we elicited perspectives from rugby and gymnastics coaches, and made available an online survey, inviting comments from individuals running sport provision, managing coaching delivery, or those directly involved in instructing young people. We also attended a number of Child Protection training workshops to view first-hand the form and content of the policy, and derived suggestions regarding practice, as cascaded down to those working directly with children and young people. We also attended a CPSU conference marking its tenth anniversary.

In total, we interviewed over 100 people and received over 100 responses from the online survey. The selection of those interviewed was representative of the gender split found within each sport and was mindful of the age profile found within the participant and coaching populations of swimming, paddlesport, and football. Most were drawn from individuals and groups located in the North West of England, as previous work had established no particular geographical variations in touching practices. In order to benefit from informed opinions and inputs from critical friends, to support and informally evaluate the project in process, we convened a steering panel, which met a number of times during the field research. This included senior academics in the field of sports coaching and PE, employees of sports' National Governing Bodies (NGBs) involved in training and the delivery of child protection workshops, and personnel from local government departments responsible for sports provision.

In addition to the fieldwork, we conducted a comprehensive review of the literature relative to the individual sports and the wider discourse on child protection within sport itself. We collected all major policy initiatives and undertook a genealogical review of key documents and seminal reports (Garratt *et al.* 2013). Beyond reviewing official documentation, we gathered newspaper cuttings, press releases, and Internet news stories relating to sport and child abuse, as these popular avenues of dissemination reflect and incite powerful discourses, and influence much of the reactive policy which became evident through the course of the project.

The greater part of the fieldwork was carried out by Bill Taylor, as the ranking coach on the project team, but all members contributed to the substantial interviewing commitment. Ongoing and summative analysis of data was conducted by the full team within a reflexive and iterative framework; monthly meetings and informal discussions helped us generate analysis, and construct themes, as data were gathered. As particular themes were developed, we returned to policy documentation and previous writings on the subject to identify patterns or anomalies. The process of thematically categorizing the data was completed via a process of intra-analysis; all involved in the project reviewed interview transcripts and other data forms, to establish initial themes. By coming together we formed a shared and collective understanding and formulated categorizations which revealed particular insights, doing justice to the data while allowing us to accommodate the variations inherent in the sports, and among the many respondents.[2]

This project was the first substantial attempt to focus on the consequences of child protection policy on UK coaches' and PE teachers' practice, and their relationships with young people they work with *in loco parentis*. Previously, research on child protection in sport had not dealt with the wider consequences of policy, and the manifestation of increased regulation and the growth of a moral panic. In consequence, the role of the coach and PE teacher as the central actor in the nexus of regulation and policy, professional duty, and sporting and educational interaction, has tended to be marginalised. Our own priority was to explore and highlight their experiences, perceived realities, and practice. We were particularly interested in issues of touch, trust, the changes in practice deemed necessary to comply with guidance and regulation, and thus in the thoughts and doubts impacting on coaches' delivery. The research was conceived and conducted at a time when the UK government, via its central sporting organizations, was pursuing a professionalization of the sports coaching agenda (Taylor and Garratt 2008, 2010). In fact, in order to draw down central funding, all sports' NGBs had to be seen to comply with directives relating to child protection, risk management, and the regulation of delivery. This trend towards increased governance was, in turn, being cascaded down to the individual coaches, who in order to practice were now required to have current certification in terms of holding a first aid award, being a member of the relevant NGB, having been checked by the Disclosure and Barring Service (formerly the Criminal Records Bureau – CRB) and, if working with under-18-year-olds, having attended a child protection training workshop.

## Research themes

An outline and summary discussion of key themes in the research data follows. As stated, these overarching themes also resonate with the previous research findings in relation to teachers and carers (Piper *et al.* 2006), and we draw on some of that data to illustrate this point. However, before presenting these themes it is worth noting some obvious shortcomings of any blanket application of policy across various practices and pedagogical space, which can never take into account the nuanced and varied nature of sports instruction. The response favoured by those organisations and managers keen to rely on policy and codes of practice in dealing with any inappropriate action is to increase control, and issue more restrictive definitions of what is deemed problematic practice. The intrinsic limitation of this approach is exposed in the comment from the manager of a large outdoor activities centre:

> And at 11 o'clock in the morning, little Johnny will be, you know, with a young, female assistant instructor, who will be doing an absolutely textbook job of making sure that everybody's putting their harnesses on properly, because that's something that everybody's really aware of, right, they've all got loads of ideas about it, and they've all talked about it. But then it'll actually be one of the reception staff, who will just be some sort of well-meaning matriarch who, you know, a bit old school, who actually hasn't been involved in any of this . . . or one of the cleaners, who hasn't done any of the child protection training, who will then be going into somebody's bedroom on their own, in an evening, where you kind of think 'oh hell, you know, I've left everything wide open there'.

While it could be argued that this example could be countered by a more inclusive training regime, it remains true that in sports contexts there has been a disproportionate focus on the behaviours of the sports coach. In reality, coaching contexts are complex and populated by a wide range of personnel; totally managing risk out of such situations appears an unattainable goal.

### *Doubting self*

As with other studies considering the impact of the wider child protection discourse on professionals' practice, our research unearthed feelings of self-doubt and guilt among those observed and interviewed (Piper *et al.* 2013b). The internalising of 'the right thing to do as a professional' was married with an uncertainty and self-doubt which sometimes led to individuals resorting to the most restrictive and curtailed practice and, at the same time, engaging in conversation with themselves about whether their next interaction could be justified. This internal self-doubt was often collectively expressed in the focus groups and during the child protection workshops we observed. In one particular training event, the research log notes:

> The members of the workshop seem keen to seek confirmation from others attending training. When the workshop leader gave various touch related scenarios for the group to discuss after offering 'this is what I would do in this situation', the contributors would often engage in sideways glances to check if any collective support and acceptance was offered. If the workshop leader cast doubt on the appropriateness of the suggested action, the individual tended to clam up for the rest of the evening.

While there was little evidence of this lack of confidence being restricted to any one sport, coaches whose main interaction with young people was through swimming seemed to frame their actions within a particularly self-critical approach. Christine, a 42-year-old part-time coach working in a local club, went on to say:

> I am always thinking about what I do before I do it. I'm always thinking about, I wouldn't say covering my back, but I'm always thinking how is this gonna look, before I do something. You've really got to make sure you cross every t and dot every i before you do anything. There's no room to do anything wrong. I don't think we have any parents here that would get upset, but if you did do something wrong, particularly with a swimmer who's not got many clothes on, what would they say?

The additional concerns of self-doubt and professional uncertainty are exemplified by 'not many clothes on' and 'watching parents' and might be explained by some of the high profile cases that have been brought against swimming coaches, and thus the sport of swimming itself (see Garratt *et al.* 2013). This notion of being a 'risky sport', possibly targeted by those with ill intent, where simple incident is turned into accusation, was reflected by an NGB official who admitted that her first response to any media report of a child abuse in sport incident is: 'Christ, I hope it's not swimming!'

Self-doubt can take a variety of forms and these findings relate to a statement submitted by email to the previous project (Piper *et al.* 2006):

> I can feel though, with . . . my step daughter of 12, a definite hesitation and suspicion of myself that's very much an implanted awareness . . . Potentially more serious though is a feeling that this implanted awareness alerts any

proclivity I have towards 'the taboo'; that it might awaken otherwise non-existent desires. It feels like this awareness acts like a carrier of an 'infection' to abuse . . .

This reflection from a male step-parent on the way that self-doubt is engendered, and its potential effects, matched comments from sports coaches throughout the research.

### Doubting others' perceptions and fear of accusations

The wider perception of having to be on one's guard, and constantly needing to think about each and every action, relates not only to the delivery of a coaching or physical education lesson, but to whom, and by whom it is delivered, in the aforementioned relational sense. While the spectre of doubt always haunts male coaches who choose to work with younger female athletes, the emergence of the child abuse moral panic in sport has sharply focussed individuals' concern. Michael, a highly qualified football coach (Level 4), explains how working with females was no longer a situation which could be taken for granted. He went on to express a new reluctance to administer first-aid on the pitch, something he was once happy to do:

> I think in terms of when I'm coaching, this is gonna sound, it might sound silly, but when I'm coaching the girls, I'm more aware of it. It sounds . . . you know, I don't understand it but because of the . . . whether it's I'm more aware of the gender or I always seem to be a bit more reluctant to do that. Obviously, maybe it's the age group I do, because I do the under-14s, so they're between 12 and 14.

Goode (2010) suggests that males working in a range of environments such as education, social care and sports, particularly with young girls who are entering and navigating puberty, are subject to additional imputed risks: being challenged and being subject to 'whispers of suspicion' or false allegations. During the project we found no evidence to suggest that when working in the sports arena, individuals were more subject to misapplied or false allegation than any other setting where intergenerational interaction is commonplace. However, the number of allegations, false or otherwise, is not where the conditioning of coaches and physical educationalist behaviour is founded; it is the fear of being involved in any allegation that prompts a coach to be normalised (Foucault 1977) or change their practice. Indeed, this is where a discourse of fear conjures the practice of which it speaks. Michael, later in the same interview, suggested that he often asked himself if it was worth coaching the girls because whatever he did, or did not do, the shadow of doubt and questioning by others and of himself was constant. As Foucault (1977: 201) might say 'the surveillance is permanent in its effects, even if it is discontinuous in its action; that the perfection of power should tend to render its actual exercise unnecessary'.

Ewan, an experienced coach across a number of sports, suggested that when comforting a worried youngster, nervous about a sea canoeing trip, he firstly thinks about the ramifications of his actions. He went on to express the following:

> So, you know, when I'm in that situation, you face a very difficult decision . . . do you give that support? Or do you say well, that potentially puts me in the line for criticism in the future? And, of course, in the way that I work, it's important I don't lose my qualifications, it's important that I'm . . . that there isn't any accusation. So personally, I'm extremely careful and I . . . and I hesitate before doing that. And really, it has to be pretty . . . pretty extreme before I go that far.

It is interesting to note here that, as quite commonly evidenced in such interviews, the path of reasoning leading up to undertaking such an action is not centred on the best interests of the young person, but on the self-interest of the coach. Ewan has focused on 'not putting himself in the line for criticism' and voices concern for his professional standing, 'it's important I don't lose my qualifications' and 'it's important . . . that there isn't any accusation'. The carrying out of the act of caring for those under your charge becomes a decision-making process which involves an increasingly complex path of consequences and 'what ifs'. The prevalence of moral hazard has escalated to the point where an arm around a young person, to comfort their fear of something new, is now deemed to be something that could end a coaching career. The displacement of the self from the self, a corrupted logic of placing the coach's needs and protection before the needs of the young person, seems complete.

The way in which an insignificant action can set off a hazardous chain of events, which are given fuel by others, was a common consideration for respondents. Reg remembered, when working in a school setting, being challenged by a young person during a PE session:

> But when I worked in secondary education, I seem to recall a student telling me, after I'd tapped him on the shoulder for attention, turning round to me and going 'you can't do that, you're not allowed to touch me'. And I was like well, 'show me where, show me why I can't'. And it was a perception of the student that they thought they were better than the teacher, going 'I know the rules and regulations'. You know, they thought they did but it was quite definitely, you cannot touch me, you shouldn't have done that, in front of all of the pupils in the class.

Child protection measures conceived as encouraging other adults to watch out for inappropriate action are now promulgated to children, to empower them to challenge adults' actions. While this engagement of the young person as an active agent, protecting their own safety, may obviously be regarded as creditable, without extensive training and due consideration the suspicion held by both generations about each other's true intent can potentially undermine a positive educational relationship. The consequence of such an atmosphere of doubt is that the benefit of sport instruction is diminished by the taken for granted assumption that the default position should be one of mistrust and fear. Reg went on later in the interview to indicate that, while he was concerned not to give any reason for doubt, he refused to 'give in to the pressure to withdraw'; his personal and professional belief was that the positive nature of extensive pastoral care in any educational setting should override permanent and pre-emptive caution.

The previous research with teachers and carers (Piper *et al.* 2006) similarly included many examples of professionals fearful of the consequences of what was once routine practice. One respondent described how a routine action of his thirty-year teaching career (loosening pupils' ties for singing lessons) became the subject of internal disciplinary inquiries:

> And that is me saying . . . you loosen your tie because it gives you a little bit more freedom . . . you might want to undo the top button and sit in a relaxed way, don't have your legs crossed, don't flop, and don't sit rigid, because it's putting it in context. If the implications weren't so serious it would be quite funny . . . once a rumour has been discussed and documented it's there in print, there's no smoke without fire.
>
> (Retired music teacher)

This teacher was found not guilty of sexual misconduct following enquiries by school managers, but chose early retirement after pupils greeted him each morning in the playground with cries of 'pervert'. Such experiences exemplify and model the doubt and anxiety around others' perceptions and the risk of misplaced allegations reported by sports coaches.

### Doubting self and others: Providing witnesses

A common theme across the three sports was that the culture of fear and self-doubt had changed both the manner in which respondents coached and interacted with young people, and the way they perceived others. Within their own practice, they sought to make the once private and individualised input with athletes open and public, observable and thus legitimate, witnessed, and safe. In Foucauldian terms, this welcoming of the disciplinary gaze serves to manage, control and displace behaviour, subtlety rendering it a collective responsibility, itself subject to correction and control. This process of surveillance, and means of 'correct training', carries a range of subtle and insidious applications (Foucault 1977, 1982; Rabinow 1984). Lesley, a canoeing and swimming coach, stressed this need to been *seen*:

> But yeah, you just have to make sure everything's done in view . . . it's really drilled into you in swimming that you can't like touch them, you can't . . . like even if you want to support their head, like you can't just have a hand under their head, and you definitely can't have one underneath their tummy or underneath their back.
>
> (Lesley three years' experience)

Kim, also a swimming coach, encouraged junior coaches to focus on parents' perceptions in justifying not just what they do but what they are *seen* to do:

> When you're coaching them, and we always tell our coaches . . . if you need to touch them in any way, shape or form, you have to get them out of the water to do it. You wouldn't dare put your hand in the water, because the parents obviously can't see what you're doing with your hand.
>
> (Kim two years' experience)

The fear of being alone, unscrutinised, changes the way that coaches and PE teachers behave, and also the experiences they feel comfortable in delivering. Max, a young soccer coach, recalled a dilemma while working in an after-school setting:

> Like last Friday . . . they said . . . 'there's an after school club and I need you to cover it'. So I went up and I think one girl turned up . . . and it was just me and her. So I texted my line manager . . . 'there's only one kid here . . . what shall I do'? And it . . . was in a sports hall, tucked away at the back of the school. And I didn't really want to be there by myself, and he texted me back, saying 'oh you've just got to do something with her'. So because I wasn't comfortable me being in there with her alone, I just went to the primary school, to the headmaster and said 'you're going to have to ring her parents . . . to come pick her up'. And that made me think, you know, that it's not right for me to have to decide that off my own back, I didn't get any advice from the club or anything like that, saying we don't really want you in that situation.
>
> (Max two years' experience)

The decision to cancel the session seems less surprising than the need to refer to others before making it. Self-policing (Foucault 1988) and self-doubt combined to undermine self- confidence; the perceived danger of the situation is paramount, and the isolation is resented. This concern at being solely accountable corrodes individual professional judgement, and also undermines intergenerational relationships.

Even in observing the performance of an athlete, to provide formative feedback to help them improve, the curtailment of once normal coaching behaviour is evident. Kathy, an experienced swimming teacher, recounted her changed thoughts on her coaching practice over the years:

> . . . you just feel a little bit more conscious, they haven't got a lot of clothes on. And when you're looking at them, you know, as you make eye contact . . . and do not drop your eye too low [laughs]. That's fine, but when you look at them elsewhere . . . you can't look at the chest, you can't look down here. So you have to be very conscious . . . in the eye, yes, in the eyes. If you think about it, it's my job, our job is to look at their bodies all the time, when they are in the water. I am looking at their bodies . . . that's my job . . . I think.
>
> (Kathy eight years' experience)

A perverse effect of the need for witnesses and for intense caution and regulation is that those responsible for PE education may be brought into disrepute and considered critically. An extension of the child protection discourse is concern about the use of photography and social and visual media. Again, the swimming pool was a site for close regulation, as a swimming coach noted:

> And I know that their legislation is . . . not legislation, rules are, if a parent wants to take a photo of their child swimming, they have to notify us at the beginning and they can either take it at the beginning of the session or the end of the session, but they cannot have any other children in the pool . . . not in view of the camera. And there has to be a member of staff present to make sure they are with the child and that it is just their child that they're taking pictures of. It really is silly, these are just photos after all . . . aren't they?
>
> (Jane five years' experience)

Beyond the doubt and confusion about where such rules and regulations come from is the recognition that they require the provision of a worst-case scenario in order to appear sensible or proportionate. This again illustrates Nancy's (1991) point that the concept of being in life is logically meaningful only as co-appearance, not as an absolute for itself, but in the sense of being-*with*.

In the previous research (Piper *et al.* 2006), similar all-encompassing caution was evident. An early years manager responded:

> When working with young children they are bound to touch us but we must ensure that we respond appropriately, knowing *we are overlooked* . . . We constantly draw attention to each other so that if an issue crops up *we have a witness* that can protect us. (Our emphasis)

Adults working in a range of *in loco parentis* contexts have learnt to initiate and welcome surveillance, creating the potential for an irrational spiral. Who witnesses the witness, and how many levels of scrutiny are sufficient?

### Some difference and diversity

We would not wish to suggest that the individuals we interviewed and engaged with during the study were totally passive and docile in dealing with the insidious advance of regulation and policy. Many of the coaches and PE teachers voiced concerns regarding how they felt their professional autonomy had been eroded and undermined. In Foucauldian terms (1977: 184), the idea of 'erosion' is linked to an understanding that power does not fall evenly upon its subjects, but rather circulates to produce 'the techniques of an observing hierarchy and those of a normalising judgement. It is a normalizing gaze, a surveillance that makes it possible to qualify, to classify and to punish', and hence separate 'good' compliant coaches from more recalcitrant ones. One noticeable feature which did emerge was an age-related split in the manner in which individuals perceived the wider child protection discourse and the resulting advance of policy, prescription and proscription. Those below the age of around twenty-five years seem to have a general acceptance of the necessity for child protection courses, defensive practice, and 'being careful of what you do'. When interviewed, this younger cohort often recounted stories of fellow coaches or athletes who had been involved, to some degree, in incidents surrounding child protection or abuse. The emergence of these elements of experience and discourse, and the way they coloured younger coaches' thinking and everyday talk about their practice, was initially surprising. An explanation may be that this age group have never been aware of different ways of thinking and acting. The observational apprenticeship that most coaches go through while being coached themselves means that defensive practice and an avoidance of touch has come to be seen as commonplace, best practice, the natural order of things.

Those teachers and coaches aged over twenty-five, or thereabouts, often compared the constraints of their current practice with earlier experiences, when the moral compass was invested in the individual and not imposed from outside. An officer from the ASA offered her thoughts on the divide:

> I think . . . it's so much a part of the training scheme now and our qualifications that people do understand. So, I think the newer qualified teachers and coaches are far more aware and far more able to understand the safeguarding line involved in that . . . But I think you always have that element there, because some coaches, like myself, were taught very differently as to what was safe to teach young people.

Notwithstanding this apparent age divide evidenced in the data, there were cases where both individuals and institutions resisted child protection policy and regulation relating to individual action. Martin, the manager of a high profile sport centre, articulated a strong desire to counter the wider pressure and to support individual staff and their personal judgment. Asked about the relative absence of policy at his centre to guide staff, he responded:

> I don't want to stifle the individual decision making that goes on, and are people doing what they believe is the right thing? I do believe really, really strongly in empowering staff . . . if I have to have policies for all those kind of things, then they're employing the wrong staff; they should be employing people who are all big enough and ugly enough and grown up enough to make their own decisions about that sort of thing.

Later in the interview, Martin admitted he often struggled to defend this position when challenged, but felt that his duty was to give staff the freedom to do what is best for the teaching of sports skills and the development of the sportsperson. Increasingly the pressure to conform, just in case, meant that Martin worried about the outcome and consequence of any complaint or incident.

When talking to clubs and organisations that sit outside NGB control, there appeared to be additional variation in the way policy was perceived and acted upon. We visited a swimming group which focused on the social and physical benefits of people with disability being involved in the sport. Here the realities of dealing with individual needs and situations overrode the notion that no-touch should be the default position. The head coach explained:

> I'll call them swimmers, even though some of them might not be able to swim to start with, but they obviously need more personal touch then, don't they, because they need to be . . . they need that assistance to help them float and . . . so I think, what we tend to do is try and put a male with a male, female with female to start with. Although we don't always stick to that ruling.

The realities of working with swimmers who required additional physical support, and employing mainly volunteer coaches, meant that in this club the pressure to comply was put to one side in favour of local practice. The head coach, himself not qualified within the NGB scheme, argued that it was unfair to ask the club's coaches to undertake additional child protection training and cover the cost themselves. His attitude was that he and his colleagues had come to coach, give time back to the sport, and encourage disability swimming; attendance on courses took away from these priorities.

Again, examples from the previous research (Piper *et al.* 2006) reiterated similar resistance to adopting no touch and similar restrictive guidelines:

> To attempt to introduce guidelines . . . would be counter-productive and a step away from the high quality of care offered by the professional carers, far better they use judgement and trust. (Nursery manager)
>
> I know there are horrible people out there but I do find it sad when I hear school staff tell me that there is no physical contact with the children . . . What kind of adults are we bringing up? (Manager of Out of School Club for young children)

Again, such resistance was particularly evident in contexts working with individuals with special needs.

## Training for child protection

Whatever the particular themes and arguments drawn from the substantial dataset, the real but variable effect of generalised anxiety and fear among coaches was starkly manifest. Obviously, coaches and all adults operating *in loco parentis* should be mindful of the welfare of their charges, but the data beg the question of how this risk-conscious climate has been induced and how the high profile of abuse and protection has been channelled into the coaching context. Reference was made earlier to observation notes from a child protection training workshop where a lack of confidence was demonstrated. In order to understand more clearly how coaches' awareness of, and perspectives on, issues around touch, abuse, and protection in working with other people's children have been formed and influenced in recent years, a number of three-hour workshops were observed, delivered under the aegis of sports coach UK. These sessions were delivered by approved tutors, to groups numbering between fourteen and twenty. Attendees covered a broad spectrum: the group at a university sports facility consisted of students with limited coaching experience, qualified at Level 1 in a number of sports; at an open access event at a gymnastics club, there were both novice coaches from a range of sports and also others with years of experience, treating the workshop as CPD, necessary to demonstrate the currency of their qualification and commitment. Responses to an invitation to introduce themselves and their reasons for attending were varied and suggestive: 'I have a commitment to protecting young children', 'I want to save my sport from the pervs', 'I was told to come here – I really don't think that I need the course', 'My three years is up and I need to get updated'. While a full account of these sessions is beyond the current brief, some summary issues can be drawn from the sample, which may help illustrate the way in which they contribute to the instigation and maintenance of unfocused anxiety:

- Ideas were presented by the workshop tutors in an uncritical and non-reflective way, with frequent dependence on simple binaries (e.g. 'good' and 'bad' coaching practice). In the absence of careful distinctions, there was confusion between desirable practices and overarching moral imperatives, neither of which were identified clearly. Ideas about child protection were conflated with ideas about 'good coaching'. Categories were left indistinct (e.g. 'normal parents would not want you to . . .', 'not all people are like us . . .') yet served to create shady 'others', 'them' as distinct from 'us'. The taken-for-granted notions of the vulnerable child and the dangerous adult, juxtaposed in terms of risk, were ever present.
- A substantial theme related to claimed legal requirements, which were never translated into referenced or detailed guidance for practice, instead resting on an implicit threat of negative consequences for transgressions of 'good practice'. Frequent but nonspecific reference was made to the Children Act (1989), which was implied or suggested to provide a welfare framework for sports coaching, a series of clear-cut legal and ethical imperatives. One tutor repeatedly referred to a 'legal requirement' to follow codes of conduct, and to coaches' 'legal duty' to follow the Children Act, which it was suggested had replaced the principle of *in loco parentis*.
- Frequent reference was made to 'experts' in child protection (usually the NSPCC), their (unspecified) research, and selected advice (e.g. 'the experts say disabled children are more vulnerable'). In addition to this lead-body role, one tutor repeatedly suggested, wrongly, that the NSPCC has statutory status, in effect implying that its word has the force of law.
- A tutor cited sports (athletics, swimming, and judo) where one-to-one coaching had apparently been banned, although without saying by whom. In each case cited, this was untrue. Another advised the group that 'if I'm their coach I can't be their friend', and that a policy of 'no-touch is the best option'.

- The child, the coach, and the act of coaching were all presented in reified, unnuanced, essentially dehumanised terms. Young people's and coaches' diverse personal histories, variable thresholds of comfort and stress, and motivations were disregarded, as were the significant distinctions in the coaching challenges and traditions associated with different sports.
- Time was spent rehearsing accounts of high profile coach/child abuse incidents and stories from the past, but also from outside sports contexts (e.g. priests, boy scout leaders, children's home care staff). Abuse and risk was presented as pervasive and ever present, beyond 'those who give sport a bad name'; after all, 'it's not all about dirty old men in macs'.
- The current situation, defined as high risk, was treated as a given; even though the need for protection policies, defensive practice, and tight regulation was sad, and regretted, 'these days we can't be too careful'. Attendees were advised to play safe and follow their NGB guidelines ('best practice'), which would provide protection against allegations of abuse.

On the basis of these observations, some tentative conclusions may be drawn. The workshops appear to be not really about training, but more about raising awareness (or, less charitably, anxiety). The problem is treated as self-evident, and little is clarified with any accuracy or sophistication; beyond 'don't touch', little detailed advice is given, yet attendees are encouraged to consider their situation (their person) as inherently and obviously dangerous and risky, and thus to be frightened and careful. For relatively novice junior coaches, hearing this message from an authoritative, confident, experienced, senior coach in an 'educative' professional accreditation or development context, is likely to have a significant impact.

When preliminary outcomes from the project began to be publicised: that the legitimacy and rationality of practices once treated as normative and unexceptional have been disturbed and rearticulated through particular formulations of rules and guidance, leading to the institutionalisation of 'no touch', the response of agencies responsible for the regulations tended to be defensive. They suggested that any resulting negative practice, where coach and PE teacher relationships with their charges was governed by self-doubt and mistrust, was due to child protection training being misinterpreted or inadequate, or, in other cases, simply dismissed as bad practice. This was illustrated by a CPSU rejoinder to a newspaper report of the project (*Daily Telegraph* 2012), to the effect that touch had never been banned and that guidelines were being misinterpreted. As noted elsewhere (Piper *et al.* 2013a), beyond evading responsibility, such a response disregards the pervasive climate of anxiety surrounding abuse and allegations, and is disingenuous regarding the power (and observing hierarchy [Foucault 1977]) which the NSPCC is able to deploy. When coaches are told often and forcibly that they are at constant risk of being accused of abuse (through pervasive safeguarding and child protection discourses), even if they are also told that they *may* touch young people, although there may well be seriously unpleasant consequences if they *do*, there is really a *de facto* blanket injunction against touch (in terms of power via a dividing practice), and so it is not credible to argue otherwise.

## The assault on humanity and care in coaching and physical education

Throughout the research we came to consider the term, 'touch' as a metaphor for a range of activities, which are now seen as risky and problematic. These individual coaching behaviours, once commonly used in sport and physical instruction, have now been (re)defined as signifiers of abuse, and possible individual acts of abuse. The redefinition and inclusion of these coach/athlete interactions and pedagogical engagements have been formalised within new codes of best practice, child protection courses, and an ever-increasing ratcheting up of regulation. The result is a progressive layering-on of conditions and constraints as those individuals and agencies responsible for protecting children, keen to appear vigilant, limit coaches' judgement and ability to interact with young people in their care. As well as adding to the transformation and control of practice, new anxiety-rich actions are established. Problematic practices now include texting to confirm fixtures, a coach's hands not being visible while posing for a team photograph, giving lifts to players who may have missed the last bus, standing too close to an athlete when providing individual feedback, and checking safety equipment by testing buckles and harnesses. A quote from a sports coach UK officer represents this wave of new concern:

> You know, 10 years ago, you never would have worried about a mobile phone in class, or text bullying or grooming. These are all new terms that we have to, you know, consider. And . . . there'll be a whole new raft of things in another 10 years, I would imagine.

Support for the belief that the work of discovering new inappropriate forms of behaviour is never complete was emphasised by a senior member of the CPSU. When asked about the continued need for the unit to issue guidance on individual activities and situations, the response was that there were always new ways paedophiles sought access to children and thus the work of the unit would never be complete. The logic of this response seems to be that it only takes one incident for bodies such as the CPSU to cast doubt on the intentions behind all incidences of a once normal and wholesome act of sports' instruction. The listing of such new and problematic behaviours rarely sees a reverse swing of the pendulum, where a more liberal understanding turns back the wave of misgiving and doubt, and where the practicalities of sports instruction are once again regarded without suspicion.

Our research findings from talking with respondents from the three sports, and others more widely associated with coaching and PE, indicate beyond argument that the coaching environment and intergenerational coaching in particular has experienced intense scrutiny and pressure in recent decades, with some damaging results. Why those involved in the act of sport instruction have been particularly subjected to this intrusive gaze and concern is unclear, and it is beyond the remit of this chapter to explore the issue at any length, although we have addressed this more fully elsewhere (Piper *et al.* 2013b; see also the concluding chapter of this book). Certainly, there is little evidence to suggest that UK sport itself is any more problematic in terms of child safety than any other organised activity with high participation rates among young people, or that sports coaches pose a particular risk. Indeed, research by Fasting *et al.* (2000) suggests that the increased confidence associated with success in sports involvement may well equip young people with the skills to challenge and resist inappropriate approaches. However, in the UK, the compelling public and regulatory focus on sport, those working within it, and the act of coaching itself, may be explicable in terms of a number of conditions. The case of the Olympic swimming coach and public school teacher, Paul Hickson, shocked both the sporting and education sectors, and the call for sport to clean up its act was swift and comprehensive (Garratt *et al.* 2013). In addition, as suggested by Brackenridge (2001), sport has always been regarded as embodying a moral good and a purity of intent which would help build fortitude and a sense of purpose for all involved. Thus, those who choose to give up their time to help with this manifesto must, by implication, be trusted to look after those in their charge. When notable child abuse cases within sport itself became known, sporting organisations, eager to reclaim lost public confidence, complied with new directives emerging from child protection agencies and other moral entrepreneurs. It was easy to strengthen this dependence and to encourage sport to regard these organisations (which cannot be immune to normal institutional self-interest) not just as the experts, but also as providing the sole source of legitimate guidance and regulation. To clinch the deal, government funding streams for individual sports were often written with the condition that child protection policy was uncritically adopted.

## Bonfire of the insanities[3]

Where does this leave the counternarrative and the room for sport to adapt and reclaim the confidence and freedom that should be at its heart? There is a danger that sport (like other activities which require external funding, often from government) is unlikely to find the ontological security to resist the advance of prescriptive policy. This, of course, is exacerbated in performative contexts where different roles and responsibilities in coaching have no fixed ontological status, apart from the very acts that constitute their 'reality' (Butler 1999: 173). Indeed, those working within a PE setting in school are subject to a number of additional professional obligations that render autonomous judgement and action at the very least problematic, or even career threatening. However, most sports rely on the volunteer and their commitment to give up their spare time because of an inherent sense of collective good and community engagement, and there is a clear danger that the imposition of increased child protection training could impact negatively on those willing to make this commitment. During the research we talked to Pat, an employer of coaches working in both schools and sport centres; she referred to the effect of additional demands made of local volunteers:

> I have it in my local village; I've got examples of where people have got involved for years and help children through the local Chapel and things, to participate in sport in Sunday school and things like that. And then all of a

sudden, it's stopped because . . . they are really scared of being accused of something or putting themselves at risk, and . . . they feel to have a CRB check would be an intrusion of their privacy . . . and then they just stop, rather than going through it because they feel . . . I think . . . I suppose they feel aggrieved really more than anything else, that somebody no longer trusts them, after they've given so many years of their life to the local community really.

This palpable loss of trust between child protection agencies and sport organisations and coaches to do the right thing, between adults and the young people they coach, and between parents and the coaches looking after their child, has a long-term damaging effect, both on sport and also fundamental, human interpersonal relationships. The social contract, inherent in these relationships, which allows sport to claim to be a positive catalyst for social change and betterment, has been attacked, and remains under threat. If it is lost, if we lose touch with each other, because of a belief predicated on a misjudged response to risk, disproportionate fear, mistrust, and self-doubt, then sport will have lost the central element that binds its participants, coaches, and the activity together.

Again, similar sentiments were expressed during the earlier research (Piper *et al.* 2006) by some who were forthright in their responses:

I waited until a staff meeting to gauge other staff members' reactions before filling this in and writing back to you . . . we cannot imagine being able to do our job . . . without 'touching' a child. This is RIDICULOUS! A child has a need to feel safe . . . We are a tactile Preschool. (Manager)

NO I am not remotely interested in any involvement [in the research] UNLESS there is some thought being given to a redressing of the balance towards normality. Bear in mind the lesson of history – eccentric grumpy old ladies were burnt to death as witches . . . Not everyone should be labelled a paedophile. I am happy to help a balanced survey, but if you are 'politically correct' I'm not willing to help. (Headmaster, preparatory school)

Those who believe in the benefits of sport and coaching may hope that coaches and PE teachers become equally blunt and vociferous in response to their current situation.

## Notes

1 Without the funding from the ESRC (RES-000-22-4156), this project would not have been possible, and we gratefully acknowledge our appreciation of the award.
2 We are very grateful to the members of the steering panel, and particularly to the many respondents who contributed their opinions, experiences, and time – especially those who felt at some risk for contradicting the 'party line' defined by their governing body and/or employer.
3 This phrase is borrowed from Piper and Stronach (2008), where it described a different setting, but is just as relevant here.

# References

Bauman, Z. (1991) *Modernity and ambivalence*, Cambridge, UK: Polity Press.

Beck, U. (1992) *Risk society: Towards a new modernity*, London: Sage.

Brackenridge, C. H. (2001) *Spoilsports: Understanding and preventing sexual exploitation in sport*, London: Routledge.

Britzman, D. (2000) 'The question of belief': Writing poststructural ethnography, in: E. A. St Pierre and W. Pillow (eds) *Culture and text: Discourse and methodology in social research and cultural studies*, (pp. 27–40). Lanham, MD: Rowman & Littlefield.

Butler, J. (1999) *Gender trouble: Feminism and the subversion of identity*, London: Routledge.

Butler, J. (1997) *The psychic life of power*, Stanford, CA: Stanford University Press.

The Children Act (1989) London: HMSO/DfES. www.legislation.gov.uk/ukpga/1989/41/contents

*Daily Telegraph* (2012) 'Climate of fear surrounds children's sports coaches' (22 July 2012) www.telegraph.co.uk/news/uknews/9417560/Climate-of-fear-surrounds-childrens-sports-coaches.html (accessed 1.3.13).

Fasting, M., Brackenridge, C. H. and Sundgot Borgen, J. (2000) *Sexual harassment in and outside sport*, Oslo: Norwegian Olympic Committee.

The Football Association (2013) *The FA Strategic Plan 2011–2015* www.thefa.com/about-football-association/strategy (accessed 22.01.14).

Foucault, M. (1991) Governmentality, in: G. Burchell, C. Gordon and P. Miller (eds) *The Foucault effect: Studies in governmentality*, Hemel Hempstead: Harvester Wheatsheaf, 87–104.

Foucault, M. (1988) *Technologies of the self: A seminar with Michel Foucault,* L. H. Martin, H. Gutman and P. H. Hutton (eds), Amherst, : University of Massachusetts Press.

Foucault. M. (1982) How is power exercised? in: H. L. Dreyfus and P. Rabinow (eds) *Michel Foucault: Beyond structuralism and hermeneutics*, Brighton: Harvester Press, 216–226.

Foucault, M. (1980) Truth and power, in: C. Gordon (ed), *Power/Knowledge: Selected interviews and other writings 1972–1977*, London: Tavistock, 109–133.

Foucault, M. (1977) *Discipline and punish: The birth of the prison*, London: Penguin.

Garratt, D., Taylor, B. and Piper, H. (2013) 'Safeguarding' sports' coaching: Foucault, genealogy and critique, *Sport, Education and Society*, 18(5)615–629.

Giddens, A. (1999) Risk and responsibility, *Modern Law Review,* 62(1)1–10.

Goode, S. (2010) *Understanding and addressing adult sexual attraction to children: A study of paedophiles in contemporary society*, London: Routledge.

Hier, S. P. (ed) (2011) *Moral panic and the politics of anxiety,* London: Routledge.

Jayyusi, L. (1984) *Categorisation and the moral order*, London: Routledge.

Lather, P. (2007) Postmodernism, post-structuralism and post (critical) ethnography: Of ruins, aporias and angels, in: P. Atkinson, A. Coffey, S. Delamont, J. Loftland and L. Loftland (eds) *Handbook of Ethnography*, (pp. 477–493). London: Sage.

MacLure, M., Jones, L. and Holmes, R. (2012) Becoming a problem: Behaviour and reputation in the early years classroom, *British Educational Research Journal*, 38(3)447–471.

Nancy, J-L. (1991) The inoperative community (Vol. 76) P. Connor (ed), trans. P. Connor, L. Garbus, M. Holland and S. Sawhney, Minneapolis: University of Minnesota Press.

Piper, H., Garratt, D. and Taylor, B. (2013a) Hands off! The practice and politics of touch in physical education and sports coaching, *Sport, Education and Society*, 18(5) 575–582.

Piper, H., Garratt, D. and Taylor, B. (2013b) Child abuse, child protection, and defensive 'touch' in PE teaching and sports coaching, *Sport, Education and Society*, 18(5)583–598.

Piper, H. Garratt, D. and Taylor, B. (2011a) Hands-off sports' coaching: The politics of touch (ESRC funded project RES-000–22–4156). www.esrc.ac.uk/my-esrc/grants/RES-000-22-4156/outputs/Read/804a88f6-0da3-480a-9ef3-24a0c89da5bb

Piper, H. MacLure, M. and Stronach, I. (2006) *Touchlines: The problematics of touching between children and professionals* (ESRC funded project RES-000–22–0815). www.esrc.ac.uk/my-esrc/grants/RES-000-22-0815/outputs/Read/44bc0bba-8fad-416e-8004-d6cba6f8579b

Piper, H. and Shonach, I. (2008) *Don't touch! The educational story of a panic*. London: Routledge.

Piper, H., Taylor, B. and Garratt, D. (2011b) Sports coaching in risk society: No touch! No trust! *Sport, Education and Society*, 17(3)331–345.

Rabinow, P. (1984) *The Foucault reader: An introduction to Foucault's thought*, London: Penguin.

Stake, R. E. (1995) *The art of case study research*, Thousand Oaks: Sage.

Stake, R. E. (1978) The case study method in social inquiry, *Educational Researcher*, 7(2)5–8.

Taylor, B. and Garratt, D. (2010) The professionalisation of sports coaching: Relations of power, resistance and compliance, *Sport, Education and Society*, 15(1)121–139.

Taylor, W. and Garratt, D. (2008) *The professionalisation of sports coaching in the UK: Issues and conceptualisation*, www.sportscoachuk.org/resource/professionalisation-sports-coaching-uk-issues-and-conceptualisation (accessed 21.01.14).

# 3 Training 'safe' bodies in an era of child panic in the United States

## New technologies for disciplining the self

*Richard T. Johnson*

## Introduction

Drawing on a range of personal coaching and caring experiences and risk analysis frameworks, this chapter offers a critical reflection on related policy and practices in the United States (US), focusing particularly on the national American Youth Soccer Organization (AYSO). It develops a critique of the taken for granted imperative to protect children from all and any risks, and of how in the sport context that is conflated with the idea of protecting adult coaches from real and potential risks. It addresses the complexities of ongoing anxiety in the US about the relationships between children and adults in popular coaching settings, and the new categories of risk vulnerability that these discourses have generated.

As a professional teacher educator, the majority of my professional practice has involved working in and across diverse field experiences with other educators. Just as the family became an 'instrument, a point of application, in the monitoring of a larger group (the population)' (Baker, 1998, p. 131), families of professionals (i.e., coaches, teachers, social workers, principals) also expertly manage individuals. For example, last semester in our weekly Student Teaching Seminar one of my students, Kahea, discussed a recent incident from her field-based school practicum experience: as she walked across the playground during recess a fourth grade girl she had taught in the previous semester ran up to her and gave her a big hug, and she had warmly reciprocated this show of affection. Shortly after the child left, Kahea was taken aside by the vice principal (VP) who had informed her that she 'should never hug children at this school'. The VP then took the child aside and instructed her not to touch adults in the way that she just had.

In my own site-supervisor practicum experiences, and coaching experiences with children and adults, and from much of my previous research, I've witnessed that a seemingly simple way around many of the 'no touch' issues in the classroom or the coaching domain is through risk management (Johnson, 2013). Recently one undergraduate pre-service teacher education student in my early childhood education course noted that he will closely follow relevant 'tips' during classroom interactions with students. As a teacher, he will:

1   Never be alone with a student, male or female, without another teacher or other students around.
2   Never initiate touching a student in any manner unless they indicate in an overt manner that they don't mind. For example, a student who initiates touching you on the shoulder or arm, or offers a hug, is indicating that he/she does not mind those displays of affection or attention. Of course, certain touching is never appropriate . . . you should never touch 'areas where a bathing suit covers you'.
3   Never cover up the window on the classroom door. It prohibits administrators and other teachers from looking in and, unless you have something to hide, it's not necessary.
4   Keep the classroom door open as much as possible.
5   Send the child to the nurse if he/she has a problem (such as soiling his or her pants, etc.). If there are other problems in clothing sensitive areas (e.g., belt buckle and pants zipper), elicit the help of fellow teacher, preferably one of the opposite sex, regardless of the presence of other children.
6   Always hug from the side – avoid frontal hugs whenever possible.
7   For legal purposes, keep a critical incident file for every student.

The primacy of risk management in the US came to light for me years ago when listening to the National Public Radio daily *Morning Edition* newscast, which included an item titled 'Day Care Center Goes to Extremes to Protect Reputation,' reporting a US day-care center that implemented a no touch policy which basically said (according to the director):

> It's against our policy to pick up the kids. It's against our policy to hold them on your lap. The 'no-touch' policy is more to protect the center than the children. In the business of day care, reputation is everything, and reputation is fragile. It would be too easy, for one innocent hug or playful piggyback ride to be misinterpreted. The picking-up thing, I don't allow, because that's one of those issues where you have, you know, the direct physical contact, body to body, that could be misconstrued, so I stop it there.
>
> (National Public Radio – Morning Edition, 1994)

Various issues raised in accounts from the classroom, arising from such an approach, are also prevalent in today's youth sport coaching contexts (Johnson, 2013; Piper 2011; Piper *et al.* 2013; Piper & Stronach, 2008). I've been actively coaching my own three children and many others in our small community in Hawaii for close to twenty years, in a sport I still play: soccer. In a soccer organization where I currently coach 18-year-old boys, I'm requested to follow these guidelines to protect myself from false accusations:

- Avoid being alone with a child
- Stay within sight of others
- Respect privacy

- Hug from the side
- Avoid sexual jokes, comments or gestures
- Do not use corporal punishment, and
- Set and respect boundaries

Before I can coach for each soccer season, I'm also required to take an online risk management course, and must successfully pass a test that demonstrates my ability to adhere to and abide by the *Touching and Supervision Guidelines* promulgated by the AYSO (2001 1a). Their policies inform me that touch must:

- Be in response to child's, not adult's needs
- Be done with child's permission
- Respect resistance
- Never include breast, buttocks, or groin
- Be in open, not in private
- Be brief in duration
- Change with age and development

Broader AYSO (2011b) policies detail the role of volunteer coaches like myself, who:

> are the lifeblood of AYSO. To ensure the safety of both children and volunteers, each volunteer is required to take a short in-person or online training session called Safe Haven®. It focuses on safety and appropriate behavior with children . . . first aid and other on-field issues. Agreeing to a background check is also required . . . Every volunteer with an application . . . is subject to a national sex offender registry check . . . coaches are put through a 'targeted' background check where all criminal history is reviewed.

Clearly, this particular form of 'lifeblood' is considered to warrant suspicion, carrying significant risk and properly subject to frequent checks for purity, to avoid system damage.

## Risk awareness: Analysis and reflection

The everyday discourses of risk dominate our lives and the prevalence of risk in the personal and public spheres within which we operate is staggering (Frankenberg, 1992). Each day when I begin my sacred ritual of reading the local paper over a bowl of breakfast cereal, risk asserts its all-encompassing presence. The old press-room adage 'if it bleeds it leads' is certainly part of this media hype, as I identified on a particular day, June 12, 2007. The front cover page of our major state newspaper, *The Honolulu Advertiser*, had six out of six headlines focused on risk in one form or another and with various degrees of detail (i.e., 'bleeding'). The lead headline, with the largest font, read 'State Fights Damage to Reserve', followed just below by a smaller subheading, 'Community Keeps

Watch on Crime'. Another headline spinning directly off that read, 'Community Patrols Team up with Police to Lower Oahu's Crime Rate', while another read, 'Deadbeat Parents Targeted in Hawai'i'. Lastly, and positioned lowest, was 'Early Sun Exposure, Not Just Burns, A Risk'. In the next section, risk reared its head again. The mid-page article entitled 'Keeping Kids Safe Online' informed readers in the subhead that 'Sex predators remain "big problem," despite efforts to catch them', and advised parents how they might potentially safeguard the experiences of their child(ren) in a popular medium that more and more dominates lives in the US and beyond (*The Honolulu Advertiser*, 2007).

The news on June 12, 2007 was not unlike much of the news most days in this particular newspaper and, I'm assuming, most like it around the US and globally. As an example on the same day, when my online search moved some 2,500 miles east I found the *Los Angeles Times* headlines were 'Close and Deadly Contact: The Killing of an Iraqi Teen Offers a Rare Look at How U.S. Military Action in an Urban Setting can be Fatal to Civilians', and 'Agent in TB Case Retires' (*Los Angeles Times*, 2007). In *The New York Times*, 2,500 miles further east, stories of risk were again readily encountered: 'Effort to Advise On Risky Loans Runs Into Snag', 'U.S. Warns Iraq That Progress Is Needed Soon', and 'As Breeders Test DNA, Dogs Become Guinea Pigs' (*The New York Times*, 2007).

Leaping ahead a few months to September 9, 2007 and focusing on a more specific professional media outlet, *The Chronicle of Higher Education* was quite similar. On this particular day all the lead stories on page one could readily be interpreted through the lenses of risk, comprising: 'The First Close Look at Colleges' Digital Pirates', 'Virginia Tech was Slow to Respond to Gunman, Panel Finds', and 'Study-Abroad Investigation Raises Alarms' (*The Chronicle of Higher Education*, 2007). In our local Oahu newspaper a few days later, a film advertisement informed parents that, 'Maybe *Spider-Man 3* is too violent for your kids. Perhaps the visuals of *Pirates of the Caribbean* are a bit too frightening . . . regardless, if you have children there are a myriad of reasons to skip the Hollywood machine'. The advertisement goes on to boast about how the Kids First! Film Festival, presented by the Coalition for Quality Children's Media, would 'ensure wholesome fun showing a variety of age-appropriate film [as] every show is guaranteed to be free of gratuitous violence, race, gender or religious bias, and free from condescension' (*Honolulu Weekly*, 2007).

Local or global, national or transnational, risk constantly and consistently prevails as an instrumental part of our existence(s). When I leave my house and venture out into the world I take further risks. The once mundane acts of buying groceries, purchasing toys for my kids and their friends' birthday parties, buying prescription drugs or vitamins all impact my very being in *risky* ways, so the professional literature reports to me and the wider community. This has very practical and attention-grabbing effects. Thus in a related current US example, the elementary, secondary, or physical education teacher, under the 'No Child Left Behind' (NCLB) government legislation, must ensure that each pupil makes adequate yearly progress (AYP), based on raised test scores from the beginning of the year to mid- and end-point dates. The terms and implementation of NCLB places teachers at significant new risks, including lowered pay and the possibility of job loss if they don't raise student scores.

When I reflect deeply on my personal experiences as a soccer coach, I readily visualize the implications of these popularized risk issues, and this assists in understanding my reconfigured identity as a caregiver and sports coach in the contemporary situation. Reflection on my personal interactions with children speaks to me about how my body (Turner, 1992) truly does not fit in with contemporary coaching and caregiving as those fields have been and are being redefined (Johnson, 2010). My body, which had strong emotional, social, and physical connections with young children, easily recalled from memories, pictures, and images of me and the children I once cared for and coached, has been (mis)appropriated and weakened by others, by myself, and by popular discourses in the media, in sports management, and through professional development practices in education (Jones, 2001). This (mis)appropriation has influenced my subjectivity so much that it is no longer recognizable by me and others (Johnson, 2011).

## Risk management, the child panic, and identity

To develop this discussion I now address the effects of 'child abuse' anxieties and risk management, their impact on the training of masculine pleasures, the surveillance practices in different coaching contexts, and how once-'normal' interactions with and among children have been reread and recategorised in pathological terms. These trends are related to the manner in which child abuse has been discovered or invented since the 1960s, creating a situation in which the fear of child abuse ('child panic') is now a dominant mechanism in shaping the work and training of sports coaches, counsellors, youth workers, psychologists, and teachers, and also in understanding children's daily interactions with adults and peers. The nature of this disciplinary shaping is exemplified and interrogated through personalized reflection on the impact on my identity as a coach and caregiver.

My own experiences suggest that, instead of promoting any deep critical analyses of no touch and the infusions of the abuse policies and professional procedures, in fact we are more apt to run away from the issue, purposely plead ignorance, and refuse to face it. We can only face it if we can mask it within a protective stance that purports to guard us and make both us (adults) and the children safe. This protective stance we are all part of is embedded in a discourse named and institutionalized as *risk* management (Douglas, 1966; Taylor-Gooby, 2000; Lupton, 1999; Walsh, 1998). Through a critique of this redefinition, whereby the subjectivity, body, and person of both the coach and the child have become abject, a forward-looking estimate of alternative ways of being and serving can be developed. A brief review of exemplar web-based Risk Management education opportunities assists in introducing this critique.

A course titled *RiskAware® for Managed Care* has the goal of assisting physicians in handling liabilities associated with managed care. As advertised, when this course is completed participants will:

1 Distinguish characteristics of five types of managed care organizations.
2 Recognize how the doctor-patient relationship is formed and terminated in managed care.
3 Be able to reconcile sources of interpersonal conflict in managed care settings.
4 Know how to handle potential liabilities associated with cost containment.
5 Be able to apply defensible charting techniques to their own documentation practices.
6 Understand how their liability is determined when they participate in managed care. (MedRisk®, 2013)

A similar company, A&E Groups, offers to save organisations billions of dollars each year in lost revenue, inventory, and personnel. The company slogan claims they will 'Shield your employees, shield your company'; serious problems can drain profits, drive away productive employees, 'and expose your company or educational institution to serious legal trouble and costly civil suits'. As protection against these perils, it provides interactive training services and preventative maintenance programs to increase workplace and school safety, enhance staff morale, reduce loss, and improve staff retention:

1 A comprehensive workplace protection program for business to teach employees and management how to work together to shield your company from problems such as theft, violence, or sexual harassment.
2 A school violence prevention program trains your students, parents, and teachers to recognize and react to the early warning signs of alienation, harassment, and threatening behaviors that can lead school violence.
3 A sexual harassment prevention program, which A&E Groups notes is a specialization area for their company as they are ' developing comprehensive sexual harassment prevention programs for companies and organizations throughout the United States', programs meant to 'Protect your students, protect your school' (A&E Groups, 2013).

Critiquing risk management and culture, Suaalii (1999) personalized her critical research by interrogating the 'insidious nature of risk and risk management' and the ways that this discourse is redistributing risk, knowingly shifting it from the state to the self through various forms of governmentality. Noting the above examples, it is not difficult to anticipate here how this redistribution of risk works, especially when a coach or teacher like me is forced to sit through mandatory in-service sessions and engage at an 'appropriate' level with easy-to-use professional development models that claim to help in managing risks. Suaalii's research assists in further understanding how this formal redistribution of risk serves to reposition the individual (i.e., the coach, the teacher, or the social worker) with new surveillance skills so she/he is now afforded refined techniques of 'self- and social observation and judgment made possible through modern measurements – allow[ing] self-examination and self-limitation to seem normal' (Wagener, 1998, p. 149). If, as a teacher or sports coach I am taught to handle liabilities, apply defensible charting techniques, minimize risk through identification and analysis, and consider the volatile world and so on, how can I not be engaged in and further embody these various forms of governmentality? As a researcher and practitioner interested in this topic, I've now used 'risk management' as an issue of my very first lecture to pre-service teachers as I alert them about what to expect, and beg them to fight it, or maybe, more smartly, get out of the overly surveillance-influenced education field, now.

This work assists me in critiquing various aspects of my normalized identity in relation to risk-based discourse. Lupton (1999) illustrates that:

> Through normalization, individuals may be compared to others, their attributes assessed according to whether they fall within the norm or outside it. If found to fall outside the norm, people are routinely encouraged (or sometimes coerced) to engage in practices that bring them closer to the norm. Risk is a pivotal discourse in strategies of normalization, used to gloss the potential for deviations from the norm. To be designated 'at high risk' compared with others is to be singled out as requiring expert advice, surveillance and self-regulation.
>
> (p. 61)

Thus our identities as coaches are impacted by definitions of acceptable risk. For instance, when people like Jerry Sandusky, the former American football coach at Penn State University and convicted serial child molester (Carbone, 2011), are highlighted repeatedly in the media for the abusive, criminal behaviour they incorporated into their daily practices, these actions and how they are critiqued are added into acceptable risk analyses for all of us who coach children and other athletes. Through the enactment of these popularized risk management techniques we implement 'structured processes to minimize potential liability, avoid harm to clients, stabilize insurance costs, and protect [our employing] agency from ruinous financial losses' (Montgomery, 1993, p. 1). The way that these processes are implemented and managed has significant impact on our actions as coaches and caregivers of children, and those we interact with. We need to understand and critically engage and continuously question how these different mandates relate to our ways of being with those who we coach or care for (Minor & Minor, 1991).

Regimes of risk management and social control like no touch diminish the quality of the lives of our children, and the adults who work with and care for them (Del Prete, 1997), yet sports coaches, like social workers, child protection specialists, teachers, administrators, academics, and parents, adults who provide various services for children, have too often sat back and allowed things to be done and said to and about us which actually require contestation (Piper, 2011). Collectively, we have been insufficiently ready to intellectualise and theorise the critical underlying issues discussed in this book and elsewhere (McWilliam, 1999). We have in effect collaborated in a multifaceted disciplinary process, with profound implications.

## The image of the child and disciplining the self

In considering the body in relation to coaching practice and related experience, I initially posit the child's physiological entity, and the notion of needs directly arises. What follows is a retreat to normative issues of nurturance (care for the body), rescue (saving children from child abuse and neglect), and normalization (education). For example, the so-called good preschool teacher provides varied physical assistance involving touch and the body: diaper changing; holding a child back from running out to a departing parent at the start of a difficult morning separation and then physically comforting them; carrying an infant to a rocking chair; or stroking a child's back while rocking them during a soothing transition time, or in assisting them in falling asleep during rest time.

As a caregiver who once cared for infants I recall that such interactions began first thing in the morning and continued throughout the day. In related fashion the 'good coach' provides similar physical assistance, as attested by my personal experiences as a child athlete mentored by different coaches: guiding a child to a spot on the pitch or field at the start of a competition; comforting them after missing a potentially match-winning penalty kick; holding a child's back and neck as they learn to float in the swimming pool while learning to swim; holding a child's hands while teaching them to hold a baseball bat as they first learn that technique; and embracing a child in a tight hug to celebrate their accomplishments in scoring a goal, hitting a baseball to win a game, or paddling a kayak to victory. I think of the physiological body first because of my real-life interactions with children and because of my conservative educational upbringing, which only looked at normative considerations and didn't push me to look beyond age-old, developmental narratives (Soto & Swadener, 2002).

Problematizing no touch in various coaching and caregiving contexts has helped me look beyond just the physiological body, the material body, the body as known, and to think more in broader terms of the discursive body. Thus I think of the body as a system of representation (Turner, 1992), within which comes alternative perceptions located in different theoretical and practical experiences. Embedded in this critical context are different depictions and different notions of bodies, as I now allow for and perceive the 'body as endlessly reconstructed and reinvented' (James *et al.* 1998, p. 150). Research in recent decades has helped increase our understandings of the 'corporeal philosophy and cultural studies of the body' (Zita, 1998, p. 1). Bodies aren't simply known, material entities that both need or provide a warm caress, a soft pat, a deliberate disciplinary spanking, or a tight, comforting hug. They are 'normative and cultural formations involving articulation, domination, resistance, and violence' (Zita, 1998, p. 1). Ussher's (1997) work illustrates that we 'need to examine both bodily processes and practices . . . constructed in the realm of the symbolic. We cannot separate the two' (p. 7). This remains the case even though traditional, normative notions of the 'pure and innocent' child's body prevail and dominate our consciousness about the nature of children and childhood.

Because our understandings and interpretations of children and childhood are dominated by rather traditional, nostalgic notions of that period in our own lives, there is a tendency for us to treat children as ever-innocent, protection-starved individuals, and to treat ourselves as benevolent, overprotective, redemptive humanitarians, always at the ready to provide needed child interventions (Robertson, 1997). Bennett's (1979) account of childhood is helpful here:

> Childhood is reminiscence and imagination . . . a child represents complete freedom to think as one pleases, to live in a world where things can and do happen for no reason at all, where good and bad, right and wrong, up and down just don't exist. Who wouldn't prefer such a place.
>
> (p. 24)

This romantic premise, through which we acknowledge children as marginalized beings and childhood as a marginalized period, in fact facilitates and supports extreme responses to risk and child protection. It assists our propensity to protect children, and thus to accept willingly the coaching stories and continued moral panic(s) generated by and accompanying extreme phenomena like the Sandusky case. As vigilant protectors, as saviors, we rush to make preconceived judgments about the sanctity of children and childhood with seemingly little concern for how that interaction impacts children's lives (Kitzinger, 1997; Sapon-Shevin, 2009). Our protective vigilance leads us, as 'child savers' to then always intervene in the lives of children. As a result, when the media interrupts our daily lives with lurid tales of sexual abuse in sports coaching contexts, in child care centers, or bullying children rampaging through classrooms, we immediately seek to counter these stories and to avoid their repetition.

With seemingly little intellectual rigor we address only the immediate problem, by rapidly creating a moral panic and then quickly eradicating it – always setting ourselves up as the vigilant, concerned adults aiming to keep the children forever innocent, therefore always in need of intervention (Brackenridge, 2010). Thus, on the relatively few occasions when child abuse is witnessed in a sports coaching context, the rapid spread of the inevitable moral panic warrants that it must be happening in all coaching contexts (Clapton *et al.* 2013). The National Council of Youth Sports (2013 np) exemplifies this: 'Although the number of athletes who are abused or exploited by coaches has never been quantified, the research on sexual abuse in general is massive and sobering'. Hence the imperative arises to implement measures to control it at all costs, for instance by implementing local soccer league policies that disallow male coaches from working with female players, telling all coaches they must have at least one colleague present at all times, and installing risk-certification practices for all coaches before each season. These control measures act to bring purification back to the coaches/caregivers, the scapegoats, so that they are effectively cleared of 'contamination and reinstated as clean in their own eyes' (Douglas, 1995, p. 14). Measures like this make us all feel good, as we then know we've acted responsibly, we've done our duty to intervene in the lives of the innocent children, and we're protecting them (as always) and their natural state (and ultimately the nation and the state), whether or not they really need our services (Chadwick, 1994; Shamgar-Handelman, 1994).

We've gone to great lengths to emphasise that children are innocent, vulnerable, and in constant need of saving, so much so that childhood is our most 'intensively governed sector of personal existence' (Rose, 1990, p. 121).

We enhance our need to intervene and to protect children by responding to reports from the front lines, which typically portray children as continually in need of protection. When research articles begin with language like, 'Young children today face a world that is more dangerous than at any time in history' (Hollander, 1992), we immediately know our redemptive place, and assume it without question. We don't question the fact that child abuse has been practiced all around the world for centuries. As Breiner (1990) notes, 'We have been killing, maiming, and abusing our children for as long as our history has been recorded' (p. 1). Similarly, Wilczynski's work (1997) notes that this systematic practice of child killing has been conducted for 'religious sacrifice, the culling of sick or deformed infants, family planning, shame of illegitimacy, commerce (in the form of "baby farming") anger and mental disturbance' (p. 5). Seeking to control childhood we only allow certain reports to surface at certain times – those times when the masses are in need of subtle reminders that our innocent children are not safe in the dark, cruel world of childhood (Leberg, 1997).

As I experienced at the start of my career in the early 1980s, representatives of many groups that serve children in various capacities, including sports coaches, have allowed their collective identities to be created, to be marked, by moral panic (Cree *et al.* 2013). The rapidly growing popularity of no touch policies, such as 'no hugging children on the soccer field', teaches coaches how to appropriately touch/not touch children in their care, demonstrating the pervasiveness and scope of this phenomenon.

## Responding to the child panic in coaching and care settings

As a collective field of specialists (i.e., sports coaches, teachers, social workers, community workers, etc.) who work with children and youth, we must balance the likelihood of child abuse in our respective environments with the costs to our profession of our overzealously preventative orientation. As committed sports coaches we should individually and collectively question what is gained and what is lost through our continued support of no touch policy in coaching practice. Children are becoming more distrustful of adults, especially coaches and teachers; we continue to betray young children (and what we know about good adult-child practices) as we submit them to a variety of inappropriate sexual abuse curricula. Caregivers are leaving the child care profession *en masse*; potentially talented male caregivers are looking elsewhere for employment opportunities; school directors are likely to spend more time and energy focused on liability and risk issues than on effective teacher professional development; and misinformed legislators funnel millions of dollars into prevention programs that could otherwise be spent on educating young people more effectively (Johnson, 2001). Sports coaching is subject to equivalent pressures, procedures, and damaging responses.

Our practical and theoretical work must be much more critically engaged and deliberate in further understanding no touch and in seeking to present alternative ways of thinking about the care and coaching of young people in sport. Instead of simply dismissing no touch as only a moral panic, I can instead interrogate why no touch influenced me, as well as other sports coaches, teachers, and other groups in particular ways at particular times. This interrogation might then give rise to further questions and lead us to critique, as Stephens (1995) notes,

> . . . other widespread public resonances as serious moral discourses on our time, and we might work towards developing the theoretical and methodological frameworks that would allow us to interpret the different kinds of truths embedded within contemporary discourses on threatened children.
>
> (p. 13)

Our critical interrogations should prompt us to think more about how no touch affects the way children connect to one another, to caregivers and coaches and teachers, to familial cultural traditions, to local places, and also to electronically mediated worlds which parents know little about (Stephens, 1995).

In our drive to implement these policies, we have in essence created an alibi for the truth, while we continue allowing trends like no touch to define who we are and govern how we operate (Foucault, 1977). Melton and Flood's (1994) research illustrates that 'the field of child protection is notable more for what is not known' (p. 3). We revise ways of being with children and adults, and we change institutional policies (from coach-athlete and classroom teacher-child interactions, to the social worker interview) on the basis of untruths. In fact, the overwhelming majority of research reveals that child sexual abuse is most likely to occur outside our practical spaces (i.e., soccer fields, teaching spaces), and away from our staff. The relatively rare occurrence of sexual abuse in coaching settings and schools (in the United States reported to occur in as few as 1 per cent of all reported child sexual abuse cases in all schools, not just early education settings, but preschool through secondary schooling), should not be allowed to define what we can and cannot do with the young people and children we serve as coaches, teachers, and caregivers (Contratto, 1986; Tomlinson & Yorganci, 1997).

Recent broader studies on child sexual abuse, not just in sports settings, suggest differing rates (Kirby *et al.* 2000). In the U.S. the Darkness to Light association noted that an 'overall prevalence rate of 7.5% to 11.7%, with the prevalence rate for girls at 10.7% to 17.4%, and the rate for boys at 3.8% to 4.6%' (2013). The Centers for Disease Control and Prevention noted that 1 in 4 women and 1 in 6 men were sexually abused before the age of 18 (2006). In recent testimony to Congress, Arias noted that the

> [t]rue number of children who are victims of child maltreatment in the United States is unknown, but in 2006 the Administration on Children & Families (ACF) reported 905,000 cases of confirmed or substantiated cases of nonfatal child maltreatment each year in the U.S. Child maltreatment includes

physical, sexual, and emotional abuse and neglect, and is believed to be underreported.

(Arias, 2008)

A 2012 article in *The New York Times* revealed a declining sexual abuse rate: 'Overall cases of child sexual abuse fell more than 60 percent from 1992 to 2010 . . . substantiated cases of sexual abuse dropped from 23 per 10,000 children under 18 to 8.6 per 10,000, a 62 percent decrease' (Goode, 2012). As these various statistics illustrate, there is disparity in categorisation and resulting outcomes in relation to prevalence of child abuse in the US, as is the case, no doubt, elsewhere. Leahy's work on sexual abuse in sport noted that 'depending on the definitions and methodologies used, the prevalence rates suggested by research reports range from 2 percent to 22 percent' (2011).

Moral panics are characterised by a language of epidemics to equate social ills with a medical model of causation, and a moral vocabulary of motive (Blaikie, 1993). The power of this medicalised discourse, so widely deployed in accounts of risk and child abuse, 'lends itself to interventionist remedies focused on the individual and is a powerful tool for policy' (Howitt, 1993, p. 22). It is so powerful that it can have dramatic and damaging consequences, as in the Cleveland case in England when paediatricians gathered more scientifically reliable data by subjecting children to reflex anal dilatation, to substantiate the prevalence of child sexual abuse (Collins, Kendall, & Michael, 1998).

As sports coaches or carers, our passive response to such powerful moral panics leads to increasing regimes of control by those outside our field (Foucault, 1977; Johnson, 2001; Stainton Rogers & Stainton Rogers, 1992; Watney, 1987). Its power is such that it has been able to (un)teach all that we know, or should know, about the importance of touch (Carlson & Nelson, 2006; Field, 1998; Hernandez-Reif *et al.* 2006). This high visibility and power assists in our dynamic construction of ignorance around no touch, characterised by Felman (1997) as 'a kind of forgetting-of forgetfulness: while learning is obviously, among other things, remembering and memorizing, ignorance is linked to what is not remembered, what will not be memorized' (p. 25). If I, a single coach, and we, as a collective mass of sports coaches, caregivers, case workers, and parents continue to passively ignore and plead ignorance, then together we knowingly allow the moral panic to gain momentum, run the debate, and continue to change our nurturing and caring subjectivities while also diminishing our technical effectiveness (Clapton *et al.* 2013).

## Conclusion: Where will this end?

My ongoing search for stories of touch and no touch makes me unsurprised at how often they appear and reappear. For example, while having a coffee some years ago I briefly glimpsed the words 'without touching her' on the cover of one of the many magazines available in the shop. Words like 'touch' readily catch my now well-trained eye; surveillance does work! I glanced through the article, and although this particular magazine story was basically a 'how to' story about seducing your adult partner, part of it actually relates to my own interests in 'no touch,' though not in seductive ways. Part of the second paragraph reads:

> Touch yourself in a place that she would want to be touched, says clinical psychologist Judy Kuriansky, Ph.D. 'You're suggesting you want to touch her. Soon you'll find her touching herself in those places, and the synchronicity creates a type of mirror, a subconscious connection'.
>
> (*Details*, 1999, p. 114)

I share this material and experience partly tongue-in-cheek (humour has helped me deal with the amazing and overwhelmingly ludicrous nature of no touch) and partly because it is profoundly related to the way(s) no touch policies are progressing. When I try to imagine the coaching scene(s) of the future, a setting which seems likely to have even less touch in it than today, I can envision where the expert suggestions in this magazine article would be helpful to me, as the kids could see me hugging myself (like I want to hug them, to console), tousling my hair, stroking my shoulder (like I want to rub their shoulder to acknowledge their presence), or patting myself on the back. According to this expert's professional advice, this mimicry might in fact be creating a 'subconscious connection', to replace what no touch policies currently disallow. If this proffered insight is correct, coaching could perhaps become easier!

When I retrospectively consider my individual and collective experiences as a sports coach and caregiver, I'm amazed at how quickly we've become 'disciplined . . . "socialized" into the [no touch] culture, such that one is both enabled and also, in a quite specific sense, "made safe"' (Green, 1998, p. 184). I remember about six years ago attending a soccer coaching clinic where we were all introduced to the newly appointed *risk manager* at the local soccer league branch of the AYSO. In my mind I positioned this person with the role of informing sports coaches like myself and colleagues what we can and can't do with the children we serve as volunteers. The AYSO website (2011b) confirms that my initial conjecturing was not far off the mark, as their Safe Haven Certification process requires that coaches modify their actions (e.g. making sure two adults are always present and never being alone with a child).

These newly implemented policies justified my skepticism over the introduction of the 'child advocate' in relationship to 'safe havens' for children. In further discussions at the coaches meeting, when I pushed the group slightly, I learned the far-reaching extent of the policy, which would soon disallow adult males from coaching *their own* female children without the additional presence of a female assistant coach. Thus the implicit message is that daughters have cause to fear their father; again, all in the name of protection.

In this era of no touch I'm shocked with what body(s) I am left with, for now (Holliday & Hassard, 2001). My maleness, my desire to coach and nurture children and adolescents, now provide and mark me with a dangerous, normalized body. Although I don't want to believe this to be true, powerful discourses clearly say it is so! What now matters is what I, what we, do with those 'other' discourses that can lead us, in some emancipatory fashion, out of the disciplinary regime within which we find ourselves un-intellectually trapped (Cohen & Weiss, 2003). Our critical interrogation of the 'techniques by which [our] lives, thoughts, and desires . . . have become microscopically examined and strategically regulated' (Wagener, 1998, p. 150), together with our ongoing critical engagement with these issues, can assist us in moving out of the dark, damaging, deeply entrenched place in which we now find ourselves.

## References

A&E Groups (2013) Retrieved from http://aegroups.com/ May 22, 2013.

American Youth Soccer Association (AYSO) (2011a) CA: Torrance. Retrieved from www. soccer.org/home.aspx May 22, 2013.

American Youth Soccer Association (AYSO) (2011b) CA: Torrance. Retrieved from http:// soccer.org/why_join_ayso/safe_haven.aspx May 22, 2013.

Arias, I. (2008) CDC Congressional Testimony: United States Senate Committee on Health, Education, Labor, & Pensions. Retrieved from www.cdc.gov/washington/testi mony/2008/t20080501.htm May 22, 2013.

Baker, B. (1998) 'Childhood' in the emergence and spread of U.S. public schools. In T. Popkewitz & M. Brennan (eds.), *Foucault's challenge: Discourse, knowledge, and power in education* (pp. 117–143). New York: Teachers College Press.

Bennett, P. (1979) *The illustrated child.* New York: G. P. Putnam Sons.

Blaikie, N. W. (1993) *Approaches to social inquiry.* Boston, MA: Polity Press.

Brackenridge, C. (2010) Myths and evidence-learning from our journey. Keynote address at *How Safe is Your Sport* conference. Retrieved from www.olympic.org/Documents/ THE%20IOC/Myths%20about%20abuse%20in%20sport%20(16%203%2010).pdf May 22, 2013.

Breiner, S. J. (1990) *Slaughter of the innocents: Child abuse through the ages and today.* London: Plenum Press.

Carbone, N. (2011, November) 'I shouldn't have showered with those kids': Sandusky admits 'horseplay' but maintains innocence. *Time Magazine.* Retrieved from http://news feed.time.com/2011/11/15/i-shouldnt-have-showered-with-those-kids-sandusky-admits-horseplay-but-maintains-innocence/#ixzz2Z3u9MFo1 June 15, 2013.

Carlson, F. M. & Nelson, B. G. (2006) Reducing aggression with touch. *Dimensions, 34*(3) 9–15.

Centers for Disease Control and Prevention (2006) Retrieved from www.cdc.gov/violen ceprevention/pdf/cm_surveillance-a.pdf June 15, 2013.

Chadwick, D. L. (1994) A response to 'The impact of "moral panic" on professional behavior in cases of child sexual abuse'. *Journal of Child Sexual Abuse,* 3(1),127–131.

*The Chronicle of Higher Education* (2007) September 9. Retrieved from http://chronicle. com/article/The-First-Close-Look-at/13153/ June 15, 2013.

Clapton, G., Cree, V. E. & Smith, M. (2013) Moral panics and social work: Towards a skeptical view of UK child protection. *Critical Social Policy 33*(2) 197–217.

Cohen, J. & Weiss, G. (eds.) (2003) *Thinking the limits of the body.* New York: State University of New York Press.

Collins, A., Kendall, G. & Michael, M. (1998) Resisting a diagnostic technique: The case of reflex anal dilatation. *Sociology of Health & Illness,* 20(1) 1–28.

Contratto, S. (1986) Child abuse and the politics of care. *Journal of Education, 168* (3), 70–79.

Cree, V. E. *et al* (2013) Moral panics for the 21st century. ESRC Moral Panic Seminar Series. Retrieved from http://moralpanicseminarseries.wordpress.com/2013/02/08/moral-panics-for-the-21st-century/ June 15, 2013.

Darkness to Light: End Child Sexual Abuse (2013) Retrieved from www.D2L.org/site/c.4dICIJOkGcISE/b.6353313/k.3F62/Darkness_to_Light_in_the_News.htm May 22, 2013.

Del Prete, T. (1997, March) Hands off? The touchy subject of touching, *The Education Digest*, 62(7), 59–61.

Douglas, M. (1966) *Purity and danger: An analysis of concepts of pollution and taboo.* London: Routledge & Kegan Paul.

Douglas, T. (1995) *Scapegoats: Transferring blame.* New York: Routledge.

Felman, J. L. (1997) *Cravings: A sensual memoir.* Boston, MA: Beacon Press.

Field, T. (1998) Touch therapy effects on development. *International Journal of Behavioral Development, 22*(4), 779–797.

Foucault, M. (1977) *Discipline and punish: The birth of the prison.* London: Allen Lane.

Frankenberg, R. (1992) Foreword. In S. Scott, G. Williams, S. Platt & H. Thomas (eds.), *Private risks and public dangers* (pp. ix–xii). Hong Kong: Avebury.

Goode, E. (2012, June 28) Researchers see decline in child sexual abuse rate. *The New York Times.* Retrieved May 22, 2013 from www.nytimes.com/2012/06/29/us/rate-of-child-sexual-abuse-on-the-decline.html?_r=0 April 22, 2013.

Green, B. (1998) Born-again teaching? Governmentality, 'grammar,' and public schooling. In T. Popkewitz & M. Brennan (eds.), *Foucault's challenge: Discourse, knowledge, and power in education* (pp. 173–204). New York: Teachers College Press.

Hernandez-Reif, M., Field, T., Largie, S., Diego, M., Mora, D. & Bornstein, J. (2006) Children with Downs Syndrome improved in motor function and muscle tone following massage therapy. *Early Child Development and Care, 176*(3), 395–410.

Hollander, S. K. (1992) Making young children aware of sexual abuse. *Elementary School Guidance & Counselling, 26*(4):305–317.

Holliday, R. & Hassard, J. (2001) *Contested bodies.* New York: Routledge.

*The Honolulu Advertiser* (2007, June 12) Retrieved from http://the.honoluluadvertiser.com/article/2007/Jun/12/ln/FP706120344.html April 22, 2013.

*Honolulu Weekly* (2007, September 15) Retrieved from www.ask.com/wiki/Honolulu Weekly April 22, 2013.

Howitt, D. (1993) *Child abuse errors: When good intentions go wrong.* New Brunswick, NJ: Rutgers University Press.

James, A., Jenks, C. & Prout, A. (1998) *Theorizing childhood.* New York: Teachers College Press.

Johnson, R. (2013) Contesting contained bodily coaching experiences. *Sport, Education and Society, 18*(5) 630–647.

Johnson, R. (2011, May) *Hands off young people! The practice, policy, and politics of touch.* Symposium presented at the Congress of Qualitative Inquiry, Urbana, IL, USA.

Johnson, R. (2010) Putting myself in the picture: Oppositional looks as sites of resistance. In M. O'Loughlin & R. Johnson (eds.) *Imagining children otherwise: Theoretical and critical perspectives on childhood subjectivity.* (pp. 111–133). New York: Peter Lang Press.

Johnson, R. (2001) Rethinking risk and the child body in the era of 'no touch'. In A. Jones (ed.), *Touchy subject: Teachers touching children* (pp. 99–107). Dunedin, New Zealand: The University of Otago Press.

Jones, A. (2001) *Touchy subject: Teachers touching children.* Dunedin, New Zealand: The University of Otago Press.

Kirby, S. L., Greaves, L. & Hankivsky, O. (2000) *The dome of silence: Sexual harassment and abuse in sport.* London: Zed Books.

Kitzinger, J. (1997) Who are you kidding? Children, power and the struggle against sexual abuse. In A. James & A. Prout (eds.), *Constructing and reconstructing childhood: Contemporary issues in the sociological study of childhood.* (pp. 157–183). Washington, D.C.: Falmer Press.

Leahy, T. (2011) Sexual abuse in sport. In D. Gilbourne & M. R. Andersen (eds.), *Critical essays in applied sport psychology* (pp. 251–266) Champaign, IL: Human Kinetics.

Leberg, E. (1997) *Understanding child molesters: Taking charge.* Thousand Oaks: SAGE.

*Los Angeles Times* (2007, June 12) Retrieved from http://articles.latimes.com/2007/jun/12/nation/na-tbinspector12 April 22, 2013.

Lupton, D. (1999) Risk and the ontology of pregnant embodiment. In D. Lupton (ed.), *Risk and sociocultural theory: New directions and perspectives* (pp. 59–85) Cambridge: Cambridge University Press.

McWilliam, E. (1999, November) Pleasures proper and improper: A genealogy of teacher/student intimacy. Keynote paper for *Hands Off? Teachers Touching Children Symposium,* Centre for Child and Family Policy Research, University of Auckland, New Zealand.

MedRisk (2013) Retrieved from www.medrisk.com April 22, 2013.

Melton, G. B. & Flood, M. F. (1994) Research policy and child maltreatment: Developing the scientific foundation for effective protection of children. *Child Abuse & Neglect,* 18(1), 1–28.

Minor, J. K. & Minor, V. B. (1991) *Risk management in schools: A guide to minimizing liability.* Newbury Park, CA: Corwin Press.

Montgomery, B. (1993) Risk management. *ARCH Factsheet,* 17, 1. Retrieved April 28, 2014 from http://archrespite.org/images/docs/Factsheets/fs17.pdf

National Council of Youth Sports (2013) Retrieved from www.ncys.org/childsafety.html April 22, 2013.

National Public Radio-Morning Edition (1994, January 4) *Day Care center goes to extremes to protect reputation.* Washington, DC. Retrieved from www.highbeam.com/doc/1P1-28260989.html April 22, 2013.

*The New York Times* (2007, June 12) Retrieved from www.nytimes.com/2007/06/12/business/12counsel.html?pagewanted=all&_r=0 April 22, 2013.

Piper, H. (2011) Daring to criticise child protection policies. *Spiked Online.* Retrieved from www.spiked-online.com/index.php/site/article/10969/ September 14, 2012.

Piper, H., Garratt, D. & Taylor, B. (2013) Child abuse, child protection, and defensive 'touch' in PE teaching and sports coaching. *Sport, Education and Society,* 18(5) 583–598.

Piper, H. & Stronach, I. (2008) *Don't Touch!: The educational story of a panic.* London: Routledge.

Piper, H., Taylor, B. & Garratt, D. (2011) Sports coaching in risk society: No touch! No trust! *Sport, Education and Society,* 17(3) 331–345.

Robertson, J. (1997) Fantasy's confines: Popular culture and the education of the female primary-school teacher. In S. Todd (ed.), *Learning desire: Perspectives on pedagogy, culture, and the unsaid.* (pp. 75–96). New York: Routledge.

Rose, N. (1990) *Governing the soul: The shaping of the private self.* New York: Routledge.

Sapon-Shevin, M. (2009) To touch and be touched: The missing discourse of bodies in education. In H. Svi Shapiro (ed.), *Education and hope in troubled times: Visions of change for our children's world.* (pp. 168–184). New York: Routledge.

Shamgar-Handelman, L. (1994) To whom does childhood belong? In J. Qvortrup, M. Bardy, G. Sgritta & H. Wintersberger (eds.), *Childhood matters: Social theory, practice and politics*. (pp. 249–265). Hong Kong: Avebury.

Soto, L. D. & Swadener, B. B. (2002) Towards liberatory early childhood theory, research and praxis: Decolonizing a field. *Contemporary Issues in Early Childhood, 3*(3) 38–66.

Stainton Rogers, S. & Stainton Rogers, W. (1992) *Stories of childhood: Shifting agendas of child concern*. Hemel Hempstead: Harvester Wheatshef.

Stephens, S. (1995) Children and the politics of culture in 'Late Capitalism'. In S. Stephens (ed.), *Children and the politics of culture* (pp. 3–48). Princeton, NJ: Princeton University Press.

Suaalii, T. (1999, October) Collective responsibility, neoliberal conditions, and sexual risk: Theorizing Samoan events of 'toso teine'. Paper presented at the *Annual Pacific Islands Studies Conference*, Honolulu, HI.

Taylor-Gooby, P. (ed.) (2000) *Risk, trust and welfare*. New York: St. Martin's Press.

Tomlinson, A. & Yorganci, I. (1997) Male coach/female athlete relations: Gender and power relations in competitive sport. *Journal of Sport and Social Issues, 21*(2) 134–155.

'Turn her on without touching her'. *Details* (1999, August) Retrieved from http://back issues.com/issue/Details-August-1999 April 22, 2013.

Turner, B. S. (1992) *Regulating bodies: Essays in medical sociology*. New York: Routledge.

Ussher, J. M. (1997) Introduction: Towards a material-discursive analysis of madness, sexuality and reproduction. In J. M. Ussher (ed.), *Body talk: The material and discursive regulation of sexuality, madness and reproduction* (pp. 1–9). New York: Routledge.

Wagener, J. R. (1998) The construction of the body through sex education discourse practices. In T. Popkewitz & M. Brennan (eds.), *Foucault's challenge: Discourse, knowledge, and power in education* (pp. 144–172) New York: Teachers College Press.

Walsh, J. (1998) *True odds: How risk affects your everyday life*. Lansdowne, PA: Silver Lake Publishing.

Watney, S. (1987) *Policing desire: Pornography, AIDS, and the media*. London: Methuen.

Wilczynski, A. (1997) *Child homicide*. London: Oxford University Press.

Zita, J. N. (1998) *Body talk: Philosophical reflections on sex and gender*. New York: Columbia University Press.

# 4 Should we be worried? Risk, fear and the 'greyness' of touch

## Experience in Aotearoa New Zealand physical education and school sport

*Clive C. Pope*

## Introduction

Teachers and coaches in schools work in a social environment that incorporates a climate of fear and anxiety. This is prompted by sporadic but poignant events and now characterises not only many school policies and practices but also the thoughts and behaviours of those charged with working alongside students. Since the Aotearoa New Zealand [ANZ][1] Government introduced *Tomorrow's Schools* in 1989 (Taskforce to Review Education Administration, 1989) which devolved governance to individual school Boards of Trustees, there has been an increasing culture of managerialism in all schools in ANZ. Part of this self-governance landscape includes the management and assessment of risk for activities and events that fall inside and beyond the school gates. Secondary schools in ANZ endeavour to offer a full and stimulating array of experiences for their students, both within and beyond the formal curriculum. Many of those experiences fall within physical education and school sport and by their very nature are associated with human physical contact. But decades of government and policy manoeuvring towards a regime of heightened risk prevention have resulted in an overdose of risk aversion and a perceived need for caution in many schools (Brown & Fraser, 2009).

This chapter is organised around three foci. First I offer a personal reflection based on many years of teaching and coaching in New Zealand secondary schools before becoming a researcher and university teacher of sport pedagogy. Because my school teaching was principally at secondary level I focus primarily on this sector, which is arguably underrepresented in the touch and risk literature. Secondly, wherever appropriate, I draw from other levels of education. A number of contextual and theoretical perspectives are used to support my personal reflections on teaching and coaching. Finally, I draw upon numerous visual ethnographic projects that I have completed in recent years, to employ selected images that collectively reveal the shades of grey associated with the double-edged and contested characteristics of safety and touch, which often emerge in sport and physical education contexts. The camera can reveal how touch and safety must be kept in focus while also foregrounding the ambiguity that can pervade the grey spaces of teaching and coaching, inviting conversation, reflection and, perhaps most importantly, reason.

## Contextual considerations

During the 1980s and '90s neoliberalism appeared on the political landscape of ANZ as 'Rogernomics' and 'Ruthanasia', named after two ministers of finance for the implementation of successive 'neoliberal experiments', considered to be 'the most radical in the Organisation for Economic Co-operation and Development (OECD), if not the world' (Kelsey, 1998, p. 62). Although this political shift triggered massive economic and social change, Rogernomics and Ruthanasia were eventually judged to be economic failures (Hazeldine, 1998). Despite such concerns, politicians on both sides of parliament continue to embrace and endorse the neoliberal model. Over a decade later and following what became known as 'the New Zealand experiment' (Kelsey, 1996) a new education landscape, dominated by a neoliberal ideology, accompanied sweeping reforms to governance, school management and a reconstituted Ministry of Education. The government's mandate, awarded under the mantra of *Tomorrow's Schools,* encourages each primary and secondary school to tailor its mission and operation according to local needs, in effect to be more market-responsive. Accordingly there is some flexibility for schools to make choices as to their particular priorities and to structure what occurs within their remit. Juxtaposed to the decisions that schools make are the inevitable 'checks and balances' that must be addressed under the guise of accountability. Schools have become responsible and publicly accountable for financial and educational performance.

In summary, after more than two decades of neoliberal reform, supporting the principle and practice of schools operating in a market, education in ANZ is preoccupied with managerialism and what can be produced and measured. Schools have ostensibly become small businesses marked by accountability and efficiency, while teachers have become managed professionals (Codd, 2005). They have also become increasingly stressed as their roles are subjected to increased responsibility, workloads and working hours. The rapid and progressive change in the nature and meaning of teaching is directly affecting those in the profession, and those considering a vocation working with young people.

## Teacher education

Under the influence of New Right policies, governments around the world have vigorously pursued the technocratic modernisation of teacher education (Young, 1998). In ANZ, teacher education has traditionally been divided between universities and colleges of education, but this arrangement has come under increasing attack on cost efficiency grounds (Openshaw, 1999). This domination of politics by New Right perspectives was to have a significant impact on the nature and operation of ANZ teacher education. In 1989 as *Tomorrow's Schools* was being wheeled out across the education landscape, I left secondary teaching to commence a career in teacher education. The imperatives of the new education environment soon directly affected me, as my institution became the first teachers' college to amalgamate with a university. This was a period of significant change as the professional ethos of teacher education came up against, and was increasingly usurped by, the academic culture of the university. One consequence was that the structure and programmes of teacher education underwent a major adjustment.

Large scale political and policy change was not only reflected at an operational and philosophical level, it also had consequences at a demographic level. The implementation of the New Right project amplified a growing trend in teaching – a shift in gender profile. Over the course of ten years the declining number of male teacher education students enrolled in my classes reflected a widely held view that teaching had become less appealing as a career choice for young men. This observation aligns with national data. The 2012 education census revealed that 33,692 teachers are female, a figure that has been trending up since 2004. This compares with 13,600 male teachers, a figure that has been trending down since 2004 (Education Counts Statistics, 2012), although this trend is less significant for the secondary area (Dench, 2009).

Teacher education in ANZ has also mirrored trends of our wider education sector and many English-speaking countries in the diminution of male teachers, in particular at early childhood and primary levels (Mills, Martino & Lingard, 2004). In 1971, 37.7% of primary teachers were male. By 1997 that number had almost halved to 20.7% (Farquhar, 1998). In 2013 in the education faculty of my institution, the primary initial teacher education student cohort was 84% female and 16% male. The contrast is even more pronounced in the early childhood programme where males make up only 3% of the student intake. A smaller secondary programme partially counters these numbers, with 56% female and 44% male students. In general there is still salience to Farquhar's (1998) questioning of whether teaching was becoming a women-only profession. Previously Farquhar (1997) had described the changing balance of teacher gender as a problem of serious professional and political concern. Yet despite the unease, fifteen years have since passed and this process of change still continues. The feminization of many levels of the teaching profession is a cause for concern, since it is arguable that the needs of young people must be answered with a balanced and appropriate diversity of adults, particularly in sport and physical education, who can provide the sporting experiences their charges seek.

If the figures for secondary education reflect a disproportionate imbalance of teacher gender that is less dramatic, then it is appropriate to ask 'what's so different about secondary teaching through the eyes of practicing and aspiring male teachers'? One perception that has circulated amongst teacher educators and researchers internationally is that many secondary teacher education students want to coach (Chu, 1984; Templin, Woodford, & Mulling, 1982), although this perception has been challenged (O'Bryant, O'Sullivan, & Raudensky, 2000). Until recently, in ANZ at least, teachers coaching sport has been an integral and widespread characteristic of secondary schooling.

## Secondary school sport

One of the most challenging tasks for educators in ANZ has been to respond to the wants and needs of students who seek a more diverse sporting experience, as considered appropriate to the twenty-first century (Grant & Pope, 2007). While a robust community club sport system continues to work, albeit within an environment of strained resourcing, escalating costs and diminished membership, many young people turn to the high school for their sporting experiences. Secondary school sport involves over 140,000 students and it is overseen by the ANZ Secondary Schools Sports Council (NZSSSC), which governs and facilitates over 180 national and North Island or South Island events involving nearly sixty different sporting codes (NZSSSC, 2012a, 2012b). Following the Council's inception in 1995, there was a steady increase in the number of students playing sport and in the number of teachers and/or other adults involved in coaching, but in more recent years the participation rates have fallen away (Grant & Pope, 2007). The NZSSSC conducts an annual census of all 444 secondary schools in the country, and while overall participation has followed an international trend of reducing numbers, it appears the degree of fall-off has been reduced by the provision of more sports and by schools being creative about how sport can be facilitated. As a result 53% of all secondary school students represent their school in at least one sport at a competitive level. This figure has dropped from 55% in the last five years but still appears high by international comparisons. It could be interpreted that sport is alive and well in the secondary school and should students wish to participate then there is the opportunity to do so. But these affirming figures mask a more disconcerting factor: the role and participation of teachers.

Since the turn of the millennium the support by teachers acting in a range of sport leadership roles has progressively diminished. There is no clear evidence or acknowledged link between this reduction of teacher support and the previously discussed issue of diminishing numbers of male teachers entering teacher education programmes. However, there is a clear need to investigate the salience of teacher participation beyond the formal curriculum, and how this is affected by gender issues. Teachers, coaches, sports co-ordinators and adult family members are the significant adults for young people playing or wanting to play sport in schools. They hold the key to providing opportunities and have the responsibility for managing the quality of the sporting experience. Thus, a decline in the number of coaches involved in school sport is of concern (Sharp, 1999) and something that has been consistently raised in successive NZSSSC Annual Reports:

> The continued decline in the percentage of teachers involved in school sport continues to be a concern, as we know that sport leadership provided by teachers is a critical element in student participation. It must also be of concern in schools, as it is well understood that the relationships formed by teacher involvement with students outside the classroom can significantly enhance the relationship inside it with all the benefits that can bring.
>
> (NZSSSC, 2012a)

In 2000, 5,434 secondary school teachers (43% of the total) were coaching at least one secondary school sports team (NZSSSC, 2001). By 2012, that figure had decreased to 20%. The concerns and espoused values iterated by NZSSSC are poignant. However, while the imperatives to recruit and retain suitably qualified coaches is recognised and emphasised by NZSSSC, in keeping with the neoliberal mantra it is officially the responsibility of individual schools to draft and codify an appropriate code of conduct for school coaches as well as ensure students always participate in a safe environment.

Working with students in a sporting context can be a rewarding and enjoyable aspect of teaching. During the 1980s as a secondary physical education teacher I coached and managed numerous sports at a variety of levels. Coaching was part of the weekly routine, including evenings and weekends. The school year melded into a series of practices, meetings, games and tournaments beyond the school day. Fundraising gave players the chance to work collectively to ensure that everybody could travel to tournaments, mostly in a minivan or bus that I drove to reduce costs. Travelling with and coaching boys was perceived as unproblematic, but my experiences of coaching girls' volleyball teams were framed differently. Whenever I was in contact with players collectively or individually, I was always reminded of my first day of teaching and a conversation with the principal. All new staff were cautioned about risk and about the way we interacted with our students, particularly those of the opposite gender. The assumptions being applied to teachers' sexuality aside, that conversation was both profound and enduring in that it framed many of my teaching and coaching experiences for the ensuing decade. My wife, a physiotherapist, would accompany our female or mixed-group teams away to tournament and the policy became 'no chaperone – no go'. Fortunately we always had parents ready to join and support us, and in terms of both sport and social relationships, the 1980s are remembered as a rich, rewarding and exciting time. Such arrangements, involving teachers committing to many extra-curricular hours with the support of pupils' parents, were not uncommon during this time; however, in the new regime of certification and surveillance there is a concern that those working in such supporting roles could be marginalised.

During the latter part of that decade I became a teacher in charge of sport and observed that the issues of risk, safety and touch would often enter the parlance of colleagues. Conversations often focused around issues of trust and risk, compounded by the particular characteristics of the physical education teacher's role. On reflection I do not think the notion of touch was as sensitive an issue as it is today. Some aspects of the physical education curriculum required elements of touch, especially gymnastics and dance. It was a time when non-competitive games and trust activities, both of which required physical contact, were part of the programme. Touch meant safety, acknowledgment, correction and combination. Sometimes functional, sometimes instructional, and in teaching and coaching contexts it was sometimes emotional, but above all I believe it was both sanctioned and appropriate. It did not have the high public profile it has since acquired.

Coaching has always been an unpaid part of teaching for a significant proportion of ANZ secondary teachers. However, the decline in support by teachers has become a growing concern for principals and administrators as an aging teaching force has responded to escalating workloads, increasing audits, growing internal assessment and occasionally a viewpoint that 'I've done my time in coaching; it's time some of these younger folks took over.' The latter perspective is seen as lamentable and significant, as younger staff are not prepared to volunteer their time to the same extent, meaning students either miss out or schools must pay to have suitable adult leadership for sports activity (Sharp, 1999, 2004).

My personal reflections may be anecdotal or even aberrant, but they are clearly pertinent to this chapter and to the book; they illustrate significant tensions and contrasts. Reflecting back over three decades of professional practice and accumulated experience and awareness, I now question whether the relatively relaxed perceptions I once held about touch and teaching were innocently naive or sensibly rational. Certainly they appear indicative of a time when ideas about vulnerability and victimhood were different; it contrasts with the ongoing contemporary moral panic and what McWilliam and Jones (2005) refer to as 'the new tyrannies of teaching' (2005, p. 110), energized by heightened awareness and anxiety. Declining cohorts of male teachers newly entering the profession now need to be more 'risk aware' (Jones, 2007). There is an obvious paradox, 'that in a period when children are perhaps safer than ever, there is a crescendo of social concern about childhood and children, and an accompanying dramatic intensification of (self)-regulation of those professionally involved with children' (Jones, 2001, p. 9).

The impact of this change on teaching and coaching sport with children and young people is manifest in the daily experience of all involved. While the work of Jones (2001) amongst others has focused on teachers touching children in an ANZ context, it also highlighted an issue that has gained prominence in several Anglophone countries including the UK (Piper & Stronach, 2008), US (Hansen, 2007) and Australia (McWilliam and Jones, 2005; Scott, 2012). Fletcher's (2013) recent research has highlighted how many secondary school physical education contexts in the UK have become more pressured, less stable and increasingly marked by coaches being positioned beneath a cloud of suspicion or accusation, as touch is actively discouraged as part of the coaching process. In ANZ, Jones (2001) highlights a new level of perceived risk and the associated anxiety touch generates, especially when fuelled by widely publicized court cases. Two such cases that occurred in the 1990s have arguably underpinned public suspicion about males working in educational contexts with young people.

What became known as The Christchurch Civic Childcare Centre abuse case (see Hood, 2001) was particularly significant in sensitizing the media and the wider public. Although Peter Ellis, a male worker in the early childhood centre was sentenced to ten years in prison for sexual abuse, his conviction has remained controversial (Francis, 2007). The allegation of sexual abuse of her son from a female parent, a counsellor specialising in sexual abuse, against Ellis started a series of events that eventually led to Ellis' conviction in 1993. This controversial case has been the subject of two books, two formal appeals, a ministerial inquiry, a parliamentary inquiry and three formal requests for a pardon. Successive governments have resisted calls for a Commission of Inquiry. It would appear all legal options have been exhausted for those advocates seeking justice for Peter Ellis.

The impact of the case was to prompt a changed educational environment as regulation intensified and suspicion escalated. The profile of the case was huge and it highlighted, amongst other things, the vulnerability of young children. The moral panic that followed, coupled with the implementation of *Tomorrow's Schools,* made teachers much more sensitive about and accountable for their actions while promoting a 'reduced acceptance of teachers' professional integrity and judgment in how teachers respond to children's behaviour and interact with them' (Farquhar, 2001, p. 91). In this context, cases of child sexual abuse in schools and early childhood centres come to light every year, fuelled by intense media coverage and scrutiny, but none have impacted the educational landscape and raised public concern more than the Ellis case. Similarly one case has impacted more on the secondary school context than any other.

## Black is black: The dark side of touch

Like every other instrument and activity humans have invented, sport can be used for good or evil purposes. The changing culture of sport, and the power conferred on the coach, can certainly promote an environment conducive to, and tolerant of sexual exploitation (Brackenridge, Bringer & Bishopp, 2005; Donnelly & Sparks, 1997). Moreover, some researchers have conjectured that sexual abuse in sport is associated with the deliberate presence of paedophiles and coaches with a 'predator' mentality (Bringer, Brackenridge & Johnston, 2002), typically men, placed in and exploiting a position of trust, intimacy and power. In common with schools and organized religion, sport can be attractive to potential abusers; access to children is relatively unproblematic, and the locus of responsibility for particular spaces and activities is not always clear. However, regulatory responses, codes of conduct and ethics for coaches, as well as policy guidelines covering the prevention of sexual abuse of athletes in sporting environments appear inadequate to protect athletes from abuse (David, 2005; Leahy, Pretty & Tenenbaum, 2002). In confronting this issue, secondary school sport in ANZ has been tainted by a lasting example of abuse by a teacher and sports coach.

Thomas Leigh was the metalwork teacher at Mahurangi College, a public co-educational school in a rural town for more than twenty years. He was a popular member of the staff and the local community, drove the school bus, was an active fund-raiser and a coach of several sports teams. He was also a paedophile who, over the course of his career, elicited yet eluded a stream of complaints from students and staff about his behaviour towards female students. He posed as a physiotherapist and threatened some students with expulsion from his hockey team unless they complied with his requests. Over the years Leigh developed a frightening trail of intricate deception, creating and exploiting ambiguous situations, cloaking his sexual intentions with seemingly 'acceptable' behaviours. Physical touching was couched in terms of 'sports coaching', 'massage', or 'medical advice' (O'Reilly, 1998). The Board of Trustees of the school responded to complaints in a manner that was at best apathetic and at worst flippant. One student who formally complained about Leigh's behaviour was asked by Board of Trustee members to leave, and to attend another school. Eventually the rising tide of concern led to a formal complaint of sexual harassment in 1995, which culminated in a police investigation where other women who Leigh had abused were approached. He was eventually charged with twenty-eight counts involving rape, sexual violation and indecent assault, and in 1996 was given a seventeen-year sentence after pleading guilty to charges relating to twenty-one female students, although a far greater number were probably affected by his actions (Hansen, 1996; Sarney, 1996). Three years into his sentence he died of an illness associated with a heart and brain condition.

Despite a visit to Mahurangi College by the Education Review Office (ERO) during the period when Leigh was committing these offences, their appraisal and report were positive and found no cause for concern. ERO supported the school's position that it was blameless. Community and parental dissatisfaction at this result led to a complaint to the Commissioner for Children which in turn led to a full review of the case that, among other findings stated:

> Overall there was a high level of awareness amongst staff members, school administration and adults in the wider community that there were suspicions about Thomas Leigh's relationships with female students. The fact that no individual or group acted on these suspicions is a sad fact to be noted and which has implications for schools, communities and adults providing safety for children. There appeared to be a clear expectation that the school was charged with the responsibility of ensuring students' safety.
>
> (O'Reilly, 1998, p. 16)

Arguably, staff and those in positions of power were unable to act on initial suspicions without a formal accusation being presented to them. Self-governing schools working under the mantra of *Tomorrow's Schools* were responsible for the formulation and enactment of any policy aimed at addressing safety of its students. This case has had a lasting impact on how schools in ANZ run sport programmes, the policies they have put in place and how coaches are 'vetted' before working with students in schools. It is now commonplace for schools to document and promote codes of conduct and conduct police checks of any adults working with their students. Such practice is complemented by similar codes of conduct advocated by teacher union groups.

The effect was not merely formal and limited to teaching professionals; during a later research visit to a secondary school I was reminded of the extent of the impact of the Leigh incident in a conversation with a teacher who coached one of their school cricket teams. He recalled that after the media frenzy over the case, a parent suddenly began observing team practices from a distance, standing on a nearby bank and monitoring movements through a pair of binoculars. The coach asked his players if anybody recognized the observer and one of the players replied that it was his dad, who had become very concerned about 'how easy it was for these creeps to become coaches!' After coaching school cricket for twenty years as a member of the school staff, the coach was made very aware that nobody was above suspicion. Regardless, he continued to coach until retirement. This recollection endorses McWilliam and Jones' (2005) assertion that 'teachers now work in a climate of suspicion, characterized in part by sensational media revelations of priestly and teacherly impropriety' (p. 111).

Clearly Thomas Leigh was a 'dangerous teacher' (Castel, 1991), a predator who lurked in the shadows, casting a cloud over his colleagues both close and distant. But trying to predict who 'dangerous teachers' might be is virtually impossible prior to the problem becoming explicit, and the societal response has been to create a category of person likely to place young people 'at risk', too easily understood as in effect any teacher or coach. The inherent potential for danger within sport and physical education settings places the teaching and coaching professions in a vulnerable position once they have been categorized as a group deemed likely to put children 'at risk' (Castel, 1991; Tate, 2001). However, the idea of intervening to control the intentions and behaviours of all coaches through policy and regulation, to avert the risk from the minority with abuse in mind, appears ill-conceived, amounting to nothing more than a symptom of moral panic (Altheide, 2009; Farquhar, 2001; Furedi, 2011, Piper & Smith, 2003). Castel (1991) argues that anything can be a risk or perceived as such; the boundaries and potential are limitless. Thus behavioural or performative guidelines miss the point. Touch is not a black and white issue; rather, it is shrouded in greyness. How risk is interpreted and how touch is perceived will often be determined by informed interpretation or even speculation. They reinforce what Piper, Taylor and Garratt (2011) refer to as 'the grey zone' that characterizes and colours the blurred issue of coach and athlete interactions. Eva Heller proclaims grey is neither warm nor cold, neither material nor spiritual. With grey, nothing seems to be decided (Heller, 2009), and some aspects of human life, including the inevitability of risk and the essential nature of trust, are the same.

## The conundrum of colour: Picturing the greyness

Visual depictions can reveal the complexity often associated with the many derivations of risk, and more specifically touch, in sport. As a concept, (visual) representation is laced with complexity and ambiguity. Yet despite its ubiquity in media reporting of the sporting world the potential for meaning-making and more sensitive understanding of sport, the emotion, the tensions, the intensity, the challenges, the release, the friendships associated with sporting settings and its participants, appears until very recently to have been untapped. Visual representations of sport ethnography work, if not in a state of ascendancy, should at least be seen as a viable and legitimate alternative to relying solely on the written word (Azzarito & Kirk, 2013; Phoenix & Smith, 2011). According to McQuire (1998) researchers need to focus on the 'promiscuity and ambiguity of the image' and an associated epistemological shift in the meaning of the meaning of images (p. 47). For current purposes, I employ images from ethnographic projects of youth sport settings (Pope, 2009, 2010a, 2010b, 2013) to explore how images could make real the meanings of touch in sport. Much of my research now focuses on youth sport and youth culture, and has often involved spending prolonged periods of time in relevant settings, understanding the local culture. This facilitates and often provides a blueprint for social action, achieved through prolonged, regular and intensive observation of a designated group. Interaction with the group offers insights into meanings and motivations of those observed, following intensive analysis and attention to fine-grained detail that can often be extracted from images. Jones *et al.* (2013) recently employed visual research to explore the politics of touch by coaches. Their work advocates the potential of visual research methods (in this case photography) to 'highlight different aspects of, the often problematic (darker?) corners of social practice' (p. 9). The irony of the image is discussed as Jones *et al.* (2013) highlight its ambiguity, and the tension of balancing between showing and telling the reader while concomitantly presenting the ambiguity of the issue (in this instance touch and proximity) and thereby helping to 'unravel coaches actions as related to touch' (p. 11). Their images and discussion highlight how the care that coaches express towards athletes varies and is inflected according to how a range of factors such as gender, age and trust are mediated through perceived gaze and codified policy. Images such as photographs can simultaneously combine the material and objective with the subjective and symbolic, but perhaps more importantly they can help capture everyday environments and the relationships of people within them. They can be tools for new narratives and new counternarratives (Harrison, 2004; Poddiakov, 2004).

The behaviours of coaches (and the points made here also cover teachers in a physical education context) are both complex and fleeting. How can the camera capture, explore and interpret the sensitivity that is associated with touch? In essence, and at risk of presenting a simplistic explanation, images can effectively facilitate discrimination between the technical and the expressive. Before recognizing the wider socialization potential of coach-athlete interaction, working with young people within a sporting context requires using strategies that help the development of skill. Traditional learning modes often follow the three-step process that commences with a verbal/cognitive phase where information is exchanged between player and coach. That information is then processed into meaningful movement components. This phase is usually manifested through explanation, demonstration and instruction, so the athlete can process the information. The picture or schema that the athlete forms is then practiced and refined to establish consistency, correctness and efficiency. This phase is often supported by coach feedback and guidance as the skill is progressed to a level of automaticity. During this process the coach may employ strategies from their pedagogical toolbox to both facilitate and progress the learning of targeted skills or movement patterns. This sometimes includes a 'hands on' approach, particularly if the athlete is still developing his or her processing skills, or if the coach's instruction is unclear or has created confusion. This is sometimes best ameliorated through gesticulation, guided support, or even manipulation (see Figures 1, 2, 3 and 4). Coaching, like teaching, involves a highly complex and ongoing series of decisions, and the underlying consideration for the decision-making process should always be athlete learning, safety and contentment.

*Figure 1*

*Figure 2*

*Figure 3*

*Figure 4*

But of course coaching is not a technical process that occurs in a vacuum. Rather it is eclectic, driven by multiple social, moral and technical considerations. Each and every coaching action is based on a combination of those composite considerations in varying proportion, based in turn on the coach's decision as to which consideration should prevail and why. The integrity and effectiveness of the coach should be demonstrated through her or his behaviour. In a perfect world a coach would allocate the correct proportion of social, moral and technical emphasis to their behaviour, but coaches are human and fallible. However, if athlete learning and safety are acknowledged as overriding considerations, then acceptable coaching behaviour mediated through the aforementioned considerations should be seen to be unproblematic.

Balanced with the technical aspect of coach behaviour is the expressive element. The affective domain of coaching is profoundly influenced by emotions that can shape cognition and performance as well as interpersonal functioning (Hanin, 2000). Coaching, like its pedagogical cousin teaching, is an emotional practice and good teaching is charged with positive emotion (Hargreaves, 1998). Hargreaves contends that 'we must acknowledge and even honor the centrality of the emotions to the processes and outcomes of teaching, learning and caring' (p. 850). This perspective supports that of Eisner (1983), who asserts 'teachers need the psychological space and the permission to maintain a sense of excitement and discovery for themselves as teachers so such excitement can be shared with their students' (p. 12). Emotion and cognition, coach and context, instruction and learning, ethical judgment and purposeful action: they are all intertwined in the complex reality of coaching or teaching and should themselves be protected from risk. The emotions of coaching are shaped by the moral purposes (Denzin, 1984) of those who coach and the degree to which they are permitted to fulfil those purposes, and it is therefore important that coaches are able to be themselves, allow feelings and emotions to be expressed periodically and understand their players through emotionality. Emotion is central to sport; many coaches' relations with their players are significantly emotional in nature (Figure 5), and

*Figure 5*

all who participate in sport as players, coaches or officials will invariably experience the intensity and complexity of emotions. They collectively demonstrate and endorse the humanness of sport. In coaching, emotion is purposefully absorbed, channelled, expressed and shared – often through touch (Figure 6). Emotions are also properly regulated, suppressed and substituted according to societal expectations and controls, but in the contemporary panic around children the emotional practice of coaching (as in many sport forms) is at risk of being supplanted by overpowering seriousness and scrutiny. This process can only impoverish coaching and the experience of adults and children involved, instead of enriching it.

While coaching has been addressed here as comprising discrete technical and expressive forms, they are of course unified. Cognition, emotion and action are inseparable; 'minds without emotions are not really minds at all. They are souls on ice – cold, lifeless creatures devoid of any desires, fears, sorrows, pain or pleasure' (Le Doux, 1996, p. 25). Any representation of coaching or teaching will be constituted by a combination in varying forms.

The images presented in this chapter portray how touch is a constitutive part of the coaching process but none are presented with captions or text to direct the reader's attention to the meaning of each image. Rather, they highlight the ambiguity and elasticity of meaning, in the event, the production and the viewing. Like most photographs, each image has 'extraordinary power and a slippery way of making their point given the recurring confusion about photographs and reality' (Harper, 2006, p. 114). The meanings within each image are created in the act of viewing; hence the ascription of 'abusive' or 'grooming' to any of the depicted coach behaviours is indeed an act of the viewer. Perception is constructed and

*Figure 6*

attained amidst a greyness of subjectivities through which the images are viewed. Perception and reality are weighed-up by the reader (or the observer in the live setting) who then decides whether touch is appropriate or inappropriate (black or white) or, whether it portrays the 'it depends' (greyness) perspective that often frames the anxiety associated with touch. Fine-grained judgment is thus essential, but it is notably absent from the approach which has gained ascendency, in which the appropriateness of touching in teaching or coaching is scrutinized in a way that 'essentialises "touch" as a discrete phenomenon, and disconnects it from other bodily and discursive practices [that] is far too narrow, and renders interaction incomprehensible and unmanageable' (Piper & Stronach, 2008, p. 144). Building on this insight, I would argue that a topic such as touch can be addressed fruitfully using the transformative power of the visual (Pink, 2007) to transport the fear and anxiety, increasingly experienced on a discursive and abstract level, to a world where touch can be represented as contextualized and seen as an important part of human functioning.

## A final comment

Teachers in ANZ secondary schools have traditionally been the backbone of an enviable and highly rated school sport system, characterised by opportunity and access. However, that level of teacher involvement is diminishing and international trends associated with risk and anxiety highlighted throughout this book reveal a conundrum of how to preserve and protect physical education and school sport while concomitantly keeping the shades of grey in focus. A better solution to this problem is essential if the escalating number of teachers choosing to disengage from such settings is to be checked or at least be eased.

## Note

1  As an acknowledgement of the bicultural status of our country the term Aotearoa New Zealand has been adopted throughout this chapter. However, in the interests of brevity ANZ is used unless reference is made to a specific document or agency that uses New Zealand only.

## References

Altheide, D. L. (2009) Moral panic: From sociological concept to public discourse. *Crime, Media, Culture*, 5(1), 79–99.

Azzarito, L. & Kirk, D. (2013) *Pedagogies, physical culture, and visual methods*. London: Routledge.

Brackenridge, C., Bringer, J. D. & Bishopp, D. (2005) Managing cases of abuse in sport. *Child Abuse Review,* 14(4), 259–274.

Bringer, J. D., Brackenridge, C. H., & Johnston, L. H. (2002). Defining appropriateness in coach-athlete sexual relationships: The voice of coaches. *Journal of Sexual Aggression*, 8(2), 83–98. doi: 10.1080/13552600208413341.

Brown, M. & Fraser, D. (2009) Re-evaluating risk and exploring educational alternatives. *Journal of Adventure Education & Outdoor Learning,* 9(1) 61–77. doi: 10.1080/14729670902789529

Castel, R. (1991) *The Foucault effect: Studies in governmentality.* London: Harvester/Wheatsheaf.

Chu, D. (1984) Teacher/coach role orientation and role socialization: Are they the same? *Journal of Teaching in Physical Education,* 3(2) 3–8.

Codd, J. (2005) Teachers as 'managed professionals' in the global education industry: The New Zealand experience. *Educational Review,* 57(2) 193–206.

David, P. (2005) *Human rights in youth sport.* London: Routledge.

Dench, O. (2009) *Education statistics of New Zealand: 2009.* Wellington: Ministry of Education Retrieved 16 April 2013 from www.educationcounts.govt.nz/publications/schooling/2507/80221.

Denzin, N. (1984) *On understanding emotion.* San Francisco: Jossey-Bass.

Donnelly, P. & Sparks, R. (1997) Child sexual abuse in sport. *Policy Options,* 3, 3–6.

Education Counts Statistics. (2012) *Tables: Full time teacher equivalent by designation (grouped), gender and age group in state and state integrated schools, as at April.* Wellington: Ministry of Education Retrieved 19 April 2013 from www.educationcounts.govt.nz/statistics/schooling/teaching_staff

Eisner, E. W. (1983) The art and craft of teaching. *Educational Leadership,* 40(4) 4–13.

Farquhar, S-E. (1997) Are male teachers really necessary? Paper presented at the *New Zealand Association of Research in Education [NZARE] National Conference,* Auckland.

Farquhar, S-E. (1998) Teaching: A women-only profession? *New Zealand Annual Review of Education,* 7, 169–180.

Farquhar, S-E. (2001) Moral panic in New Zealand. In A. Jones (ed.) *Touchy subject: Teachers touching children* (pp. 87–98) Dunedin: University of Otago Press.

Fletcher, S. (2013) Touching practice and physical education: Deconstruction of a contemporary moral panic. *Sport, Education and Society,* 18(5) 694–709.

Francis, R. (2007) New evidence in the Ellis case – II. *New Zealand Law Journal,* 11(December), 439–444.

Furedi, F. (2011) The objectification of fear and the grammar of morality. In S. P. Hier (ed.) *Moral panic and the politics of anxiety* (pp. 90–103) Abingdon, Oxon: Routledge.

Grant, B. & Pope, C. (2007) Sport in secondary school: Sport for all or sport for some. In C. Collins & S. Jackson. (eds.) *Sport in New Zealand Society* (pp. 246–262) Palmerston North: Dunmore Press.

Hanin, Y. L. (ed.) (2000) *Emotions in sport.* Champaign, IL: Human Kinetics.

Hansen, J. (1996) In the line of fire. *Metro* (Auckland, NZ), May, 68–76.

Hansen, J. (2007) The truth about teaching and touching. *Childhood Education,* 83(3), 158–162.

Hargreaves, A. (1998) The emotional practice of teaching. *Teaching and Teacher Education,* 14(8) 835–854.

Harper, D. (2006) Cultural studies and the photograph. In P. Hamilton (ed.) *Visual research methods Volume III* (pp. 211–228) London: Sage Publications.

Harrison, B. (2004) Photographic visions and narrative inquiry. In M. Bamberg & M. Andrews (eds.) *Considering counter narratives: Narrating, resisting, making sense* (pp. 113–136) Amsterdam: John Benjamins Publishing Company.

Hazeldine, T. (1998) *Taking New Zealand seriously: The economics of decency.* Auckland: Harper Collins.

Heller, E. (2009) *Psychologie de la couleur-Effets et symboliques*. (French translation). Paris: Pyramyd.

Hood, L. (2001) The Christchurch Civic Centre abuse case: How could it have happened? In A. Jones. (ed.) *Touchy subject: Teachers touching children* (pp. 74–86) Dunedin: University of Otago Press.

Jones, A. (ed.) (2001) *Touchy subject: Teachers touching children*. Dunedin: University of Otago Press.

Jones, D. (2007) High risk men: Male teachers and sexuality in the early years contexts. *International Journal of Adolescence and Youth,* 13(4) 239–255.

Jones, R. L., Bailey, J. & Santos, S. (2013) Coaching, caring and the politics of touch: A visual exploration. *Sport, Education and Society*, 18(5) 648–662.

Kelsey, J. (1996) *The New Zealand experiment: A world model for structural adjustment?* London: Taylor & Francis.

Kelsey, J. (1998) Privatizing the universities. *Journal of Law and Society,* 25(1), 51–70.

Leahy, T., Pretty, G. & Tenenbaum, G. (2002) Prevalence of sexual abuse in organised competitive sport in Australia. *Journal of Sexual Aggression,* 8(2) 16–36.

Le Doux, J. (1996) *The emotional brain.* New York: Simon & Schuster.

McQuire, S. (1998) *Visions of modernity: Representations. Memory. Time and space in the age of the camera.* London: Sage.

McWilliam, E. & Jones, A. (2005) An unprotected species? On teachers as risky subjects. *British Educational Research Journal,* 31(1) 109–120.

Mills, M., Martino, W. & Lingard, B. (2004) Attracting, recruiting and retaining male teachers: policy issues in the male teacher debate. *British Journal of Sociology of Education,* 25(3) 355–369.

New Zealand Secondary Schools Sports Council. (2001) *Annual Report.* Christchurch: New Zealand.

New Zealand Secondary Schools Sports Council. (2012a) *Annual Report.* Oakura: New Zealand.

New Zealand Secondary Schools Sports Council. (2012b) *Census of sport participation.* Oakura; New Zealand: New Zealand Secondary Schools Sports Council.

O'Bryant, C., O'Sullivan, M. & Raudensky, J. (2000) Socialization of prospective physical education teachers: The story of new blood. *Sport, Education and Society,* 59(2) 177–193.

Openshaw, R. (1999) Forward to the past in New Zealand teacher education. *Journal of Education for Teaching,* 25(2) 111–122.

O'Reilly, L. (1998) *Report of an inquiry by The Commissioner for Children: Mahurangi College.* Wellington: Office of the Commissioner for Children.

Phoenix, C. & Smith, B. (2011) *The world of physical culture in sport and exercise: Visual methods for qualitative research.* New York: Routledge.

Pink, S. (2007) *Doing visual ethnography* (2nd ed.). London: Sage Publications.

Piper, H. & Smith, H. (2003) 'Touch' in educational and child care settings: Dilemmas and responses. *British Educational Research Journal,* 29(6) 879–894.

Piper, H. & Stronach, I. (2008) *Don't touch! The educational story of panic.* London: Routledge.

Piper, H., Taylor, B. & Garratt, D. (2011) Sports coaching in risk society: No touch! No trust! *Sport, Education and Society,* 17(3) 331–345.

Poddiakov, A. (2004) Photographs and counter-narratives. In M. Bamberg & M. Andrews (eds.) *Considering counter narratives: Narrating, resisting, making sense* (pp. 137–142) Amsterdam: John Benjamins Publishing Company.

Pope, C. C. (2009) Sport pedagogy through a wide-angled lens. In L. Housner, M. Metzler, P. Schempp & T. Templin (eds.) *Historic traditions and future directions in research on teaching and teacher education in physical education* (pp. 227–236) Morgantown: FIT Publishing.

Pope, C. C. (2010a) Talking T-shirts: A visual exploration of youth material culture. *Qualitative Research in Sport and Exercise,* 2(2) 133–152.

Pope, C. C. (2010b) Got the picture? Exploring student sport experiences. Using photography as voice. In M. O'Sullivan & A. MacPhail (eds.) *Young people's voices in physical education and youth sport* (pp. 186–209) London: Routledge.

Pope, C. C. (2013) Visualizing the social landscape of high school Waka Ama and the apotheosis of visual ethnography. In L. Azzarito & D. Kirk (eds.) *Physical culture, pedagogies and visual methods* (pp. 212–228) London: Routledge.

Sarney, E. (1996) Broken trust. *New Zealand Listener,* April 13–19, 18–21.

Scott, C. (2012) The Australian situation: Not so touchy? *Sport, Education and Society,* 18(5) 599–614.

Sharp, P. (1999) Can New Zealand afford the loss of teachers' voluntary support for secondary school sport? Unpublished position paper. *New Zealand Secondary Schools Sports Council.* Christchurch.

Sharp, P. (2004) Secondary school sport in New Zealand and the roles of sports administrators. Paper presented at the *Young People, Sport and Physical Activity National Conference,* Hamilton, New Zealand.

Taskforce to Review Education Administration, *Administering for Excellence: Effective Administration in Education,* Chairman Brian Picot, Government Printer, Wellington, 10 May 1989.

Tate, G. (2001) 'No touch' policies and the government of risk. In A. Jones. (ed.) *Touchy subject: Teachers touching children* (pp. 39–49) Dunedin: University of Otago Press.

Templin, T., Woodford, R. & Mulling, C. (1982) On becoming a physical educator: Occupational choice and the anticipatory socialisation process. *Quest,* 34(2), 119–133.

Young, M. F. D. (1998) *The Curriculum of the future: From the 'New Sociology of Education' to a critical theory of learning.* London: Falmer Press.

# 5 The pedagogical consequences of 'no touching' in physical education

## The case of Sweden

*Marie Öhman and Carin Grundberg-Sandell*

### A story to begin with

As one of the authors of this chapter, I (Marie Öhman) have worked in a university physical education (PE) teacher training programme for twenty years and, amongst other things, have taught gymnastics, dance and motor skills movements. Some years ago, a new and unexpected topic of conversation surfaced during gymnastics, acrobatics and massage lessons, a session in which I was teaching students handstands, cartwheels and different kinds of vaulting exercises and showing them how to assist and support these movements by physically helping someone to cope with the exercise. The students also undertook acrobatics and created 'body pyramids', necessitating standing on each other's shoulders. At the end of the lesson we massaged each other's shoulders as a way of relieving the tension in the muscles. At the end of the lesson one of the students said: 'When I become a PE teacher, I'll never do any of the things we have done in class today'. I was rather taken aback, and asked the student why he had said this. The response was: 'You can't touch pupils today, they might think I'm a paedophile or a "dirty old man"'. A third of the class agreed with the student and I, somewhat confused, asked myself: When, how and why did supporting a student attempting handstands, acrobatic movements and massaging become sexual harassment or sexual abuse? It also made me wonder what are the consequences of this 'new' way of thinking (feeling) and how might it reflect in Swedish PE teachers' work.

### Introduction

The chapter takes as its point of departure the public discourses concerning the 'politics of touch' and the child protection policies that are prominent in society. Through a Foucauldian lens, it highlights the potential risks and consequences for PE teachers' practice that may result from public discourses concerning child protection and sexual harassment, and discusses how strict codes of conduct concerning 'no touching' in policy documents might influence PE teachers' pedagogical work. It is a matter of problematising teachers' pedagogical interactions in the practice of PE and pointing to the harm arising from the absurd situation of PE becoming a 'no touch zone'; here we want to argue the importance of 'not losing touch'.

This chapter is divided into five parts. In the first we briefly examine research in the field of the politics of touch, where we attempt to make an important distinction and define our position. In the second, we turn to a particular Swedish context illustrating how the politics of touch has changed in the wake of high profile cases and public anxiety about paedophilia and sexual harassment. Public discourses concerning the politics of touch are exemplified by policy documents published by the various organisations dealing with children and young people and which thereby reflect a certain official discourse and regime of truth (Foucault, 1990). In the third part, we demonstrate our use of Foucault's body of work, especially the relation between particular discourses and specific ways of thinking and acting. Utilising Foucault as a theoretical lens it becomes possible to reflect and critically examine what is often regarded as self-evident and taken for granted. In the fourth part we consider PE video recorded lessons from a pedagogical point of view and illustrate different types of situations in which physical contact seems to be pedagogically relevant and reasonable in a PE context. Finally, these pedagogical situations are discussed in relation to 'no touching policy', and issues relating to children's rights are problematized.

One thing that separates school education from other activities in the community in which children take part is that schooling is compulsory. Schools have to offer a functioning everyday life for children with different needs and abilities. At the same time, every child has the same right to be met and treated in the context of the school's overall mission to inspire, support and monitor learning and growth. By focusing on PE, a compulsory school subject where the overarching aims and objectives of education entail significant differences from other sports contexts, the chapter contributes to the literature and empirical body of work on 'the politics of touch'.

## Research on sexual harassment and abuse

Sexual harassment[1] and sexual abuse are not new social phenomena, although research on these issues in a sports context has only been highlighted in the last two or three decades.[2] Brackenridge (2001) claims that sexual abuse in sport was a known problem a decade before it began to receive attention from scholars studying sports coaching in the 1980s.[3] Volkwein *et al.* (1997) and Fasting (2005) demonstrate that the world of athletics, for example, is no different from other social domains when it comes to occurrences of sexual harassment. According to Fasting (2005), elite female athletes in Norway are exposed to the same amount of sexual harassment as other female groups in society. Moreover, Fasting *et al.* (2004) suggest that sexual harassment occurs in every sporting group. In most of the initial research in this field, the focus has mostly been on the relationship between coaches and athletes, especially female athletes (exceptions being Hartill, 2008 and Toftegard Nielsen, 2004). Much of the research, however, has approached these matters from two different perspectives: initially empirical and descriptive investigations which highlighted and revealed harm and abuse in sport settings, and recently through a more critical approach. There is a growing body of research which emphasises the consequences of strict codes of conduct in relation to child protection, and problematises how child protection is conceived and manifests itself in practice.

From the empirical and descriptive perspective, research focuses on athletes' experiences of sexual harassment by investigating and highlighting the risk factors and emphasising the importance of clear guidelines and interventions. It has focused on the athlete's experiences of sexual harassment by coaches (Brackenridge, 1997; Martin, 2011; Fasting *et al.* 2002). In line with this, Fejgin and Hanegby (2001) examined what kind of behaviour female athletes perceive as sexual harassment, with Toftegard Nielsen (2001) describing the experiences of coaches' behaviour in order to establish where the boundaries between acceptable and unacceptable behaviour could be drawn. The exploitation of power and positions of authority is often given as explanations for sexual harassment (Brackenridge, 1997; Fasting, 2005). Researchers from this perspective have also identified some of the risk factors associated with sexual harassment (Brackenridge and Kirby, 1997; Brackenridge, 2001; Fasting *et al.* 2002). In doing so they have highlighted the importance of preventing sexual harassment by the use of clear guidelines, educational workshops, intervention programmes and implementing codes of conduct in order to guarantee a safe learning environment for all participants (Volkwein *et al.* 1997; Toftegard Nielsen 2001).

An example of the increasing interest in the politics of touch in sport, from a critical perspective, is the Special Edition of the international journal *Sport, Education and Society*, titled 'Hands off! The practice, policy, and politics of touch in sport and educational settings' (Piper *et al.* 2013a). The edition, the genesis of which was a UK Economic and Social Research Council funded research project conducted by the editors, explores how sports coaching/teaching has responded to wider concerns in relation to touch. In the particular edition, a number of researchers and authors claim that the emergence of the issue of sports coach abuse has led to a widespread fear of touching – that coaches and PE teachers are fearful and confused about how to be around the children and young people they coach and teach (Piper *et al.* 2013b). This means that it is the widespread fear, dealt with in different ways, which is becoming the focus of attention, rather than the issue itself. Earlier, Piper and Smith (2003) showed that fear of child abuse ('child panic') is a dominant feature in the daily work of teachers, coaches and carers in general. They drew attention to these dilemmas in the UK over thirteen years ago, and pointed a cautionary finger at the extent that many schools and childcare settings have now become 'no touch zones'. The complexities of, and anxieties about, the relationships between children and adults in early childhood education settings in the US is also highlighted by Johnson (2012), while McWilliam (1999), writing about Australia, outlined the discursive context in which child abuse and moral panic have appeared, and the new categories of vulnerability that these discourses have produced.

There has thus been a growing interest in research questions addressing sexual harassment in relationships between sports coaches and athletes, although in this context there is still a lack of research regarding PE teachers' and pupils' relationships (see Taylor and Garratt, 2010). Teachers' work in PE is mentioned in some of the studies indicated above, but is not particularly emphasised. An exception is Fletcher (2013); drawing on interviews with PE teachers in England, he identifies their growing experience of fear and shows that this fear and confusion have resulted from moral panic. His data demonstrates how teachers have tried to avoid 'problematic incidents' and their associated risks.

Researchers have thus approached the same research area in different ways. Our own research is in line with those who are interested in discussing this complex issue from a critical perspective. From this critical position, which mostly draws on the work of Foucault, we contribute to this body of literature by focusing on the risks and possible consequences if PE practices become 'no touch zones'.

## Public discourses of child protection – the case of Sweden

We now turn to the Swedish context to illustrate how the politics of touch has changed in the wake of heightened awareness and concern in relation to paedophilia and sexual harassment. Public discourses in this area are exemplified by policy documents published by a number of organisations dealing with children and young people.

According to Fasting (2005), policies and codes of practice for the prevention of sexual harassment in sports settings have been developed in some countries, although in a worldwide perspective many countries still ignore this issue (or may choose to deal with the issue in other ways). In comparison with many other countries (e.g. the UK, US, Canada), problems concerning the politics of touch and child protection in organisations and associations involving children and young people are relatively new in Sweden, and have not been highlighted to any extent. It is only in recent years that the debate has blossomed and led to a series of policy documents and 'Child Protection Tool Kits'. The reason why discussions about physical touch, sexual harassment, abuse and sanctions for 'good and bad' interactions between children and adults have become more prevalent in Sweden is due to influences from other countries and the growth and internationalisation of the concern and resulting discourse. However, scandals in sports and the Swedish scouting movement have also recently come to the surface and contributed to a higher profile. For instance, the recent report that Patrik Sjöberg, the former world record holder in the high jump, was sexually abused by his coach caused a public outcry and considerable reflection. The news item was widely published, and was debated extensively by both sports organisations and the media. After the release of Sjöberg and Lutteman's (2011) autobiography *Det du inte såg ('What You Did Not See')*, more stories emerged about sexual abuse in sport. Johansson (2012), backed by the Swedish Sports Confederation, argues that when this particular case came to light, the lack of knowledge and the need for established procedures to prevent and deal with sexual abuse in sport became clear.

In recent years, many Swedish institutions, associations and organisations have published documents on child protection and no touching policy, including right and wrong ways of treating young people in sports, guiding and scouting settings.

In 2005, the Swedish Sports Confederation published a policy document opposing sexual harassment in sport, the aim being to provide guidelines and raise awareness of sexual harassment. In 2012, the same organization published the document 'Skapa trygga idrottsmiljöer' ('Creating safe sporting environments'), and Johansson (2012) did a systematic review 'Sexuella övergrepp – I relationen mellan tränare och idrottsaktiva' ('Sexual abuse – in relationships between coaches and sportsmen and women'). These documents, together with the Child Protection Tool Kit developed in 2007 by World Association of Girl Guides & Girl Scouts (WAGGGS) and the European Scout Region, had a great impact on the topic of child protection policy, providing practical information and sample forms. These documents have in turn influenced other organisations working with children and young people in Sweden and reflect a certain discourse. We refer to some within the chapter to illustrate how public discourses concerning child protection are expressed.

The main purpose of these documents is to protect children from harm and abuse at all times by creating safe environments. This is indicated in the following extracts: '. . . we need to ensure that all adults take their responsibility for the protection of children and young people seriously and that appropriate policies and practices are developed to guide this' (Child Protection Tool Kit, 2007:1), and '. . . sexual abuse is unacceptable and sport organisations are responsible for actively deterring and preventing this' (Johansson, 2012: 47).

In many cases, the documents include guidelines for good practice. These codes of conduct, like the Child Protection Tool Kit (2007:8), tend to advocate a very restrictive use of physical contact between adults and young people, as is illustrated and discussed later. Directive recommendations, which are in effect warnings and instructive guidelines, are increasingly common. Many institutions and associations, particularly in Western countries, have started to implement child protection policies that guide and advise on practice and ethical standards in the guise of good child protection. As Foucault (1990) states, policy documents can be regarded as 'texts written for the purpose of offering rules, opinions, and advice on how to behave as one should' (p. 12). Policy documents relating to child protection can thus be seen as advice to individuals who engage in particular regimes of training and adopt specific technologies to shape and conduct themselves as 'good' teachers, leaders or coaches (McCuaig *et al.* 2013). In line with Foucault (1970), we note the significance of the extent to which, in the policy documents described above, and also in some of the more conservative research studies, there is a degree of regularity in the language used to describe the topic (e.g. abuse, protection, security, safety, risks, codes of conduct and avoid touching). Policy documents like these produce a dominating discourse, an 'official text' that reflects a particular view of 'reality' and a specific way of thinking, acting, and of reporting incidences (Foucault, 1970).

## The power of discourses – specific ways of thinking and acting

In order to be able to discuss how public discourses on child protection and sexual harassment may influence teachers' professional work in PE, we turn to some of

Foucault's writings. The specific language usage referred to above can be seen as an example of how the world is created. The language here is not arbitrary, but follows patterns and systems, or discourse, that is, a certain way of speaking, thinking and acting in a particular area (Winther-Jørgensen and Phillips, 2002). Discourse can be seen as an accepted and dominant way of looking at and talking about the world that influences our understanding and actions. When talking about discourses in a Foucauldian manner – focussing on regular language rules that allow certain statements and actions to be made – an important question to ask is what the political, individual and social consequences of the discursive practice might be. The moment something is uttered, other versions are excluded. In this sense, Foucault's concepts of discourse and power relations are fruitful for understanding the governance and control of the human body and its relationship with other bodies (Foucault, 1976/1980, 1982, 1994a).

It is a matter of how dominating discourses in society impact discursive practices in terms of facilitating or restraining action. As Foucault points out: 'The only important problem is what happens on the ground' (1980/1991:83). Hence, the proper focus of interest and analysis is 'identifying the ways in which human beings are individuated and addressed within the various practices that would govern them' (Rose, 1999:43). Garratt *et al.* (2013: 616) also refer to Foucault, and suggest: 'discursive practices are relational modalities, with networks and connections, whose "dispersion" across the boundaries of different professional domains gives rise to new practices'. Thus, discursive practices and new ways of talking and acting in a specific area affect not only the practices in that specific field, but those in other domains as well. Foucault, when considering power, goes on to suggest:

> But in thinking of the mechanism of power, I am thinking rather of its capillary form of existence, the point where power reaches into the very grain of individuals, touches their bodies and inserts itself into their actions and attitudes, their discourses, learning processes and everyday lives.
>
> (1975/1980:39)

Even if many of the discussions about safeguarding and child protection arise in specific areas (e.g. sport, scouting, childcare) they should, as Garratt *et al.* (2013) point out, be linked to other connected domains, such as the context of PE (see also Fletcher, 2013). It is important to highlight that individual schools in Sweden do not always have their own child protection documents with guidelines and regulations, but PE teachers in Sweden are often engaged in other activities with children and young people outside school, including scouting and sport clubs. In these contexts, such documents are common, and probably affect teachers' work in school. An example of this is the student teacher who spoke and reacted in the example provided at the beginning of this chapter. The development of child protection discourses in general may be expected to have an impact on PE. It is against this background that we discuss the risks and consequences for PE teacher's pedagogical work that may follow from these public discourses. However, in order to be in a position to discuss this further, we need to look at compulsory schooling in general and PE in particular, and clarify what schooling is about.

## Compulsory schooling in general and PE in particular

What is schooling about? The National Swedish Agency for Education (2011:11) states that the task of the Swedish school is to promote learning by stimulating the individual to acquire and develop knowledge and values. The school is expected to promote the personal development of pupils into active, creative, competent, and responsible individuals, and to be concerned about each individual in its care. The Agency emphasises that education involves an understanding and compassion for others, and claims that: 'The school should promote understanding of other people and the ability to empathise. Concern for the well-being and development of the individual should permeate all school activity' (p. 9).

However, the Swedish curriculum does not provide guidelines and instructions for teachers' pedagogical work, or make any specific statements about the role of the teacher, although in a report on sustainable teacher education (State Official Report, 2008) concepts like care and relationships are central. Here, education is essentially regarded as a question of encounters between people, and teachers are exhorted to develop warm and close relationships with their students. A good relationship is considered important for the child's development, although the report notes that an excessive reliance on the teacher impedes the development of students' independence (see also McCuaig *et al.* 2013). As McCuaig (2012) demonstrates elsewhere, the PE profession has increasingly advocated caring teacher-student relationships (see also Larsen and Silverman, 2005; Owens and Ennis, 2005; Rovegno and Kirk, 1995). For Armour and Jones (1998), the importance of care in the work of PE teachers, in a UK context, is 'inextricably linked to the ideal of using physical education, and particularly sport, as a form of social and moral education' (p. 108). Many commentators draw attention to PE teachers' capacity to shift the student-teacher dynamic from the 'impersonal, vertical, highly regulated relationship of teacher and student toward a more personal, horizontal relationship in which there is an exchange of equals' (Brown and Evans, 2004, p. 55). This change of dynamics allows 'meaningful and caring relations between students and staff to be established' (Armour and Jones, 1998, p. 120). The PE profession has long argued that this provides its teachers with the foundations on which they can undertake the social and moral shaping of future citizens (McCuaig, 2012; McCuaig *et al.* 2013).

According to the Swedish school syllabus, the aim of PE is to develop students' physical, mental and social capacities and the acquisition of skills that will enable Swedish youth to adopt healthy lifestyles (NSAE, 2000). Among other things, the subject is expected to stimulate the capacity for, and enjoyment of, movement, and also to encourage responsibility for one's own physical exercise. It is important to mention that since the 1980s the school subject of physical education and health has been co-educational, which means that male teachers have taught female students and female teachers have taught male students. This has created a situation in which the implications of heightened sensitivity regarding touch and potential abuse, in the PE context and more generally, can be expected to have been made more pressing. Against this backdrop, we now draw on research data from video-recorded PE lessons, to illustrate and consider different types of situations in which physical contact and touching seem to be pedagogically relevant and reasonable in the PE context, and where PE teachers can make distinct choices. We then discuss the risks and possible consequences for PE teachers' pedagogical work of heightened anxiety around the issues discussed here, and their significance in the PE environment.

## What is going on in the gym?

The empirical material we draw on consists of fifteen video-recorded lessons in Years 2 to 9 in five upper-secondary Swedish schools. The study has a rich geographical spread, in that it includes schools in large cities, medium-sized towns and rural areas throughout Sweden. Twelve teachers – four women and eight men – of varying ages took part in the lessons. The data was collected in conjunction with a national evaluation of PE in Swedish upper secondary schools (Quennerstedt *et al.* 2008). For the purpose of this chapter, a selection of lesson transcripts and recordings from the study are used to illustrate when physical contact and touching appear as integral components of PE teachers' pedagogical work and pupils' learning situations. We have selected particular incidents, which are appropriate to inform and develop the current discussion.

The various activities conducted during the recorded lessons were: ball activities and ball games, in eight lessons; activities in the form of fitness, strength and cardio training, in seven lessons; gymnastic exercises, in three lessons; and dancing, in two lessons. In order to judge whether this subject content is 'typical', we compared it with several other studies dealing with the content of PE. The results of an evaluation of PE in Swedish schools (Eriksson *et al.* 2005) and other research (Quennerstedt *et al.* 2008) show that teaching is dominated by activities like ball games and different kinds of ball activities, followed by fitness and strength training, and gymnastics.

So, what is going on in the Swedish gym? What happens when it comes to physical contact and 'touching situations'? Physical contact or touching primarily and most frequently occurs in gymnastics lessons, and there seem to be two reasons for this. First, teachers guide and support a correct movement, through 'spotting' a handstand, a somersault, or a flip, thus physically helping pupils to complete the movement, or 'get it right' in a corrective sense. It is about bringing the body into the *right position* to create a sense of the movement itself. Second, physical contact is about *preventing injury* when doing movements that seem risky, such as a somersault on a trampoline.

Physical contact (touching) also takes place in fitness and strength training. Here teachers often *correct bodily movements* by supporting a specific part of the body with their hands. This might be to stop someone from overdoing a sit-up or a squat, or to show that in press-ups your nose has to stop just short of the floor. Correcting bodily movements by touching pupils when they are working with muscle training is about making the exercises as effective as possible.

When it comes to dance activities, physical contact occurs when a teacher *demonstrates* the steps of a dance and puts his or her hand on a pupil's shoulders or their arm around the pupil's waist, as one does in ballroom dancing. Although physical contact between teachers and pupils is not very common in ball games, it does sometimes occur. One example is when a teacher demonstrates what a foul in basketball looks like by 'hitting' the pupil on the arm or jostling (pushing) to get the ball.

Touch seems to be a natural part of teaching practice, in these examples, when it comes to correcting body movements, preventing injuries, making exercise effective and demonstrating how to perform exercises in learning situations. However, physical contact also occurs in other pedagogical situations; for example, when a 'naughty' child needs to be calmed down the teacher puts his or her hand on the child's shoulders. Alternatively, when a pupil has overcome a difficult challenge, the teacher and the pupil give each other a hug or a 'high five', or when the lesson is over and a pupil goes up to the teacher for a 'goodbye' hug. It would seem that in this general pedagogic context physical communication in PE is a natural part of the sporting culture, and integral to a subject in which body and movement are central concerns. However, this touching culture or atmosphere is not always obvious or straightforward, and can take various forms in the different lessons. We would like to illustrate two completely different situations – dealing with fear and injury – in which physical contact (or not) can (or should?) be a natural part of humanity. These two situations illustrate the complexities of physical touch.

In the first situation (in Year 2), a student was afraid of doing a gymnastic movement on the beam and did not want to do it. He was close to tears, and the teacher put his arm around him, patted him on the back, and encouraged him to try again. When the teacher reassured the pupil that everything would go well, his arm remained on the pupil's shoulders. The boy then successfully performed the exercise with the aid of the teacher. In the second pedagogic situation, this time in Year 3, a soccer tournament was in progress. Everyone seemed to be engaged and taking part and many of the pupils were encouraging each other. Suddenly, one of the girls was hit in the stomach by the ball. It obviously hurt because she cried out and made her way to the bench to rest. The teacher, who was standing only a metre in front of the girl, said: 'You need to watch out. Come on, stop it now, the ball hits everyone sometimes. Rest for a while'. These two examples show how two teachers deal with critical and emotional situations in different ways, involving a pedagogic interaction with or without physical contact, and arguably with different degrees of warmth and empathy.

From considering these recorded teaching sessions, it seems that although, in many physical activities, physical contact in the form of instruction-based touching, spotting, supporting, risk prevention, encouraging and comforting, is a useful, helpful and valuable part of PE practice, this is no guarantee that it will be applied. In the context of the powerful discourses referred to earlier, teachers have to make choices, which may in turn influence their effectiveness in technical and more broadly significant areas.

## 'No touching' – the weakening of pedagogical practices

The selected illustrations from the PE lessons show that physical contact between teachers and students takes place in a variety of pedagogical situations. In some situations, physical contact seems to be both relevant and reasonable as an integral component of pupils' learning, development and growth. As an educator any interactions with pupils involves both a human and a professional encounter.

We have previously indicated that the codes of conduct that appear in many of the policy documents advocate a restrictive use of physical contact between adults and young people. A key example includes for instance:

- Where physical contact is necessary, be sensitive and always avoid touching the children and young people yourself,
- Where physical contact is unavoidable, ensure that another adult is present[4], and
- When a child is upset, try to seek ways to provide comfort and support without unnecessary or excessive physical contact (Child Protection Tool Kit, 2007:8).

If PE teachers follow these guidelines in practice, and 'always avoid touching the children' (an approach that the student teacher indicated in the story at the beginning of the chapter had clearly absorbed) much of the educationally and developmentally valuable content in PE will either be lost, or will need to be changed. This may result in many of the teachers' pedagogical practices being weakened.

If PE practice becomes a 'no touch zone', what will be the risks and potential consequences for teachers' pedagogical work and for students' learning? We believe that certain learning situations will be impossible to deal with in an effective way, and the risk could be that teachers will find it difficult:

- To develop students' motor skills and physical abilities ('to get it right'), and to convey the desired body movements. Some learning situations will be lost and the pupils will lose some key skills,
- To prevent injuries and deal with 'risky' situations when pupils carry out complex physical activities,
- To cope with social situations involving behaviour and manners, where many students need physical contact in order to understand what is going on. Not all students have the ability to listen to verbal reprimands, and
- To spontaneously express joy when pupils have successfully carried out a specific exercise.

In PE, where body and movement are central, it is important to ask whether it is possible to learn about the body's potential and body movements by verbal communication alone. However, it is not just about physical abilities. It is also about the general goals of education in terms of developing students' personalities, their capacity for empathy, and social and moral shaping. Noddings (2002), in her discussion of the holistic nature and responsibility of education, points out that the relationship between teacher and student is crucial for learning to take place. This relationship has a special quality in that it involves a reciprocal giving and receiving of care.

During lessons pupils sometimes become sad and upset. As noted, the Child Protection Tool Kit advises teachers that: 'When a child is upset, try to seek ways to provide comfort and support without unnecessary or excessive physical contact', and the implications of such advice deserve consideration. In one of the illustrated lessons, the teacher puts his arm around a pupil and speaks in a friendly and comforting tone. In another, when a ball hits a student in the stomach, the teacher maintains distance and only uses verbal communication. Is the second approach reasonable or appropriate, one might wonder, in a situation in which a child is in pain and is upset? What happens here to the educational goal concerning 'the ability to empathise' and to the social and moral shaping of future citizens? Schooling is a matter of developing knowledge and values, as well as personal development and an ability to empathise. It also includes social and moral shaping, in which care and warm relationships need to characterise teachers' pedagogical work. In an educational engagement, pupils learn about society and their own place and importance in it – being a citizen in a democratic society. Few of us would deny that the capacity for empathy and care and developing as a human being includes physical interaction. In some learning situations, might non-verbal communication in terms of physical interactions be more significant and relevant than words? The defensive approach encapsulated in 'no touching' in such situations might mean that teachers are unable to implement and develop some of the general goals of the curriculum, which can lead to an erosion of teachers' pedagogical work in PE practice.

Finally, when highlighting the risks and consequences of 'no touching' policies, it is important to discuss children's rights. The documents that we have referred to in this chapter have a specific approach to children's rights, which is that children and young people have a right to feel safe and protected. It is of course important to highlight the problems of abuse, harm and sexual harassment in terms of the protection and rights of children; for many, the issue of children's rights appears to be merely a matter of protection. But contrary to this idea, we must not override other significant rights associated with childhood, namely the rights to learning, socialisation, personal development and physical contact. It is a social and human right to have an education whose content and approach help one to develop and grow – where physical touch does not only have an instrumental value but is also a personal value that can help to develop the student's full potential and thus lead to a good life (Hägglund *et al.* 2013). In this matter, Piper and Smith (2003: 890) suggest: 'A moral panic has led to the production of guidelines that are concerned with protecting children from abuse and adults from false allegations, but where the needs of children are lost.' We share this concern and argue that a caring and interpersonal relationship is built on mutual respect and exchange. This includes touch as an action in its own right, as well as one that is a fundamental part of reciprocal gestures and social intercourse.

Thus, it is very important that we not only continue to discuss the necessity of child protection, but also the risk that striving for children's rights and security could create a social practice that lacks sound pedagogical and caring physical interactions. If the learning objectives stated in the curriculum are to be achieved, we have to make visible the tensions, contradictions and implications of our zeal to protect, secure and safeguard. We also need to be aware of the consequences of restricting PE teachers' pedagogical actions by strict codes of conduct on touch. Has it gone a bit too far when supporting a handstand in PE is even conceivably interpreted as sexual harassment?

## 'Do not throw the baby out with the bath water'

The tensions that arise between the protection of children and problems of abuse on the one hand, and charitable and pedagogical interactions on the other, are of course important to highlight. Even though the huge majority of people consider the protection of children as essential and non-negotiable, it is still necessary to take up the challenge issued by Nealon (2008:71) and seek to distinguish between different responses, different practices. We should particularly be attuned to register those taken-for-granted social practices that appear beyond reproach, like the defensive response to the theoretical potential for abuse which lies behind the culture of 'no touch', since 'power becomes more effective while offering less obvious potential for resistance' (McCuaig *et al.* 2013). The moment we work to protect children by securing the relationships between children and adults in a normative and prescriptive way, we also create concern about relationships between children and adults. Johnson (2012) refers to this as the production of new categories of vulnerability out of public discourses around 'no touching policies'.

Using a Foucauldian inspired approach makes it possible to reflect on and critically examine the consequences of dominating discourses that produce 'realities' and specific ways of thinking and acting. It is a matter of looking critically at those things that are taken for granted and appear to be beyond question. Taken-for-granted assumptions can make us blind to the existence of other 'truths' and 'realities'. It is thus 'a matter of introducing a critical attitude towards those things that are given to our present experience as if they were timeless, natural and unquestionable' (Rose, 1999:20). In his later work, Foucault (1994b) encourages us to attend to those 'strategies by which individuals try to direct and control the conduct of others' (p. 298). In line with this, the well-known injunction, 'do not throw the baby out with the bath water' refers to the importance of retaining the positive things when seeking to clear away the bad. In our eagerness to improve and develop, there is a danger that we forget to retain and protect what is good. We argue that if in the commendable struggle for children's rights and security the body becomes forbidden, and as a result generally sexualised, an inhuman social practice will be created that both contradicts the established educational goals of PE teaching, and renders sound pedagogical and caring physical interactions taboo.

Thus we must argue the case for 'not losing touch'. The professionalism of PE teachers is built on notions of caring, mutual respect and educating young people to engage in positive social and sporting interactions, and embraces the social and moral shaping of future citizens. All this important work involves interpersonal touch, contact and trust.

## Notes

1 The concept 'sexual harassment' is used throughout the text. A general definition is 'unwanted sexual attention', and we include sexual abuse as part of the concept of sexual harassment. In some cases, we use the term as used by a certain author (see Brackenridge 1997; Fasting 2005; and Toftegard Nielsen 2001 for discussion of the different definitions).
2 See Fasting (2005) for a detailed overview of research on sexual harassment and abuse in sport.
3 The growth of interest in the issue of child abuse and protection, through diverse contexts including childcare, teaching and sports coaching, can be traced back to the identification of the 'battered child' in the 1960s (Kempe *et al.* 1962).
4 It seems impractical, even absurd, to always have to fetch another adult when physical contact is necessary, especially as physical education teachers are often alone with the class, and the gym may be located several hundred metres away from the main school building.

## References

Armour, K. M. & Jones, R. L. (1998) *Physical education teachers' lives and careers: PE, sport and educational status.* London: Falmer Press.

Brackenridge, C. (1997) 'He owned me basically . . .': Women's experience of sexual abuse in sport. *International Review for the Sociology of Sport* 32(2) 115–130.

Brackenridge, C. (ed.) (2001) *Spoilsports: Understanding and preventing sexual exploitation in sport.* London: Routledge.

Brackenridge, C. & Kirby, S. (1997) Playing safe. Assessing the risk of sexual abuse to elite child athletes. *International Review for the Sociology of Sport* 32(4) 407–418.

Brown, D. & Evans, J. (2004) Reproducing gender? Intergenerational links and the male PE teacher as a cultural conduit in teaching physical education. *Journal of Teaching in Physical Education* 23(1): 48–70.

Child Protection Tool Kit (2007) The Europe Region World Association of Girl Guides & Girl Scouts (WAGGGS) and the European Scout Region. The World Organization of the Scout Movement European Region, Geneva. Accessed 5 January, 2014 at www.scout.org/en/information_events/library/child_protection/child_protection_tool_kit

Eriksson, C., Gustavsson, K., Quennerstedt, M., Rudsberg, K., Öhman, M. & Öijen, L. (2005) *Idrott och hälsa – ämnesrapport NU-03.* [The national evaluation of compulsory school 2003 – physical education]. Stockholm: Fritzes.

Fasting, K. (2005) Research on sexual harassment and abuse in sport. *Idrottsforum.org.* [*Nordic Sport Science Forum*] Accessed 5 January, 2014 at www.idrottsforum.org 2005–04–05.

Fasting, K., Brackenridge, C. & Sundgot-Borgen, J. (2004) Prevalence of sexual harassment among Norwegian female elite athletes in relation to sport type. *International Review for the Sociology of Sport* 39(4) 373–386.

Fasting, K., Brackenridge, C. & Walseth, K. (2002) Coping with sexual harassment in sport – experiences of elite female athletes. *The Journal of Sexual Aggression* 8(2) 37–48.

Fejgin, N., & Hanegby, R. (2001) Gender and cultural bias in perceptions of sexual harassment in sport. *International Review for the Sociology of Sport* 36(4) 459–478.

Fletcher, S. (2013) Touching practice and physical education: Deconstruction of a contemporary moral panic. *Sport, Education and Society* 18(5) 694–709.

Foucault, M. (1970) *The order of things: An archaeology of the human sciences.* New York: Pantheon.

Foucault, M. (1975/1980) Prison talk. In Colin Gordon (ed.), *Power/Knowledge, selected interviews & other writings 1972–1977*, p. 37–54. New York: Pantheon.

Foucault, M. (1976/1980) Two lectures. In Colin Gordon (ed.), *Power/Knowledge, selected interviews & other writings 1972–1977*, p. 78–108. New York: Pantheon.

Foucault, M. (1980/1991) Questions of Method. In G. Burchell, C. Gordon & P. Miller (eds.), *The Foucault effect. Studies in governmentality*, p. 73–86. New York: Pantheon.

Foucault, M. (1982) The subject and power. *Critical Inquiry* 8(4) 777–795.

Foucault, M. (1990) *The use of pleasure: The history of sexuality* (Vol. 2). Random House Digital Inc.

Foucault, M. (1994a) *Power: The essential works of Foucault 1954–1984* (Vol. III). J. D. Faubion (ed.), R. Hurley and others, trans. London: Penguin Books.

Foucault, M. (1994b) *Ethics: subjectivity and truth: The essential works of Foucault 1954–1984* (Vol. I). In Paul Rabinow (ed.), R. Hurley and others, trans. London, Penguin Books.

Garratt, D., Piper, H. & Taylor, B. (2013) 'Safeguarding' sports' coaching: Foucault, genealogy and critique. *Sport, Education and Society* 18(5) 615–629.

Hägglund, S., Quennerstedt, A. & Thelander, N. (2013) *Barns och ungas rättigheter i utbildning* [Children's and Young People's Rights in Education]. Malmö: Gleerups.

Hartill, M. (2008) The sexual abuse of boys in organized male sports. *International Review for the Sociology of Sport* 12(2) 225–249.

Johansson, S. (2012) The Swedish Sports Confederation (2012) Kunskapsöversikt: Sexuella övergrepp – i relation mellan tränare och idrottsaktiv. (Systematic review: Sexual abuse – in the relationship between coaches and sports active') FoU-rapport2012:5. Stockholm: Riksidrottsförbundet. Accessed 5 January, 2014 at www.rf.se/ImageVault/Images/id_27851/scope_0/ImageVaultHandler.aspx

Johnson, R. T. (2012) Training 'safe' bodies in an era of child panic: New technologies for disciplining bodies. Paper Presented at the *Annual American Education Research Association Meeting*, Vancouver, Canada, April 2012.

Larsen, A. & Silverman, S. (2005) Rationales and practices used by caring physical education teachers. *Sport Education and Society* 10(2) 175–193.

Kempe, S. H., Silverman, F. N., Steele, F. B., Droegemueller, M. D. & Silver H. K. (1962) The battered child syndrome. *Journal of American Medical Association* 181(1), 17–24.

Martin, M. (2011) Don't be mistaken – this does concern you! *Qualitative Inquiry* 17(9) 864–874.

McCuaig, L. A. (2012) Dangerous carers: Pastoral power and the caring teacher of contemporary Australian schooling. *Educational Philosophy and Theory* 44(8) 862–877.

McCuaig, L., Öhman, M. & Wright, J. (2013) Shepherds in the gym: Employing a pastoral power analytic on caring teaching in HPE. *Sport, Education and Society* 18(6) 788–806.

McWilliam, E. (1999) *Pedagogical pleasure.* New York: Peter Lang.

Nealon, J. (2008) *Foucault beyond Foucault: Power and its intensifications since 1984.* Stanford, CA: Stanford University Press.

Noddings, N. (2002) *Educating moral people: A caring alternative to character education.* New York: Teacher College Press.

The National Swedish Agency for Education (NSAE) (2000) Grundskolan. Kursplaner och betygskriterier Idrott och hälsa. Lpo 94. [Curriculum for the compulsory school system, the pre-school class and the leisure-time centre: Assessment and grades in physical education and health]. Stockholm: Fritzes. Accessed 5 January, 2014 at www.luthag ensskolor.uppsala.se/dokument/kursplaner.pdf

The National Swedish Agency for Education (NSAE) (2011) Curriculum for the compulsory school, preschool class and the leisure-time centre. Stockholm: Skolverket. Accessed 5 January, 2014 at www.skolverket.se/publikationer

Owens, L. & Ennis, C. (2005) The ethic of care in teaching: An overview of supportive literature. *Quest* 57(4) 392–425.

Piper, H., Garratt, D. & Taylor, B. (2013a) Hands off! The practice, policy, and politics of touch in sport and educational settings. *Sport, Education and Society* 18(5) 575–582.

Piper, H., Garratt, D. & Taylor, B. (2013b) Child abuse, child protection, and defensive 'touch' in PE teaching and sports coaching. *Sport, Education and Society* 18(5) 583–598.

Piper, H. & Smith, H. (2003) 'Touch' in educational and child care settings: Dilemmas and responses. *British Educational Research Journal* 29(6) 879–894.

Quennerstedt, M., Öhman, M., & Eriksson, C. (2008) Physical education in Sweden – a national evaluation. *Education-line.* Accessed 5 January, 2014 at www.leeds.ac.uk/educol/documents

Rose, N. (1999) *Powers of freedom: Reframing political thought.* Cambridge: Cambridge University Press.

Rovegno, I. & Kirk, D. (1995) Articulations and silences in socially critical work on physical education: Toward a broader agenda. *Quest* 47(4), 447–474.

Sjöberg, P. & Lutteman, M. (2011): *Det du inte såg* [What you did not see]. Stockholm: Norstedt.

State Official Report (SOR) (2008) Lärarutbildningsutredningen: *Sustainable teacher education* [Teacher education inquiry: Sustainable teacher education]. Stockholm: Regeringskansliet. Accessed 5 January, 2014 at www.regeringen.se/sb/d/10005/a/116737

Taylor, B. & Garratt, D. (2010) The professionalisation of sport coaching: Relations of power, resistance and compliance. *Sport, Education and Society* 15(1) 121–139.

Toftegard Nielsen, J. (2001) The forbidden zone. Intimacy, sexual relations and misconduct in the relationship between coaches and athletes. *International Review for the Sociology of Sport* 36(2) 165–183.

Toftegaard Nielsen, J. (2004) Idrættens illusoriske intimitet. PhD thesis. Universitetet i København, Institut for Idræt, Denmark.

The Swedish Sports Confederation (2005) Riksidrottsförbundets policy mot sexuella trakasserier inom idrotten [The Swedish Sport Confederation policy against sexual harassment in sport]. Stockholm: Riksidrottsförbundet. Accessed 5 January, 2014 at www. rf.se/ImageVault/Images/id_16622/scope_0/ImageVaultHandler.aspx

The Swedish Sports Confederation (2012) Skapa Trygga Idrottsmiljöer [Creating safe sporting environments]. Stockholm: Riksidrottsförbundet. Accessed 5 January, 2014 at www.rf.se/Allanyheter/2012/Nyttstodmaterialskagetryggareidrottforbarnochungdomar/

Volkwein, K.A.E., Schnell, F. I., Sherwood, D. & Livezey, A. (1997) Sexual harassment in sport. Perceptions and experiences of American female student-athletes. *International Review for the Sociology of Sport* 32(3) 283–295.

Winther-Jørgensen, M. & Phillips, L. (2002) *Discourse analysis as theory and method.* London, Sage.

# 6 'It's not what you see, it's how it feels'

## Touch in the tactile context of Cypriot track and field sport

*Maria Papaefstathiou*

## Introduction[1]

Human rights movements and social inclusion campaigns have evolved significantly in recent years. In particular, children's rights and child protection (CP) are now central concerns among nations and their social institutions. Within the context of sport, recent European projects and conferences have brought together national sport advocates, to accumulate and share practices and knowledge around the problem of abuse, including sexual violence against children in sport (Chroni *et al.* 2012). This growth of interest in athlete welfare at international policy, research, and practice levels is likely to influence national and local activity relating to CP in sport settings. Nevertheless, culturally sensitive research and knowledge around the understanding of these elements, especially in the field of sport, remains scarce. The aim of this chapter is to focus on the understandings of actors in Cypriot track and field sport as a way of highlighting their uncertainties and fears around notions of 'touch' and other related social practices. It is suggested these fears are double-edged, in that there are uncertainties attached to learning to read touch (anew) within a largely tactile Mediterranean culture, and there are fears that guidelines based on international practices may be too heavy-handed for the local context. First, I briefly describe both the specific culture of sport and that of Cyprus, to set the background for the rest of the chapter.

## The physiognomy of sport

The distinct historical and sociocultural physiognomy of sport constitutes an exceptional case, making CP development particularly sensitive and challenging. Traditionally, the engagement of children in sport has been typically perceived as an enjoyable activity, often associated with inclusion, a tool for healthy development, and goals related to achieving or promoting peace (e.g. UN, 2011). Due to the largely positive perceptions of sport, it often remains an autonomous and unregulated field (Brackenridge, 2001) establishing a strong 'moral status', deeply embedded in people's views. This contrasts with other institutions, for instance education and health, where welfare measures to protect and nurture young populations have been more clearly defined and prescribed.

Sport also tends to set itself apart as a unique case because of some distinct social characteristics, including the close coach-athlete (often professional) relationship, where physical and emotional bonds are often cultivated due to the nature of training practice (Chroni *et al.* 2007; Rhind & Jowett, 2010). For example, in track and field sport the frequent one-to-one training, involving physical contact as part of the improvement of technique, massages, and demanding physical checks, can make the coach's role appear unique, as well as critical and sensitive. Within this training environment power imbalances can occur, which can lead to aggressive behaviours, even crossing into abusive practices (Brackenridge, 2001; Hartill, 2009). This physiognomy of sport generates more concern when a particular culture of sport – a hierarchical, masculine, gender-based culture of 'obedience' – is highlighted (Brackenridge, 2001; David, 2005). Therefore, the 'exceptional' place of sport in society is now being replaced by the idea that sport can exhibit the same problems found in other social institutions and activities (Chalip, 2006; Brackenridge *et al.* 2007) especially as the sporting body and its physicality is central to this field. While aspects of the sport environment may be unique, it is also similar to other fields in terms of how touch can be necessary yet appear risky at the same time. When this tension is overlaid with local traditions and cultural features which are also notably tactile, another dimension is added to the setting of this chapter.

## Historical and sociocultural parameters of Cypriot sport

Prior to the accession of the Republic of Cyprus into the European Union (EU) in 2004, the country was historically subject to diverse ruling systems, including being a British Crown Colony from 1925 until the inauguration of the Republic in 1960. This history resulted in the country's ongoing efforts for independence, the development of a sense of identity, and the sustenance of traditional values. The 1974 Turkish invasion (which followed continuing political problems since the country's independence in 1960), imposed a *de facto* division of the island and the separation of the Greek-Cypriot and Turkish-Cypriot communities. Together with the recent economic recessions, this upheaval strengthened efforts in the Greek Cypriot community (in the area of the country under the effective control of the Cypriot government) to preserve and foster a strong sense of national Greek culture and orthodox Christianity. This priority is embedded across several fields including the educational curriculum, illustrating a substantial commitment to patriarchal, religious, and family bonds (Office for the Commissioner of Children's Rights, 2011).

When it comes to the care of children, while relevant legislation is in place, the family's responsibility has been prioritized, with the state intervening only when basic needs provision is deemed insufficient. This context, I suggest, can create and support a situation in which a sense of community and close knit, almost familial relationships can be cultivated and replicated across institutions, including sport. The country's small geographical scale helps sustain this environment in that individuals can easily acquire knowledge about each other (e.g. home, origin). Thus, in sport a coach can constitute a well-known individual for the child athlete's family and can often be perceived as a second parent figure by the child athlete. The positive contribution of family relationships including facilitating affection, attention, support, and care for children in diverse forms (pedagogy, health, food), can communicate in environments outside the family, with adult professionals frequently acting as *in loco parentis* figures. From a Northern European perspective, Mediterranean cultures can appear to be characterised by more demonstrative, sensuous and, controversially, perhaps less 'rational' human interactions. Such everyday interactions are not just in the personal realm, but also extend into wider political, legal, and sociocultural arenas that influence how institutions like sport, and particular organisations, view touch in practice. Such elements have a significant impact on the way Cypriot sport settings are organized, and how human relationships function within them.

When Cyprus joined the EU, directives and laws were introduced, problematising its patriarchal and hierarchical characteristics, reflected in the macro level down to micro everyday lived experiences, with changing meanings and approaches towards children and young people's participation and protection becoming increasingly dominant and influential. Whereas previous emphasis would heavily rely on cultivating the child as a member of a *community*, recent approaches tend to celebrate the idea of empowering the child as an *individual* (Mapp, 2011, Thukral, 2011). Such moves have gathered momentum with the establishment of the National Office for the Commissioner of Children's Rights in 2007, alongside NGO establishments responsible for monitoring children's rights issues in all areas under the control of the Government of Cyprus (Office for the Commissioner of Children's Rights, 2011).

Cultural views of childhood, which previously tended to be defined in traditional terms are now strongly informed by, and intersect with, global discourses on children's rights (Spyrou, 2008), often leading to opposing definitions and understandings between traditional and contemporary approaches (Howe, 2010). For instance, physical punishment, which had been socially acceptable as part of developing the child's discipline, is now questioned, having been prohibited since 1994 (Office for the Commissioner of Children's Rights, 2011). Nevertheless, it continues to be tolerated at times (Georgiades, 2009), revealing the multiple layers of contradictory discourses on childhood and indicating that strong cultural norms can change very slowly even when legislation is established (Mapp, 2011). Significantly, however, the problem of child sexual harassment and abuse began to constitute a central public concern, particularly following the promotion of the Europe-wide campaign *1 in 5* (Council of Europe, 2014). The sensitivity around this 'taboo' issue has been further increased as several cases of sexual abuse of children and national level research and statistical findings began to be reported in the media (e.g. Politis Online, 2011). While the recognition and tackling of a sensitive, difficult, complicated, and sad problem constitutes a positive step, heightened awareness can too easily create a moral panic amongst the public (Parton, 2006; Piper *et al.* 2013). Despite the media's positive contribution in making the problem public (Boyden, 1997), the nature of media reporting and campaigning can be greatly influential in moulding the public's understandings of child sexual abuse (Garratt *et al.* 2013).

Against this backdrop, in the Cypriot context much of the knowledge around problems of child abuse provided through media can sound sensational, vague, or superficial, since culturally sensitive formal debate, training, or education in these issues is scarce. The largely family centred approach to welfare provision, indicative of the historically rooted elements mentioned earlier, remains strong, particularly since the country's recent financial situation might not permit child welfare provision by the state to extend beyond basic needs provision (including education, training, funding of welfare organisations, and Criminal Records Bureau [CRB] checks). Nevertheless, the media remains the sole powerful source of information and the fact that it currently adopts the pathological–individual narrative is strongly influential, particularly on parents/carers and adult professionals interacting with children, as well as on the children themselves. One area affected is the utilization of touching, and related practices. For instance, the frequently promoted emphasis of *1 in 5* on 'Touching: if it does not feel right it isn't right', while accompanied by elaboration on its meaning, can cast suspicion on the largely positive and culturally contributive tactile practices between adults and children in the Cypriot context. This can result in changing the meanings of touch, from largely positive to largely negative connotations that can be harmful to local tradition and culture. While any attempt to protect children from actual abuse is to be welcomed, a 'superficial' awareness of the problem is striking in Cypriot sport settings. However, no educative guidelines or information sources are in place, even though the Cyprus Sport Organization (CSO) has signed on to European agreements which recommend the development of measures for safety and health of children and young people in sport (e.g. EU, 2007). It may therefore be that Cypriots find it easy to accept the *goal* of child protection while being less accepting of the *methods* which are prescribed for achieving it.

In the context of this climate of cultural change and uncertainty, this chapter considers current experiences and opinions of actors engaged in Cypriot track and field sport, exploring their perspectives on touching and other 'risky' practices characteristic of sport, such as offering lifts, texting, and socializing. This empirical work is introduced later as it appears useful to first outline a framework to support understanding of what has been happening, of how actors have experienced it, and of what they think about it.

## Disciplinary power and touch: Technologies of domination and of the self

To situate the findings of my research within a theoretical framework I use the notions of 'disciplinary power' and 'Panopticon' (Foucault, 1977) as developed and discussed in Foucault's later work on 'bio-politics'. They illustrate the findings in a number of ways. Touching practices in Cypriot sport can constitute 'technologies of the self' since they can be perceived as moral and ethical actions (Markula & Pringle, 2006) comprising acceptable and normalized types of 'micro-technique[s]' (Fraser, 1981, p. 276). Further, I suggest that the current pathological narrative made visible through media coverage, together with authoritative recommendations (International Olympic Committee [IOC], 2007), comprise types of 'macro-strategies' (Fraser, 1981, p. 276). They appear indicative of a mode of governance resembling the neoliberal model, and shape the population's thinking about, and response to, matters of CP and abuse as constituting an individual rather than a social problem (Markula & Pringle, 2006; Fletcher, 2013).

These 'global' narratives can be 'located in a macro risk society context' (Johansson, 2013, p. 3), which with 'an ensemble of multiple regulations and institutions [. . .] take the generic of "police"' (Foucault, 1980a, p. 170). Indeed, the research findings discussed later make visible the types of self-regulation enforced in a situation of neoliberal governance in order that certain expectations are met, including child health and well-being (Markula & Pringle, 2006). Nevertheless, a number of unforeseen consequences occur, including the cultivation of an ambiguous, often suspicious and insecure, climate among individuals in sport. Such approaches, I suggest, can be culturally insensitive, presenting the need for developing culturally friendly, 'light-touch' guidelines to reflect the simultaneous intent and fear around the facilitation of CP measures, and their implications for Cypriot sporting culture.

Foucault (1980b) established a view of the developmental procedures of knowledge in relation to power and discourse which can be 'at work in modern societies' (p.148). These procedures create 'relations of domination which have their own configuration and relative autonomy' (Foucault, 1980c, p. 188). In these relations of domination, individuals become objects and simultaneously are produced as subjects, resulting in their becoming 'tied to particular identities' shaped by social institutions (Markula & Pringle, 2006, p. 8). Foucault (1977) articulates a form of disciplinary power found in internal and local spaces (contexts) through the application of daily practices, which results in obedient, docile bodies, which in turn illustrate a form of 'knowing how to be'. In his genealogical work, Foucault articulates the relations of power between individuals as productive in a spatial environment, resembling Bentham's architecture of the 'Panopticon' through the use of 'technologies of control' including 'hierarchical observation', 'normalizing judgment' and 'examination' (ibid., p. 170), which result in individuals exercising self-regulation since 'inspection functions ceaselessly' (ibid., p. 195). For Foucault (1977), the 'Panopticon' constitutes a 'marvelous [architectural] machine' (p. 202) where the effects of dominant (state) power can transmit silently and indirectly 'since each individual has at his [sic] disposal a certain power, and for that very reason can also act as the vehicle for transmitting a wider power' (Foucault, 1980d, p. 72).

The effectiveness of the 'Panopticon' in local institutions as discussed by Foucault (1977) extends to a description of the level of (political) governance, utilized as a useful means for managing the public (Fraser, 1981). This system of politics is characteristic of neoliberal states with 'a nexus of common interest between various forms of contemporary capital and the contemporary state' (Ball, 2012, p. 3) placing 'people under surveillance to subject them to some exemplary penalty' (Foucault, 1980e, p. 38). In this situation, 'the government is enabled to govern at a distance' (Piper *et al.* 2013, p. 594). While freedom and autonomy celebrate the system's democratic element, nevertheless individual responsibility and self-regulation is integral, an 'individualizing culture of surveillance, accountability, and resentment' (Silk & Andrews, 2012, p. 6), and can be coercive and repressive.

When it comes to CP in sport, critical research suggests that similar modes of governance can function within contemporary contexts such as the UK (Piper *et al.* 2013). Most particularly, organizations providing policies and guidelines relating to awareness, monitoring, and evaluation of child abuse can create types of self-regulation among individuals (ibid.). This type of governance can develop 'regimes of truth' (Foucault, 1980, cited in Garratt *et al*, 2013, p. 616) that can 'lock individuals into a particular identity' (Markula & Pringle, 2006, p. 138). In this manner, a collective management of public groups and organisations is maintained via an indirect control exercised by the state.

The influence on the Cypriot public regarding child (sexual) abuse exercised by media and international interventions is also illuminated through this framework. In Foucault's words media can constitute a similar mode of gaze, serving the needs of particular politics. 'Media would necessarily be under the command of economical-political interests' (Foucault, 1980b, p. 162). Thus, the way that child sexual abuse is presented in Cypriot media can 'act as powerful forms of public pedagogy' (Silk & Andrews, 2012, p. 5) proposing the prevalent narrative around the problem, which in turn influences greatly how the Cypriot population conceive the problem and individuals self-regulate themselves. Likewise, dominant views of the problem as presented in statements and 'moral campaigns' (Markula & Pringle, 2006 p. 46) can exercise a particular understanding on child abuse problems. However, critiques of current approaches suggest that while the sensitivity of the problem creates a response that is well intentioned, it might allow no space for disagreement and criticism; as such a response would be conceived as uncaring (Piper *et al.* 2013). This situation can resemble a type of gaze in which 'the ones doing the looking [i.e. media/campaigns/ other international movements] are giving themselves the power to define' (Mita, 1989, p. 30). Nevertheless, definitions can be often subjective and culturally insensitive, particularly when it comes to such a complex issue such as touching (Grosz, 1994 cited in Chare, 2013, p. 670), leading to particular problems since 'disciplinary institutions do not always produce their intended outcomes' (Foucault, 1977, cited in Markula & Pringle, 2006, p. 47), in this case the child athlete's welfare. This situation can also raise questions regarding the legitimacy and capacity of nations' regions to control their own institutional systems, since international guidelines and policy 'is being "done" in new locations, on different scales, by new actors and organisations' (Ball, 2012, p. 4). Some consequences of this situation are illustrated in the section that follows.

## Research outcomes and themes

The data discussed here was produced during doctoral research conducted over twelve months: an ethnographic case study exploring the meanings of child athlete protection/abuse within the context of Cypriot sport. The research was conducted by the author, and funded by her university, where the work was approved by the relevant research ethics committee in 2011. Semi-structured discursive interviews were conducted with ten respondents heavily engaged in track and field sport in Cyprus: four coaches, four athletes, two administrators, some of whom had experience in different roles, with equal gender representation and a range of ages. From a consideration of the interviews, key themes were identified which provide headings for subsequent discussion. Obviously this is a limited sample, subject to the normal conditions of mainstream qualitative research.

### *Touching and related practices: Acceptable, normal, and important*

The first theme communicates that the occurrence of 'touching' practices seems to be perceived as normal and acceptable in Cypriot track and field sport, and also as important and necessary for the holistic development of the athlete and child. In a Foucauldian sense these practices can form moral acts generated by the coach with the intention of being a positive contribution for the child athlete (Markula & Pringle, 2006). The views of Michalis, an experienced coach, illustrate his relationship with a number of 14-year-old to 16-year-old athletes in his charge:

> I am like a second parent for my athletes. The children ask for attention not only for their performance. A few days ago, during the training an athlete gave me her leg to have a look. She said that she felt pain. When I placed my hands she did not feel any pain the next day.
>     . . . When the training finishes, if it is convenient for me to drive an athlete home then I do, sometimes. They often organise social gatherings at their place and invite me as well. So, I have a very close relationship with the athletes other than the athletic one, and their parents as well. We go out for pizza or to the athletes' houses. I see each one of them as a unique individual so I want to educate them as individuals not only as athletes. For this reason, I sacrifice personal time for each one of them. Many times the athletes wake me up at 2am saying 'Coach, I can't sleep' asking 'What can I do?' I will respond to the athlete and I need to find a key word to make her sleep.
>     . . . Caressing and affection are necessary for the child. Sometimes the athletes themselves seek a hug, which I will give with affection, like when a parent cuddles their child. (Michalis, coach, 60)

Michalis describes core culturally accepted elements and practices found in Cypriot sporting and social engagement, acts such as the coach giving a hug to an athlete with spontaneity and emotion indicating a social and moral obligation to look after the person and not just the athlete (Foucault, 1992). The tactile Cypriot culture allows for a touch to communicate a range of commitments, some of which may not apply in less demonstrative cultures. These may include asking for attention, showing how trust operates between adult and child, and how the placing of a coach's hand can have a therapeutic role in massaging, allowing the athlete to function again (Chare, 2013). A young athlete adds to this sense of the coach as a caring influence, expressing how a hug is perceived as reassuring and comforting:

> When the coach hugs you to say something to you, it is not a problem . . . for example; a hug to say congratulations or to explain your mistakes . . . this hug may be generated because of happiness for your success.
>
> (Maria, athlete, 17)

When the coach is viewed as a parental figure then the act of a hug, even a phone call between an athlete and the coach in the early hours of the morning, can demonstrate what Jones *et al.* (2013) refer to as 'care for athletes' (p. 4). Given the multifaceted role that the coach fulfils, coaching *in loco parentis* can be seen as a natural expression of the cultural significance of a community responsibility to offer comfort and guidance to young people within and beyond named roles. The coach here, in Maria's account, provides an act of caring for him/herself through a social practice provided to the athlete (Foucault, 1992). However, the act of 'touching' and the commitment to care is not without conflict and ethical consideration. For a number of those interviewed, touching practices occur within limits, each incident asking the individuals to judge what is inappropriate at any particular time.

### Touching and related practices: Limits and conditions

Since the athletic body is central in track and field sport this 'emphasis might make someone perceive the use of physical contacts to be natural', according to ex-athlete and assistant coach Mary (aged 43). While this is accepted by many involved in Cypriot athletics and regarded in a positive light, the respondents also suggested that critical to the positive utilization of this social practice is 'where you stop', suggesting that such practices should occur within certain limits and conditions. It is suggested by Eleni, a 31 year old coach, that setting limits in these practices helps to build 'a good communication'. It would seem that the collective sense of a Cypriot moral code makes it possible for individuals to 'determine which acts are forbidden' (Markula & Pringle, 2006). The following quotes indicate that judging what is acceptable and appropriate is constant:

> In our society, I don't think that the male or female coach will use physical contact such as a hug in a bad way . . . (Georgia, administrator, 61)

> For the athletes we might also be teachers in their schools, so we need to be doubly careful so to avoid any misunderstandings. (Pantelis, coach, 50)

The fact that a number of track and field coaches work as teachers presupposes a moral behaviour determining how the coach (also a teacher) is expected to behave (Foucault, 1992). The coaches need to preserve their teaching identity during their work on the track or pitch. While these dual roles complement each other they require at times differing senses of authority:

> A coach needs to build a certain image, so athletes will remain disciplined and motivated.
>
> (Elena, ex-athlete, 29)

Relations of trust, gender, and age modify 'the precise nature of that care' (Jones *et al.* 2013, p. 12) and alternatively compose key boundaries and factors for consideration in relation to certain practices: Eleni (coach, 31) suggests that 'When the coach is young in age, he needs to be more careful with his female athletes'. The ethical standards formulated through a network of religion, community, and family within Cypriot culture seem to act as a framework of 'prescriptions for "good" conduct' (Markula & Pringle, 2006, p. 140) for sport individuals when engaging in touch related or risky practices, including social events, transporting athletes, and the use of physical work. For instance, it was suggested that:

> These [social gatherings] are not prohibited as long as there is a relation of trust between the athlete's family, the coach and the athletes. (Mary, ex-athlete/assistant coach, 43)

> I would drive a group of athletes home, but I would avoid being alone with a female athlete in a car. (Yiannis, ex-athlete, 42)

The interviewees' accounts demonstrate an ability to assess, and feel, which behaviors have positive or negative value (Johansson, 2013). The following insight illustrates the tangible rather than visible aspects of touching, posing a significant challenge to the regulating of touching and other physical practices (Piper & Stronach, 2008).

> When the coach cuddles or caresses a female child athlete . . . you can tell if this is out of affection . . . like when a parent cuddles his child, than as something else.
>
> (Mary, ex-athlete/assistant coach, 43)

While the emphasis on the body in sport allows these practices to be beheld as normal under ethical standards and practice, there is a suggestion from some of the interviewees that this emphasis on physicality can equally constitute a sensitive element, leading to possible misunderstandings. The next theme further considers this potentiality.

### Touching and related practices: Unfamiliarity can cause misunderstandings

The following account illustrates a typical dialogue than can occur on a Cypriot track and field pitch between a male coach and a female child athlete, which could be conceived negatively by an outsider unfamiliar with the cultural context and language:

> A coach views an athlete from a professional/athletic point of view and this is why he is asking her to dress in a restricted number of clothes during the training. For example, he may ask her to remove the trousers and wear shorts. Or maybe the dialogue will continue and the female athlete might say that she did not shave and then the coach will respond jokingly saying 'I like you like that as well'. Someone like an outsider who is going to witness this incident or a child who is outside sport might misunderstand . . . if the athlete is familiar with the environment she will not misunderstand . . . but if someone joins the training occasionally and witnesses isolated incidences like this one, they may misunderstand . . . or a parent may say that inappropriate behaviours exist in Cypriot sport.
>
> (Mary, ex-athlete/assistant coach, 43)

Mary suggests that when the coach makes comments such as the above, it is perfectly normal. The coach is not hinting something further and more sinister, since the athlete is only seen from a professional point of view. Nevertheless, Mary asserts that a child or a parent who is not used to the norms of the context may easily misunderstand an incident such as the above, overlook the bigger picture of the relationships in track and field sport, and perceive the coach's behaviour as inappropriate. This account demonstrates the complexities of non-physical practices, illustrating that 'defining and establishing relationship boundaries are a highly complex matter' (Johansson, 2013, p. 2). The same incident exemplifies Chare's assertion about physical contact in sport illustrating 'the difficulty of interpreting physical contact between coaches and athletes' (2013, p. 663), raising questions around the usefulness, appropriateness, and value of regulating touching through policy formation. Similarly, the insights presented below draw attention to the complexities and microrealities of learning contexts (Jones *et al.* 2013), highlighting familiarity with institutional norms as a key element in normalizing such practices. Nevertheless the coach's role seems to become increasingly sensitive, particularly if practice is viewed by someone who is not established as a member of the culture:

> Today, I was doing this exercise with the athlete . . . when a parent comes into the pitch, he does not want to see his child in this position.
>
> (Michalis, coach, 60)

Whereas a range of tactile practices are typical elements of training and relationships on the field, this may not be perceived equally by outsiders. This suggests that coaches need to be particularly careful in order to preserve the open tactile sporting culture. The next theme considers how the changes in the understanding of children and child protection in the wider Cypriot culture can have unfortunate implications, such as viewing child athletes as 'risk'. It is argued that this eventuality can create ambiguities and dangers around these social practices in sport.

## Touching and related practices: Children as 'risk'

The cultural shift in Cypriot society from traditional towards more globally framed views about children can cause concerns in sport in relation to touching and other social practices. These conflicts are articulated by Alexis:

> Things have changed in our society. Nowadays, children are familiar with sex and their bodies. They do not have taboos. A 17-year-old athlete has the body of a female adult. During trips, the coach finds the athletes together in bed . . . there are no guidelines.
>
> (Alexis, coach, 38)

Here the coach expresses uncertainty regarding the way he should handle situations such as where child athletes appear to demonstrate a type of power generated from their sense of 'individual agency', illustrating an ability to decide and manage things about themselves (van Nijnatten, 2010, p. 7). The coach suggests the need for guidelines to cope with these occurrences. The incident below raises similar uncertainties and nervousness:

> Frequently we need to give them massage. I told an athlete to remove a piece of cloth that was placed on her back, in order to do the physiotherapy, and she removed her top in front of me.
>
> (Alexis, coach, 38)

The coach seems to be placed in a difficult position. While massage comprises a typical physical practice in Cypriot sport under ethical and moral terms, a coach can potentially come across incidences where ethical boundaries are problematised. The above quote also exposes a note of contradiction. Alexis, while explaining the normality of touching the athlete to engage in physiotherapy, calls for guidance to help him and others to navigate these problematic incidences. In addition, the act of the athlete is perceived as indicating the need for regulation to protect him from the unconsidered acts of young people. Whereas previously Cypriot morals have been functioning as a type of moral regulation for social practices in sport for both adults and children, they now seem at risk of being overwhelmed. An inevitable effect of these changes in Cypriot communicative culture is that it can lead sportspeople and administrators to be anxious about practices such as social gatherings, since individual rather than a collective good now tends to prevail (van Nijnatten, 2010):

> When socials occur, then there is no respect during training . . . these days you can easily lose balance and control. This is how other things start to develop . . . gossip is created.
>
> (Elena, ex-athlete, 29)

It is interesting to note that Elena says that 'these days you can easily lose balance and control' suggesting that the inherent confusion found in these social gatherings puts both herself and her athletes in situations where the discipline and control evident in the coach-athlete relationship may be undermined by either party. The power exercised by idle gossip is also acknowledged as a powerful and persuasive agent that can undermine trust and respect between athlete, coach, parent, and the wider community. Yiannis, a 42-year-old former athlete, emphasized the recent stress experienced by adults as an effect of the children's rights discourse, which might cause a misuse of power by the child athletes themselves, one that can be risky for the adults engaged with children, and even problematising the notion of the 'rhetorically weak and vulnerable child' (Fletcher, 2013, p. 698). This account of the changed understanding of children, and the implications for the tactile approach of Cypriot sport, is illuminating:

> Children may misunderstand because they were given rights . . . but knowledge is given in reverse since the education should be provided to the coach and not to the child . . . of course children should know their rights . . . the basics . . . because children may threaten the coach's position as they can complain against the coach.
>
> (Yiannis, ex-athlete, 42)

According to this particular view there can be a palpable imbalance between an over-emphasis upon children's rights and a 'ruthless indifference to teachers' [coaches] rights' (Scott, 2012, p. 15). While protecting children's rights can be positive and welcome, these rights can have unexpected implications if provided arbitrarily to children without reflexive, careful, and critical consideration by both adults and children. These findings also relate to Green's (2012) concern around overemphasizing children's needs at the expense of other social groups. Arguably, the nervousness felt by adults in their dealing with, and their relationship to children has allowed a situation to manifest itself where deference is shown to the child's voice because of the fear associated with being thought uncaring and not concerned (Piper *et al.*, 2013). In Cypriot sport, such attitudes can result in detrimental consequences for groups of individuals such as adult coaches, as a result of overvalorising children's needs. Given the current changes in Cypriot society, the coach above highlights the lack of relevant knowledge provided to adults on how to behave with children or what is current best practice. Once again, this situation can intensify adults' uncertainty and confusion about how to interact with young people. To inhibit this 'nervous' climate, adult respondents suggested the need for relevant guidelines; however, this idea coexists with the fear that the loss of the current tactile culture of Cypriot sport would be an undesirable outcome. The final theme explores this tension.

### Touching and related practices: Guidelines, need, and fear

Touching and other social practices are deeply embedded in Cypriot track and field culture. As a result, they typically occur:

> . . . without thinking, that he [the coach] is going to be accused [because of] his behaviour or that his behaviour will be perceived as inappropriate.
>
> (Georgia, administrator, 61)

The current international focus on, and sensitivity towards, children's rights, in conjunction with media emphasis on child protection, can foster uncertainties (Piper & Smith, 2003) amongst sportspeople. As a result, everyday culture-specific norms occurring in their particular setting can be redefined as inappropriate and unsuitable when compared to global discourses on touching and child protection. This prompts some of the coaches interviewed to propose changes to teaching and knowledge: 'It is better to receive some form of training and education' (Alexis, coach, 38). While this view illustrates the protective aspect of guidelines provision, which can be positive (Fletcher, 2013), potential problems can be identified. An 'ideology of double standards' has been described in the case of decision making in non-rich or developing countries, where often it is 'assume[d] that supposedly universal, but imperialist ethics are in fact appropriate ethics for their populations' (Garrafa & Lorenzo, 2008, p. 2225). Moreover, although this type of knowledge provision and policy transfer can be viewed by sportspeople as a form of assistance in inhibiting any concerns raised among adults for their own protection against complaints, it is striking that adults seem to prioritise their own protection instead of safeguarding child athletes. This is another unforeseen effect of child protection restrictive policy found in other contexts (Piper *et al.* 2011), but imposed universally across cultural and historical sporting traditions. Given this eventuality, questions can be raised around the manner and effectiveness of children's rights promotion within a climate that increases adults' sense of guilt and fear, producing a tendency for them to protect themselves instead of children. While guidance and education appears to be welcomed, the manner in which this training is facilitated seems to prompt criticisms from Alexis and other coaches, suggesting the need for a supportive environment which avoids contributing to a culture of suspicion and guilt:

> Education, support and assistance to the coach should be given in a friendly manner . . . not making you feel guilty and bad . . .
>
> (Alexis, coach, 38)

This comment is illuminating in this context in showing how such an established and pervasive problem as child abuse can have a changed and changing meaning in contemporary conditions. Instead of being perceived to be a social problem it is articulated as an individual one (Silk & Andrews, 2012). This individualism of action and responsibility indicates a collateral outcome of neoliberalism, a type of governance aiming to 'celebrate the virtues of individualism' (ibid, p. 7). Regrettably in sport, adults can be placed in a position where such pressures might lead them to seek ways to protect themselves instead of operating in a way that meets the best interests for the child athletes (Piper *et al.* 2013). The administrator's view below summarises this contradiction:

> If we begin to think of all the potential risks then everything will be 'framed' . . . the personal appropriate communication, which includes emotion will disappear . . . you cannot be constantly in a condition to think about everything so to avoid being misunderstood . . . you will not be able to perform

to your maximum if you need to think about all these things . . . there will be no result . . . I speak as a human . . . I mean as a human being you will not be able to function and achieve your objectives as a coach.

(Georgia, administrator, 61)

Anxiety for the loss of spontaneous expression of feelings is evident in Georgia's response. While the narrow provision of guidelines has been suggested to result in a situation such as this (Piper *et al.* 2011), additional implications may occur in Cypriot sport, including loss of trust between sportspeople, absence of the value of professional expertise, and a decline in normal human conduct and interaction. In other words, it seems that constant surveillance, fear of being accused, and pervasive self-regulation can be problematic, even negative, constraining sportspeople from behaving spontaneously, responding to the needs of the individual at any single point in time. The fear is that this will destroy Cypriot culture where locally endorsed relationships based on community trust and mutual respect will be overtaken by the application of insensitive and blanket regulation exported by bodies with little knowledge or appreciation of the centrality of the culture in which they might be imposed. Ultimately, this situation can have implications for child athlete's welfare, since the attentive and affective climate important for children's holistic and athletic development can be lost in pursuit of a 'policy designed to protect, rather than care' (Jones *et al.* 2013, p. 7).

## Reflections and conclusions

The case of Cypriot track and field sport presents an opportunity for critical thinking around practices such as touching and other social communication in tactile sporting cultures, particularly those located in relatively demonstrative and familial regions such as those of the Mediterranean. In Cypriot track and field sport, touching and other social practices constitute key interactive elements, underpinned by moral boundaries. While the familial nature of Cypriot sport relationships appears to have a positive influence in accepting and simultaneously 'regulating' this culture of touching, the nature of sporting environments lead to a situation in which touching and traditional social practices can be exploited, even obscured at times, by sportspeople in order to protect sport's moral reputation (Hartill, 2013). This situation is a significant aspect of current international initiatives around children's rights and CP in sport. Nevertheless, the findings of this research indicate the creation of confusions and ambiguities, extending into fears of adults of facing allegations in relation to the 'appropriateness' of touching practices. Given this, it is argued that the current international pathological discourse provides little assistance or encouragement to sport practitioners for real reflection on the potential for sport's sociocultural character to trigger harmful practices. As a result the real interests of CP are not being served.

Despite the acknowledgement of sport's physiognomic sensitivity in relation to the misuse of touching (child abuse), context-friendly sociocultural elements can also function as regulators in particular cultures for behaving 'ethically'. This is indicated in the case of Cypriot track and field sport which, however, may not be representative for less demonstrative cultures. The Cypriot case raises questions regarding the current development and assertive dissemination of prescriptive international guidelines and measures, which may threaten the continued positive contributions of the Cypriot tactile sport practices towards children's holistic and athletic development. Undoubtedly, the uncritical adoption of neoliberal practices of 'fixing' solutions, by borrowing from other countries, should be critically assessed. Cultural differences constitute a challenging reality, and one that policymakers should consider, as it seems that a 'one-size fits all' approach may not function efficiently. It is recommended instead that culturally sensitive research, focusing on understanding the functions of power in relation to sport in particular contexts, can constitute a first step in exploring how sociocultural influences relate to child abuse and protection in sport. The key recommendation of this chapter is to seek ways to cultivate less 'suspicious', more positive and trustful environments where adults and children interact. Good communication and reflexivity will enhance a climate of trust so that a blaming environment (Kemshall *et al.* 1997), alternatively described as a 'value of mistrust' (Furedi, 1997, p. 74), can be diminished.

## Note

1 I would like to thank my supervisors, Dr Esther Priyadharshini and Dr David Aldous, and the editor of this book for their insightful and constructive comments on an earlier draft of this chapter. Mostly I would like to thank the research participants whose experiences illuminated the findings of this study.

## References

Ball, S. J. (2012) *Global Education Inc.: New policy networks and neo-liberal imaginary.* London and New York: Routledge.

Boyden, J. (1997) Childhood and the policy makers: A comparative perspective on the globalization of childhood. In A. James & A. Prout (eds.) *Constructing and re-constructing childhood* (pp. 190–229) London: RoutledgeFalmer.

Brackenridge, C. H. (2001) *Spoilsports: Understanding and preventing sexual exploitation in sport.* London: Routledge.

Brackenridge, C., Pitchford, A., Russell, K. & Nutt, G. (2007) *Child welfare and protection in football: An exploration of children's welfare in the modern game.* London: Routledge.

Chalip, L. (2006) Toward a distinctive sport management discipline. *Journal of Sport Management,* 20(1) 1–22.

Chare, N. (2013) Handling pressures: Analysing touch in American films about youth sport. *Sport, Education and Society,* 18(5) 663–677.

Chroni, S., Fasting, K., Harthill, M. J., Knorre, N., Martìn Harcajo, M., Papaefstathiou, M., Rhind, D., Rulofs, B., Toftegaard Støckel, J., Vertommen, T. & Zurc. J. (2012) *Prevention of sexual and gender harassment and abuse in sports: Initiatives in Europe and beyond.* Frankfurt, Germany: Deutsche Sportjugend im Deutschen Olympischen Sportbund e.V.

Chroni, S., Kourtesopoulou, A. & Kouli, O. (2007) Sexual harassment consequences for female athletes and prevention in Greek sports. *Inquiries in Sport & Physical Education* 5(2) 283–293.

Council of Europe. (2014) 1 in 5: The Council of Europe Campaign to stop sexual violence against children. Retrieved 13 May 2014 from: www.coe.int/t/dg3/children/1in5/default_en.asp

David, P. (2005) *Human rights in youth sport: A critical review of children's rights in competitive sports.* London: Routledge.

European Commission. (2007) *White Paper on Sport.* Retrieved February 5, 2013 from http://ec.europa.eu/sport/white-paper/the-2007-white-paper-on-sport_en.htm

Fletcher, S. (2013) Touching practice and physical education: Deconstruction of a contemporary moral panic. *Sport, Education and Society*, 18(5) 694–709.

Foucault, M. (1977) *Discipline and punish: The birth of prison.* London: Penguin Books.

Foucault, M. (1980a) The politics of health in the eighteenth century. In C. Gordon (ed.), *Power/Knowledge: Selected interviews and other writings 1972–1977* (pp. 166–182) Hertfordshire: The Harvester Press.

Foucault, M. (1980b) The eye of power. In C. Gordon (ed.), *Power/Knowledge: Selected interviews and other writings 1972–1977* (pp. 146–165) Hertfordshire: The Harvester Press.

Foucault, M. (1980c) The history of sexuality. In C. Gordon (ed.), *Power/Knowledge: Selected interviews and other writings 1972–1977* (pp. 183–193) Hertfordshire: The Harvester Press.

Foucault, M. (1980d) Questions on geography. In C. Gordon (ed.), *Power/Knowledge: Selected interviews and other writings 1972–1977* (pp. 63–77) Hertfordshire: The Harvester Press.

Foucault, M. (1980e) Prison Talk. In C. Gordon (ed.), *Power/Knowledge: Selected interviews and other writings 1972–1977* (pp. 37–54) Hertfordshire: The Harvester Press.

Foucault, M. (1992) *The use of pleasure: The history of sexuality* (Vol. 2) London: Penguin.

Fraser, N. (1981) Foucault on modern power: Empirical insights and normative confusions. *Praxis International*, (3) 272–287.

Furedi, F. (1997) *Culture of fear: Risk-taking and the morality of low expectation.* London: Cassell.

Garrafa, V. & Lorenzo, C. (2008) Moral imperialism and multi-centric clinical trials in peripheral countries *Cadernos de Saúde Pública* [online], 24(10) 2219–2226.

Garratt, D., Piper, H. & Taylor, B. (2013) 'Safeguarding' sports' coaching: Foucault, genealogy and critique. *Sport, Education and Society*, 18(5) 583–616.

Georgiades, S. D. (2009) Child abuse and neglect in Cyprus: An exploratory study of perceptions and experiences. *Child Abuse Review*, 18(1) 60–71.

Green, M. (2012) Advanced liberal government, sport policy and 'building the active citizen'. In D. L. Andrews & Michael L. Silk (eds.), *Sport and neoliberalism: Politics, consumption and culture* (pp. 38–56) Philadelphia: Temple University Press.

Hartill, M. (2009) The sexual abuse of boys in organized male sports. *Men and Masculinities*, 12(2) 225–249.

Hartill, M. (2013) Concealment of child sexual abuse in sports. *Quest*, 65(2) 241–254.

Howe, T. R. (2010) International child welfare: Guidelines for educators and a case study from Cyprus. *Journal of Social Work Education*, 46(3) 425–442.

International Olympic Committee. 2007. IOC Adopts Consensus Statement on 'Sexual Harassment & Abuse in Sport'. Available: www.olympic.org/Assets/ImportedNews/Documents/en_report_1125.pdf [10 July 2013].

Johansson, S. (2013) Coach–athlete sexual relationships: If no means no does yes mean yes? *Sport, Education and Society*, 1–16. doi: 10.1080/13573322.2013.777662

Jones, R. L., Bailey, J. & Santos, S. (2013) Coaching, caring and the politics of touch: A visual exploration. *Sport, Education and Society*, 1–15. doi: 10.1080/13573322.2013.769945

Kemshall, H., Parton, N., Walsh, M. & Waterson, J. (1997) Concepts of risk in relation to organizational structure and functioning within the personal social services and probation. *Social Policy & Administration*, 31(3): 213–232.

Mapp, S. C. (2011) *Global child welfare and well-being.* Oxford: Oxford University Press.

Markula, P. & Pringle, R. (2006) *Foucault, sport and exercise: Power, knowledge and transforming the self.* London and New York: Routledge.

Mita, M. (1989) Merata Mita On . . . *New Zealand Listener*, 14 October: 30.

Office for the Commissioner of Children's Rights. (2011) *Report of the Commissioner for Children's Rights in Cyprus to the UN Committee on the Rights of the Child.* Retrieved July 13, 2013 from www.childcom.org.cy/ccr/ccr.nsf/All/C8605F7BFB72C6B5C22579D 000336E35?OpenDocument.

Parton, N. (2006) *Safeguarding childhood: Early intervention and surveillance in a late modern society.* Hampshire and New York: Palgrave MacMillan.

Piper, H., Garratt, D. & Taylor, B. (2013) Child abuse, child protection, and defensive 'touch' in PE teaching and sports coaching. *Sport, Education and Society*, 18(5) 583–598.

Piper, H. & Smith, H. (2003) Touch in educational and child care settings: Dilemmas and responses. *British Educational Research Journal*, 29(6) 879–894.

Piper, H. & Stronach, I. (2008) *Don't touch! The educational story of a panic.* London: Routledge.

Piper, H., Taylor, B. & Garratt, D. (2011) Sports coaching in risk society: No touch! No trust! *Sport, Education and Society*, 17(3) 331–345.

Politis Online. (2011) *Θύματα σεξουαλικής κακοποίησης: Θλιβερά στοιχεία για Κύπρο [Sexual abuse victims: Doleful data for Cyprus].* Retrieved March 17, 2011 from www.politis-news.com/cgibin/hweb?-A=205792,printer.html&-V=webcontent

Rhind, D. & Jowett, S. (2010) Relationship maintenance strategies in the coach-athlete relationship: The development of the COMPASS model. *Journal of Applied Sport Psychology,* 22(1) 106–121.

Scott, C. (2012) The Australian situation: Not so touchy? *Sport, Education and Society*, 1–16. doi: 10.1080/13573322.2012.717067

Silk, M. L. & Andrews. D. L. (2012) Sport and the neoliberal conjuncture: Complicating the consensus. In David L. Andrews & Michael L. Silk (eds.), *Sport and neoliberalism: Politics, consumption and culture* (pp. 1–19) Philadelphia: Temple University Press.

Spyrou, S. (2008) Education and the cultural politics of childhood in Cyprus. In A. James & L. A. James (eds.), *European childhoods: Cultures, politics and childhoods in Europe* (pp. 149–171). Hampshire: Palgrave Macmillan.

Thukral Ganguly, E. (2011) *Every right for every child: Governance and accountability.* Abingdon: Routledge.

United Nations (UN) (2011) World Health Organisation. Retrieved January 12, 2012, from www.un.org/wcm/content/site/sport/home/unplayers/fundsprogrammesagencies/who

Van Nijnatter, C. (2010) *Children's agency, children's welfare: A dialogical approach to child development, policy and practice.* Bristol: The Policy Press.

# 7 Teaching and touching in physical education in pre- and post-communist Romania

*Simona Petracovschi*

## Introduction

Following the end of communist government in 1989, the Romanian educational system began a process of transition from paradigms focused on directive teaching and the passing on of knowledge, to paradigms focused on creating and increasing students' skills and capabilities. This chapter considers the implications of this transition for teacher-pupil relationships and touch, and particularly touching behaviours employed in pursuit of discipline and the imposition of the teacher's will. During the communist period, the educational system was focused on the teacher and the teaching process, whereas pedagogy since 1989 has increasingly focused primarily on the student and the learning process (Miroiu *et al.* 1998; Stan, 1999; Marga *et al.* 2005). This has had implications for the role and prestige of teachers in Romanian society, and such changes take time to assimilate. The teacher-student relationship has evolved, from the teacher's authoritarian role previously imposed by communist pedagogy towards the contemporary conception of the democratic teacher. Professional contacts suggest that many teachers now avoid touching pupils, in part to avoid misinterpretation, but also because many children are very aware of their new rights under the law, and assert them. Paradoxically, if a pupil is under eighteen there is no legal restriction on them touching a teacher. This real and perceived imbalance, and the new reality of pupils recording and passing on teachers' embarrassing moments through their cell phones, has added to teachers' sense of powerlessness. Their authority, once almost absolute, is now contingent and problematic. This chapter considers how these changes have impacted particularly on teaching and learning in physical education and sport, where touching cannot be 'managed out' in the context of moulding psychomotor habits and aptitudes, and where disciplinary touch was previously routine and endemic.

The modern Romanian educational system is defined by legislation reflecting its historic legacy and wider political changes. In 1948 the communist regime implemented provision based on the Soviet model (Decree 175), which set the tone until 1989. Although revised in 1968 (Law 11) and 1978 (Law 28), each modification underlined the educational system's subordinate relationship with both communist ideology and Romanian Communist Party policy. The regime gave physical education a strong military and disciplinary character, evident in the structure of lessons, exercises, and the form of collective organization. Although physical punishments were not officially permitted in communist pedagogy, in fact they were widely used by physical education teachers. Mistakes were physically sanctioned with squats, push-ups, or even physical violence, such disciplinary interventions being conceived as educationally positive rather than abusive. Physical contact between teachers and pupils was facilitated in part by the segregation of girls and boys in physical education.

Following the end of the communist regime and the democratic constitution of 1989, the educational system was again subject to changes; in 1995 the new democratic system began a reform process to move away from the communist educational model (Law 84). Between 2002 and 2010, new laws on the promotion and protection of children's rights, equality of opportunity between the sexes, and coeducation in physical education, formally distanced physical education teachers from the intimate and private space of the students, and changed their perception of the student's body. As a result, any sort of physical contact during lessons became much less acceptable. A conception of actual or potential abuse, previously submerged by assumptions implicit in communist pedagogy, became viable and relevant. Drawing on original interview data from twenty-four physical education teachers with varied experience pre- and post-1989, the impact of this sociocultural transformation process on Romanian sport and physical education is explored later in this chapter, particularly the use and meaning of touch for physical education teachers.

## The Romanian educational context

The communist era saw the imposition of Romanian education provision based on 'Soviet pedagogy' which emphasized three characteristics: community, militarization, and authority (Boia, 1999), designed to promote the communist education of the younger generation, to form 'the new man'. Although the idea of education as a human right was promoted, the emphasis was on economic development; schools' main objective was to prepare the labour force (Stanciu, 1995). However, education during this period was not static; there were changes in content, curricula, and class organisation, especially aspects related to teaching technology and teaching methods. While Soviet pedagogy was promoted, Romania became increasingly open to Western pedagogy and, from the 1960s, authors like Piaget, Bruner, Galperin, and Skinner were studied (Stanciu, 1995). In the context of overarching communist pedagogy, increasingly a new concept drawn from Western influence was applied: creative thinking, aimed at giving the student freedom to solve problems during the learning process, through questioning and discovery (Rosca, 1972).

Within communist pedagogy, education in preceding slave, feudal, or bourgeois societies was understood as being based on principles and methods generated by types of morality (Christian, bourgeois) subservient to the interests of the ruling classes, the ignorance of the population, and the depersonalization of human beings through conformity and docility; to these ends, constraint-based violence

and corporal punishment were applied (Ceausescu, 1976). Communist pedagogy rejected such methods and adopted new directions for training, designed to
achieve ownership, interest, and affirmation of human personality, ranging from
democratic methods (conversation, discussion, ethical debate, critical analysis,
and self-criticism) to persuasion (advice, asking for help), while allowing more
coercive methods to ensure order (Dumitrescu, 1979). Foucault's account of discipline is pertinent here:

> Discipline . . . is a type of power, a way to exert it and it is built from a set of
> tools, techniques, procedures, levels of application, targets, it is a 'physics' or
> an 'anatomy' of power, a technology. And it can be taken either by special-
> ized institutions . . . or by some state apparatus.
>
> (1975, p. 251)

Central to educational provision, in accordance with communist ideology, was
its role and effectiveness in disciplining individuals and the masses across all
social spheres. The communist regime prioritised discipline in controlling the
economy and ensuring efficient organization of the group and the masses, and
initiated it through the education system. Thus, imposing order was conceived as
the prime purpose of communication with children, and at a young age detailed
explanations were considered ineffective (Ceausescu, 1976). Instead, commands
expressed in an authoritarian tone would be understood, and student compliance
achieved through persuasive force, the application of dialectical and historical
materialism as the basis of philosophy and pedagogy, and respect for teachers'
authority. If these methods were insufficiently successful, punishment could
be applied to correct deviations, ranging from reprobation, analysis, criticism,
negative feedback, or suspension; according to the age and mental particulari-
ties of individuals and the pedagogic judgment of the teacher. Corporal punishments (like smacks on the face and pulling hair or twisting ears) could be
applied in private, but physical punishments were applied in front of everyone
(like repeated push-ups or squats) and were seen as providing an example to
the wider school community. Disciplinary action and its deployment was the
preserve of the teacher, whose judgment about how to deal positively with each
individual student, improving them and avoiding harm, was to be trusted. Without giving a clear definition of appropriate pedagogical judgment, yet relying on
this quality, communist education allowed teachers to use significant physical
punishment *in extremis*; it was considered that 'a fatherly slap' could not hurt.
External involvement would risk diminishing the authority of the teacher and
encourage distrust in their professional competence, an assumption corresponding with communist principles of unity and exigency. Once the punishment was
executed, it was advised that it should be forgotten, to avoid doubt or demotiva-
tion. Although senior party bodies could intervene, investigating and resolving
matters if a teacher was considered to have committed serious mistakes, these
were considered as individual and isolated cases for which no general preventative framework was required.

The approach to child development was all-encompassing, following the Soviet model, with organizations to incorporate young people into the desired approach to education, life, and work: the *Hawks* (preschool), *Pioneers* (primary), *Communist Youth* (high school), and *The Association of Communist Students* (university). There were also specialist programmes including *Ready for Work and Defence*, and *Preparing Youth for Defending the Country* (Ionescu & Massiera, 2008). Directed physical activity pervaded the education experience, beyond physical education and sport. Thus, during the day the body was stirred up, controlled, and moulded, through exercises at the start of teaching, and also by gymnastic minutes which replaced teaching activity at unproductive times, to wake up the body through movement. Beyond education, organized sporting events, tourism, and cultural celebrations were pervasive features of life.

The directive and instructional primacy of the teacher, particularly the physical education teacher, was strongly influenced by militaristic approaches. The teacher gave an order and the student executed it; the student group was seen as a place to learn commands and the ability to react promptly and manoeuvre to order. As in the army, commands were given in a firm and strict voice, allowing no discretion and emphasising simultaneous and uniform responses in accordance with principles of communist socialization (Boia, 1999). This process of development and training required internal processes of self-regulation and self-transformation, but also external regulatory and training inputs from student-teacher interaction. Collaboration and cooperation were important, but the teacher's leadership role was central (Dancsuly, 1972), granting substantial autonomy in its performance and in directing students. Leadership was subject to the style and personality of the teacher, combined with discretion and flexibility (enabling, directive, or cooperative, depending on the situation), and taking into account the age of the students, the purpose of the particular class, the theme of study, and the objectives pursued (Potolea, 1989). However, standardised evaluation mediated this discretionary element to ensure efficiency (Pavelcu, 1968); in physical education, class tests and control standards were implemented and students evaluated according to national criteria related to age and sex. In all subjects, rulings by the state and the communist party affected classroom organization, the balance of individual and group work, and gender-based divisions, although the importance for student success of help, control, and encouragement from the teacher was considered paramount (Tarcovnicu, 1981).

Even following the influx of Western educational ideas, order and discipline still defined schooling, delivered through military-style orders and activities as the main responsibility of the teacher, whose role performance could only be authoritarian; any attempted disputation from students was illegitimate (Stan, 2009). Military-style hierarchical control was achieved through organizing the class into groups and assigning individual students as responsible for each, to maintain order and discipline and to report disciplinary breaches to the teacher, who could impose normalizing sanctions. Thus, and crucially for this chapter, promoting the superordinate goals and priorities of the system and the state, had priority over the protection of individual students, and a discourse featuring any conception of abuse, or the imperative of safeguarding against it, was essentially unachievable. This legacy, which may be shared with other post-communist societies, distinguishes contemporary discussion of appropriate interaction between teachers and their students in Romania from that evident in countries with different historic, political, and cultural experiences.

## Physical education in Romania before 1989

In common with other pre- and early-capitalist societies, physical education and sport in pre-communist Romania developed in a spontaneous and unorganized way, connected with folklore and cultural tradition. Although Romanian sports pedagogy developed valuable elements, there was no unified system (Ceausescu, 1976). The creation of the National Institute of Physical Education in 1922 supported the construction of a heterogeneous approach, in which the Swedish system (see later in this section) was dominant. However, the communist period ended heterogeneity, with the application of Marxist-Leninist concepts to continuously improve physical education goals, tasks, and resources, consistent with the advancement of the interests of the broad mass of working people. It was the physical education teacher's responsibility to train and instruct students, applying specialist, pedagogic, and psychological knowledge, in the context of an appropriate professional culture (Ceausescu, 1976). Programmed instruction permeated Romanian pedagogy, demonstrated in physical education teaching by the design of motor skills training in stages, and the application of methodical algorithms seen as improvements on behaviourism. Considering Foucault (1975) is useful here: the docile body (shaped, trained, skillful, strong, and biddable), combining the analyzable and manipulable body, was to be trained through physical exercise, subject to constraints, prohibitions, obligations, and responding to commands.

Physical education teaching acquired strong military characteristics; schooling (like other state institutions) was designed to prepare students for homeland defence (Stanciu, 1995), using military formats and commands, and battlefield exercises. Running over obstacles, marching and walking, eye-alertness, self-control, tenacity and determination, and strategy in fighting and defence, were common features (Ceausescu, 1976). This approach had important implications for the conception of the student, as person and body. Command as a social relationship between two or more individuals (Dumitrescu, 1979) was central; in physical education this equated the relationship between the teacher and the students with that between officers (who give orders) and troops (who obey them). This imperative relationship left no room for discussion, and was supported by a particular social psychology (Dumitrescu, 1979). In this approach, the primacy of command, as a concept and a practice (incorporating requests, queries, gestures, expressions, will, energy, and so on) emphasized the teacher and their ability to deal with problems. Discussions of principle, adopting the appropriate tone, applying objective assessments, and providing positive advice, were considered decisive in all 'educational work'. Thus the physical education group was controlled through continuous scrutiny and routinised coercion, to ensure adherence to expectations regarding time (rhythm, tempo, pace), space (assembly, alignment), and movement (posture, gesture), without allowance for personal style. However, as Foucault (1975) notes, tight discipline, through inculcating docility, is more effective in generating useful and strong bodies for work and economic advantage than in fostering political strength and engagement.

Romania, like other communist states, used huge mass assemblies to mark and celebrate important events, and to handle these large numbers of people, skilful leadership was essential, often provided by physical education teachers working with obedient and manageable masses, previously educated and prepared through physical education. Beyond this political utility, Romanian physical education and sport, conceived as a national education discipline, prioritized physical strength (applied with capability and skill) as the main objective, with benefits in everyday life and especially in work and labour. The building of healthy bodies, with strength to work in production and to defend the country, represented the predominant goal, to which all else was subordinate. In all aspects, direction and discipline were central, and gymnastics in particular played an important role in the instrumental encoding of the body. The late-nineteenth-century Swedish gymnastics system continued to be used because of the simplicity of the movements and the possibility of their execution in unison by the entire community. Its formal purpose was to correct poor posture, but it also placed the instructional and disciplinary role of the physical education teacher at the centre of the learning process.

Even when Western influences began to affect Romanian education during the 1970s, physical education remained characterized by discipline, authority, and control. Sanctions and punishment took varied forms, still frequently including physical punishment. However, the evolution of pedagogy away from behaviourism prompted a critique of these practices, with some physical education and sport teachers arguing that it was contradictory to use physical activity (the positive purpose of the lesson) in a negative way as a punishment. However, beyond such debates corporal punishment remained common, typically involving beating the palm of the hand, slapping the face, ear pulling, or blows to the head with an open or closed hand.

Although co-educational teaching in Romanian elementary schools was normal from the nineteenth century, and Public Law Guidelines from 1864 established the principle of gender equality in schools (Radulescu, 2003), in physical education and sports curricula, gender discrimination was pervasive throughout the communist period. From 1956, coeducation was extended to secondary schools, but physical education and sport was still conducted separately. Here, gender discrimination was more apparent than elsewhere; in production and defence the communist system favoured a mixing of the sexes at all levels but, in sport taken-for-granted gender stereotypes were applied: boys as strong and brave, and girls as sensitive, caring, and artistic (Chiru & Ciuperca, 2000). Boys were 'those who do', and girls 'those who are' (Grunberg, 1996). In physical education, 'light' sports, generally without direct contact, such as volleyball, were considered 'feminine'. Working in separate groups, especially in adolescence, was recommended by teachers for effective teaching, and avoiding discipline problems. Before 1989 if both a male and female physical education teacher were available, the female teacher would typically work with the girls, and the male teacher with the boys.

Thus the conception and performance of pre-1989 Romanian physical education teaching matches the model of the authoritarian teacher: one who, in organizing and leading, punishes, humiliates, imposes, requires in an imperative way, criticizes, applies pressure, uses a sharp voice, dominates, is harsh, and inspires fear (Moore, 1992). This conception and reality constrained the teacher to a substantial degree, as the model ordained through the communist system's approach to physical education and sport defined role performance, even when individual personality did not support such a style. As a result the teacher had to rely on status, experience, and acquired specialist knowledge to sustain their authority (Stan, 2009). In relation to touching pupils, the rigour and discipline imposed before 1989 provided the physical education and sports teacher the possibility of touching the student's body, in effect without fear of repercussions or possible critical interpretations. In principle any sort of abuse could be investigated by the school administration, but great courage was required to denounce a teacher. As a result, to help students learn and perform exercises, the teacher had no reluctance in approaching the male or female student or to touch them; the definition of unacceptable touch remained opaque and largely unconsidered. In terms of the experience, agency, and rights of the student, the impact of this approach was significant since, barring the most extreme manifestation of violence or abuse, the integrity and primacy of the teacher was taken for granted, and the power available to them in relation to the student's body and emotions was beyond what would now be considered normal or acceptable.

## Physical education and sport teaching since 1989

Following the traumatic political upheaval in 1989 and the end of communist party control, changes in Romanian society have been fundamental. While the principles and procedures of democracy have impacted across society the effect remains variable and, in some areas of culture and practice, elements and patterns from the past are still evident. Although the ideals of democracy and individual rights are commonplace and, in formal terms, the ruling educational paradigm has changed, the communist era discipline-focused approach to lesson planning and classroom organization remains operational and significant. In particular, physical education classes have changed little; battlefield exercises and group formations are still used, and students are ordered what to do (Nacu, 2002). This apparent cultural and pedagogic time lag has created significant discrepancies between those teachers with experience of the old system and the new generation of students who react against it, and between these older teachers and those trained more recently, who choose not to apply historic curricular and disciplinary approaches which they consider ineffective. These discrepancies result in tensions in the classroom, gymnasium, and sports field, but also in terms of process and administration. Thus, although age-group assessment is still formally conducted through nationally defined exams, tests, and trials, calibrated against rigid standards (Miroiu *et al.* 1998), many younger teachers choose to apply a more qualitative assessment approach, and record student progress even where outcomes differ from those centrally defined.

At the pedagogic level, teacher-student interaction in physical education has become a site of anxiety and argument. The continuing formalized approach to assessment, in a teaching context where many practices are contrary to widely accepted contemporary principles and assumptions, has created a problem of absenteeism and widespread attempts by students to obtain a general exemption from physical education as a school subject. The expectation of obtaining poor grades in a contested and incongruous teaching and assessment environment has led students and their parents to seek to avoid this difficulty, by opting out of physical education entirely. The subject area has become regarded by many as problematic and overly demanding (Miroiu *et al.* 1998) and many students choose to pursue sporting activities outside school.

However, as a pre-1989 legacy, the role of the teacher is still seen as central, and even in post-communist education the conception or myth of the 'gifted teacher' is predominant (Miroiu *et al.* 1998). It is still expected that the teacher will dominate the teaching and learning experience, and intervene in crisis situations and resolve problems on the basis of individual authority, but the regulatory environment has changed, as has the cultural context. New regulations cover teacher-pupil interaction and teacher behaviour, making it explicit that the teacher, while still expected to maintain order and discipline, must not employ corporal punishment and verbal or physical bullying of students (MEC Order no. 4925/08.09.2005). Where violation of these rules is demonstrated, teachers are subject to disciplinary sanctions, graduated depending on the seriousness of the offence. Possible sanctions run from written observations and formal warnings, to significant salary reductions, and barring for a period of up to three years from any competition for teaching positions, achieving higher education degrees, or promotion to a management position. In serious cases, payment of compensation to the injured party may be required. Those already in a leadership or management position can be subject to guidance and control or dismissal from their post, or even complete disciplinary termination of their employment (Law 128/1997 art. 115). The possibility of contravening these new regulations or being reported to have done so, creates significant stress for physical education teachers in particular, and also presents them with challenges in terms of managing relationships both with individual students and classes for which they are responsible. It also places particular pressure on, for instance, touch and discipline in sport and physical education. This variable and inconsistent reconception of policy and practice might be expected to impact differently on different groups of teachers, depending on their age and differential experience before and after the historic disjuncture of 1989.

In spite of regulatory change, gender differentiation in the gymnasium and on the sports field remains pervasive, still used by teachers from both pre- and post-1989 generations in the absence of contrary strategies and teaching methods. Without concrete promotion and implementation of anti-discriminatory practice, physical education teachers are likely to prefer to work separately, thus sustaining gender stereotypes and ignoring equality issues. The rationale for discriminatory approaches has evolved; boys aged ten to fourteen are considered competitive but not cooperative, and girls vice-versa (Chiriac, 2004). Although some recommend exercises in mixed pairs, to counter these perceived differences, in practice it remains difficult for pupils to step out of the gendered stereotypes which support teachers' assumptions and default methods. Romanian education remains structured around competition rather than cooperation and on practical skills aimed at industrial labour for boys and manual and domestic activities for girls. This gendered segregation (in both assumptions and practices) contributes to a lack of discussion or clarity concerning how teachers and students can touch during physical education classes, and about what is permitted (or not) by sporting regulations and by more general moral and ethical codes. The fear of working in mixed groups mirrors the approach adopted towards sex education (Stefanescu, 2003). More frequent working in mixed-gender groups would open new perspectives and the possibility of approaching intimacy and touching among students, as well as related problems that teachers appear not yet ready to address. Sex education and discussion of relationships, including the frameworks and implications around touch, may be included in civic education lessons, but teachers can choose to exclude it. Physical education could make a more positive contribution in support of social and sex education.

Since the more active implementation of rules prohibiting hitting or touching students for disciplinary reasons, there is more scope for varied interpretation if the student is touched. Often, teachers prefer to avoid any contact with students, minimising their intervention even in gymnastics, and requiring students to touch and support each other. Touch has been removed from teacher-student communication, and the absence of consistent sex education further restricts opportunity for open dialogue about touching, how it can be performed, by whom, and under what conditions. Significant taboos and anxieties remain unaddressed. With increasing numbers of pupil exemptions from physical education, the teaching and learning experience may become further impoverished, as teachers find new ways to teach without touching their students, typically assuming the role of activity organiser, assigning tasks but not helping ensure they are achieved. Sensitivity on these topics, and in teacher-pupil relationships, will have been increased by the recent highly publicised case (the first involving a sport and physical education teacher). A 23-year-old male teacher at the Jean Monnet School was prosecuted and sentenced to a short prison term (and also banned from teaching for life), having had sex with a 16-year-old pupil during an extracurricular activity trip in the mountains. The relationship was wholly consensual, but a complaint from the girl's father prompted the prosecution, which was widely reported in scandalous terms (Cana, 2011). International experience suggests there will be similar disclosures in the future, and that anxiety around the teacher-pupil relationship will increase.

It was to explore such tensions in the area of touch, discipline, and potential abuse, and to further understand how physical education teachers perceived and reflected on their work, particularly the use and meaning of touch, that semistructured discursive interviews were conducted with twenty-four teachers. The sample (both purposive and opportunistic) included twelve male and twelve female teachers aged between twenty-nine and sixty-two, half of whom taught during the communist period, some for many years. The interviews were conducted in February–March 2013, some in the teachers' schools and others during weekend competitions (badminton and athletics); in both situations the teachers agreed to be interviewed in a separate room, near the sports field. The purpose was to explore the personal and professional experiences of interaction physical education teachers had with students and how the conflict between historically bound behaviours and new expectations is manifested. Current teachers who began teaching during the communist era have experienced significant change in ideas about the management of bodily contact, as well as about the role of the teacher, and children's rights, suggesting useful comparison of their accounts with those of the post-1989 generation of teachers interviewed.

## Teaching physical education and sport

The data presented in this section provides evidence of a number of historical, geographical, gender-based, and pedagogical conditions and contradictions. It would seem evident that differing expectations based on age and enculturation are played out in both the structure of the physical education delivery and the paradoxical nature of personal commitment and professional expectations.

A newly qualified teacher expressed feelings of confusion and uncertainty:

> The first two years were different from everything that happened afterwards. I thought that I had to be very authoritarian, being new there. It was a matter of dominance. I was very young and I thought that the students would not be scared enough of me. Until you adjust your relationships with everyone, you have to combat the feelings of helplessness by being authoritarian. Afterwards you build a normal relationship with them. My relationship with the 8th graders was horrible . . . it was like that because they could feel I was stiff . . . They were always joking around. I had to fight this thing . . . and then I relaxed.
>
> (Maria, aged 33)

As Miroiu *et al.* (1998) suggest, the myth of the gifted teacher, although prevailing, does not seem to marry with the lived experience of neophyte teachers such as Maria. The ineffectiveness of centralized guidelines is laid bare when compared with the realities of achieving pedagogic effectiveness while getting through to the next lesson unscathed.

It was apparent that teachers operating in rural areas were afforded a certain level of prestige and respect, although this did not transfer seamlessly to the urban school setting. In addition, there seemed to be a belief that students from urban and rural areas differed in physical ability, and that in consequence teacher/student communication needed to be different. These perceptions are expressed in the following paired quotes:

> The difference between students from the rural and the urban areas was a shock to me. In the city, although students come from the so-called elite schools, they are very weak at physical education and could be completely uninterested, especially in high school. The class from the rural areas cannot be compared to those in the urban area. (Cristian, 40)
>
> For me, in terms of teaching, it was the same in both areas. The difference is how the professor is perceived and in general the respect that children show towards professors. Nowadays, it seems to me that there is too much poorly understood freedom. Ana (59)

It could be suggested that the notion of 'too much poorly understood freedom' is an example of differing intergenerational notions of ascribed and achieved status, as well as the difficulties, felt by both parties, in adjusting to new patterns of social expectation.

Disciplining any group of students is and remains a constant feature of physical education and sports classes, and it appears that a continued reliance on military-type formations is justified as the 'best' method of organizing classes. Again, paired quotes bring forward these ideas of training and compliance.

> I believe that in small classes one must use this type of organization [militaristic] to teach students what discipline is. After they grow up, especially in adolescence, it's harder if you have not done it before. (George, 46)
>
> Front and group exercises are similar to initial [military] training. If I don't do them, I cannot control the group. From what we have available, we cannot do it otherwise. Just like with a dog when you give it an order it knows what to do. When you say 'stop playing' or 'turn around' they know not to sit there and stare at you. I order all the time, even with the whistle, when I whistle the students stop and know what to do. (Veronica, 36)

A sense of nostalgia and disrespect is apparent here; the physical education teacher, whose education, training, and conditioning took place under the communist model, or were strongly impacted by its continuing influence, is seeking some sense of comfort and reassurance by training students as you would a dog. It may be expected that in the absence of alternative accepted educational models, teachers' references to past practices continue to generate tension and unease for all concerned. 'It irritates me to repeat something seven times. It is very difficult to train a child for whom the orders at school are not the same ones as from home' (Anton, 42). This is not to suggest that all physical education teachers believe that applying a military form of discipline is an appropriate solution. The promise of security, and a license to apply a more liberal model, which would come with employment tenure, was highlighted by Loredana (34):

> I do not like this communist education model but I cannot do anything about it until I finish my qualification exams and inspections, I cannot do anything else. I will be inspected and I think that if they do not see this organizational model they will not approve. But afterwards, when I become fully qualified

I would like to find other forms. Any kind of movement is more important to me than the army style.

This lack of security in generating individual teaching practices is seemingly generated by a perception that the educational establishment continues to hold true to values and structures previously endorsed by the communist model.

In terms of physical punishment, both in the form of extra physical activities and direct physical contact, the interviewees suggested that teachers still utilized them in practice. In addition, a number of respondents thought that the present insecurity of teaching as a profession and the slow transformation from a once powerful cultural commitment, had led them to modify their behaviours.

> If the punishment is squats, then we live with that. These are the only forms that I can use to punish them now. These are those who are absent all semester and when they do come to class, I grade them on what they can or cannot do. Only those who work and are responsible receive an 'A', the kid who comes and sweats. I also have students who do not gain an 'A' because they do not deserve it and they do not work to their full potential.
>
> (George, 37)

Those who do resort to direct physical violence are also caught between a system that increasingly wishes to be seen as progressive and inclusive while reference is made to a time when the personal endorsement of the communist party gave reassurance through the primacy and centrality of the teacher and their right to use physical punishment:

> I hit a student, it was before 1989. Actually, I slapped him twice for being naughty. His parents made a complaint, and it got so far that even President Ceausescu heard about it. But I stayed calm, I knew from . . . [teaching colleague's name] that he . . . had Nicu Ceausescu [the son of the president] as a student and he once slapped him so hard that his teeth almost fell out. The next day Nicolae Ceausescu came to school and said 'Brava professor, keep doing it, I would slap him myself but I do not have time'. The principal called me in his office and the only disciplinary measure was that I was no longer head professor for that particular class; a new professor came to replace me for this. Next year I had parents come up to me and ask me to be the head professor again, including the father of the complainant.
>
> (Gheorghe, 61)

Again, nostalgic referencing is evident, with the new social order being compared and contrasted with the old. The notion that physical punishment could also be justified by seeing it as a part of 'paternalistic teaching' was clearly expressed by Vasile (62) who recounted:

> A former student of mine . . . told me that all the beating I gave him when he was a student was life changing for him. He did all sorts of dumb things and

nobody could make him stop. The principal came to me to complain about him. I took him to my office and slapped him twice. Anyway, I did it because I cared about him and I knew he could be a good athlete.

The notion of the paternalistic teacher can be conceived as mirroring 'the fathering state', a state that takes care and considers what is both right and proper for all its citizens, be they teacher, student, athlete, or parent. Whilst there is an indication that the age and experience level of those interviewed had considerable influence on their everyday practice and thoughts on the use of physical punishment, through the interviews there was also a realization and expectation of change. The discourse of 'no touch' appears to be slowly emerging and is now discussed in the staff rooms and gymnasiums of Romanian schools. Violeta, a 46-year-old teacher, appears to struggle with the incipient move towards this regulation. While accepting the directive, she laments the curtailment of her practice:

> Now there is continuous discussion about touching, about putting your hand in the wrong place, and it seems crazy to me to not be able to explain 'listen, I wanted to help your child if I had not put my hand there, regardless of the area; your child could have fallen or broken something'. It is not good that we always have to think where we put our hands. I always discuss this with my colleague.

Seeking reassurance from fellow staff members of the school is echoed in other recent empirical research on practice and policy in school settings. Fletcher (2013), in his UK-based work, reports physical education teachers gaining socially shared understanding of practice, and a level of support from each other and those in similar situations. This collective security allows newly located boundaries to be drawn up to assist individual teachers so they can navigate the complexities and policy fluxes while attempting to maintain professionally accepted practice.

> For several years there have been all kinds of stories, I am careful . . . before I wasn't very careful regarding how I touch them, but now I am very careful where and how, although it is not normal to think about this when my main concern is for them to not get hurt. Instead you automatically start to think: if you do the roll on the box [reference to gymnastic equipment] where should you put your hands to help, if you accidentally touch what do you do? Do you ignore and move on so as to not leave room for discussions or on the contrary do you bring it in discussion.
>
> (Victor, 44)

Further indications of uncertainty in the face of increased variation in attitudes and intergenerational change appeared in relation to pupil (and teacher) sexuality and the challenges which can arise.

> A maths colleague told me what happened to him when he was starting his career. A student in the first row was wearing a short skirt and no panties.

This kept happening and [he] did not know what to do, especially as he felt very embarrassed . . . and did not want to show it to the class. He asked the student to review her behaviour but she kept on provoking him, saying she could do nothing about it. So he moved her to the back row and annihilated her attempts . . . What I mean is that we need to know why we do this job and if you're not careful, you can take the wrong path.

(Cristian, 40)

A supportive environment in which such tensions and anxieties might be explored and resolved is not yet in place.

From these interviews, one consideration is clearly evident: that the practices of physical education teachers and coaches working within the Romanian school system need to be seen in light of the considerable social and political upheavals experienced since 1989 and the long reach of the legacy from the preceding decades. The apparent variation in the acceptance and rate of change apparent between rural and urban schooling, those teachers and professors trained before and after 1989, the transfer from paternalistic to more technical philosophies, those newly qualified and those experienced and in tenure, and the contested and stressful emergence of a new 'no touch' discourse, are all tensions which will continue to be played out, contributing to the struggles and anxieties expressed by those interviewed. What remains to be seen is the rate of accelerated change and whether the Romanian school system can embrace notions of child protection while also selectively embracing the cultural traditions from its past.

## Conclusion

Romanian physical education and sports instruction is currently characterized by a stasis created by a diverse and inconsistent understanding and response to change in the wider society, which has made the practice of teaching and the interaction between teachers and students highly problematic. Although there are variations between physical education teachers according to their age, whether they worked under the communist system operative until 1989, and how individuals have responded to significant cultural and political changes since, in many cases physical education classes retain the shape and structure that was typical under communism. This relative consistency is also observable in terms of curriculum content and activities and also, significantly for this chapter, the assumptions and methods employed in maintaining discipline; even now, direction and control remain central characteristics of the physical education class.

For many teachers, ideas about how it is acceptable and appropriate to relate to, touch, discipline, and punish students have changed little. This is true even though both general social attitudes and also formal regulation of the teaching situation has moved in another direction, towards a recognition of the principles behind the rights of the child, and the practical reality that (approaching twenty-five years since the fall of the communist regime) students and parents are able to exercise a degree of market choice, in education and beyond. As a result, teacher behaviours once treated as normal and positive are increasingly likely to be regarded as inappropriate or even abusive. On this basis, the continued application of an approach to promoting order and discipline derived from a military model (in which control over the student and their body was in effect taken over by the teacher), can be sanctioned by students through seeking exemption from classes (full or partial) or by taking formal action against offending teachers, to secure professional disciplinary proceedings. The outcome is a situation of instability, confusion, and anxiety, arguably with negative effects for teachers and students, but also for sport and physical education itself. Where in the past the physical education teacher did not question the way she or he helped, touched, or disciplined the student (because a taken-for-granted and state-sanctioned authority bestowed professional rights and professional discretion, without the need to fear suspicion, accusation, or even critical discussion), the current situation is both more complex and threatening. Until a greater harmony is achieved between the broad sociocultural context (both public attitudes and state regulation), the formal specification of physical education as an element of the school curriculum and pupil experience (its content and expected activities), and the prevailing taken-for-granted assumptions and practices by teachers in sport and physical education, the situation will remain challenging and unsatisfactory.

## References

Boia, L. (1999) *Mitologia stiintifica a comunismului*, Bucuresti: Editura Humanitas.

Cana, P. (2011) Cazul "Jean Monnet" a fost o orgie bahica nu viol (The "Jean Monnet" case was an orgy not a rape), *Evenimentul zilei*, 11 November 2011, www.evz.ro/detalii/stiri/cazul-jean-monnet-a-fost-o-orgie-bahica-nu-viol-955736.html (Journal accessed on 31 July 2013).

Ceausescu, N. (1976) *Pedagogia educatiei fizice si sportului*, Bucuresti: Editura Sport-Turism.

Chiriac, A. (2004) (ed) Diferente de gen in cresterea si educarea copiilor, Centrul Parteneriat Pentru Egalitate, Romania., Accessed 7 June 2013 at www.cpe.ro/romana/images/stories/continuturi/ghid%20diferente%20de%20gen%20in%20cresterea%20si%20educarea%20copiilor.pdf

Chiru, C., Ciuperca C. (2000) Stereotipurile etnice si de gen la prescolari, *Sociologie romaneasca*, New series no. 3–4, 133–146.

Dancsuly, A. (1972) Relatia profesor-elev in perspectiva unei educatii moderne, in: Dancsuly A., Salade, D. (eds) *Educatie si contemporaneintate*, (pp. 46–62). Cluj: Editura Dacia.

Decree no. 175/1948 regarding the reform of educational system, http://lege5.ro/Gratuit/g42domzq/decretul-nr-175-1948-privind-reforma-invatamantului (accessed on 31 July 2013).

Dumitrescu, Gh. (1979) *Interpsihologie in activitatea sportiva*, Bucuresti: Editura Sport Turism.

Fletcher, S. (2013) Touching practice and physical education: deconstruction of a contemporary moral panic, *Sport Education and Society*, 18(5) 694–709.

Foucault, M. (1975) *Surveiller et punir. Naissance de la prison*, Paris: Gallimard.

Grunberg, L. (1996) Stereotipuri de gen in educatie: cazul unor manuale de ciclu primar, *Revista de Cercetari Sociale*, 4, 123–129.

Ionescu, S., Massiera B. (2008) L'héritage de la période communiste (1946–1989) sur l'actualité du sport de masse en Roumanie, *European Studies in Sports History*, 1(1) 94–106.

Law 11/1968 – *Education in Socialist Republic of Romania,* http://lege5.ro/Gratuit/he2daojr/ legea-nr-11–1968-privind-invatamintul-in-republica-socialista-romania (accessed on 31 July 2013).

Law 28/1978 – *Education and the Educational System,* www.lege-online.ro/lr-LEGE-28–1978-(466).html (accessed on 31 July 2013).

Law 84/1995 – The law of the educational system, http://legislatie.resurse-pentru-democra tie.org/84_1995.php (accessed on 31 July 2013).

Law 128/1997 – on the *Statute of Professors*, art. 115, www.mmuncii.ro/pub/imageman ager/images/file/Legislatie/LEGI/L128–1997_act.pdf (accessed on 31 July 2013).

Marga, A., Baba, C., Miroiu, A. (2005) *Anii reformei şi ceea ce a urmat,* Cluj-Napoc: Editura Fundaţiei pentru studii europene.

MEC Order no. 4925/08.09.2005 – *Regulation of organization and functioning of pre-university educational institutions,* http://administraresite.edu.ro/index.php/articles/554 (accessed on 31 July 2013).

Miroiu, A., Pasti, V., Codita, C., Miroiu, M. (1998) *Invatamantul romanesc azi,* Iasi: Editura Polirom.

Moore, K. (1992) *Classroom teaching skills*, New York: McGraw-Hill.

Nacu, A. (2002) *Le corps sous contrôle: aperçus du sport soviétique*, Revue: Regards sur l'Est.

Pavelcu, V. (1968) *Principii de docimologie, introducere in stiinta examinarii*, Bucuresti: Editura Didactica si Pedagogica.

Potolea, D. (1989) De la stiluri la strategii: o abordare empirica a comportamentului didac-tic, in JingaI., and Vlasceanu L. (eds) *Structuri, strategii, performanţe în invatamant*, (pp. 160–186).Bucuresti: Editura Academiei Române.

Radulescu, D.C. (2003) Invatamantul public din Romania in secolul al XIX-lea- evolutie si consecinte sociale, *Revista Calitatea vietii*, XIV (2) 1–12.

Rosca, A. (1972) *Creativitatea*, Bucuresti: Editura Enciclopedica Romana.

Stan, E. (1999) *Profesorul între autoritate şi putere,* Bucuresti: Editura Teora.

Stan, E. (2009) *Managementul clasei*, Iasi: Editura Institutului European.

Stanciu, I. (1995) *Scoala si doctrinele pedagogice in secolul XX*, Bucuresti: Editura Didac-tica si Pedagogica.

Stefanescu, D. O. (2003) *Dilema de gen in educatie*, Iasi: Editura Polirom.

Tarcovnicu, V. (1981) *Invatamant frontal, invatamant individual, invatamant pe grupe*, Bucuresti: Editura Didactica si Pedagogica.

# 8 Exploring the appropriateness of contemporary child protection measures in Danish sport

*Jan Toftegaard Støckel*

## Introduction[1]

As evidenced throughout this edited collection, the emergence of the issue of sports coaches' sexual abuse of young people involved in sport has led to a fear of paedophiles and a concern that sports activities may not be safe for children. This fear has been particularly evident in the US and a number of European countries. While sports organisations in many Western countries implement child protection policies, including mandatory criminal record checks, child protection courses, ethical standards, and restrictions on photography, there is some concern and scepticism in Western and other countries, suggesting that such efforts will not really protect children from abuse but rather, from a wider perspective, potentially do more harm than good. Moreover, it is believed by many that more rules, regulations, and controls can be interpreted as expressions of distrust, which may serve to increase the fear of false allegations, and intensify the bureaucratic activity required in sports clubs (Piper, Taylor, & Garratt, 2011). Through describing and discussing the moral panic associated with media disclosures of paedophilia in sports, this chapter considers the genesis, nature, and appropriateness of contemporary child protection measures in Danish sport.

## Paedophilia and moral panic in sport

According to Beck (1986), one consequence of the shift from an industrial society to a risk society, which he considered more generally, has been a breakdown in traditional mechanisms of social order. To counteract the resulting social insecurity and moral panic, Beck identified the formation of 'communities of anxiety', based on powerful discourses of risk. When he originally suggested the term, he could not have grasped the ramifications of the Internet and social networking, where information about anything and everything gets shared in seconds, and it can be argued that such electronic communication networks have played an important role in further facilitating and accelerating perceptions of risk and fear. In recent years discourses of fear, panic, and risk have sprung up, and have been extensively discussed in sociology and related disciplines, in response to the countless threats intrinsic to life in a globalized world. Jenkins (1998) argues that moral panic about paedophilia has been particularly evident and strident in the UK and the US, and there are different approaches to understanding how these different discourses have articulated risk and fear as a social problem, a so-called social construction. Thompson (1998) cautioned that moral panic is not just about perceived "risk", but also involves powerful discourses on fear, anxiety, collective hysteria, extreme deviation, social pathologies, and moral decay. Paedophilia and sexual exploitation in sport are not only potential and actual risks, but also constitute powerful discourses, pre-loaded with connotations and judgments. Thus, in many contexts the terms 'paedophile' and 'paedophilia' have played a substantial role in the development of a discourse which has shaped the current prevention measures, in part as a result of a significant misapprehension.

Contrary to the apparent understanding of the majority, supported by media usage, paedophilia is not synonymous for sexual offending against children, in sport or elsewhere. Paedophilia is a psychiatric disorder characterized by a persistent sexual interest in prepubescent children (American Psychiatric Association, 2013), and to be a paedophile is not in and of itself a crime, although having sexual contact with a child below the legal age of consent obviously is. Given this distinction, it is important to note that more than half of sexual offenders against children are *not* paedophilic, but act out of other motivations, such as a lack of more preferred sexual opportunities, hypersexuality, indiscriminate sexual interests, or disinhibition as a result of substance use, or other factors (Seto, 2009). It could be suggested that this makes them more like a subset of 'ordinary' adults (the majority male) rather than an easily distinguished sick minority. Further, paedophilia is too loosely applied to anyone with a sexual interest in children under the legal age of consent, when in fact it applies only to interest in prepubescent children (normally younger than thirteen years old). Different clinical labels, hebephilia and ephebophilia, apply to those interested in early pubescent children, or to children later in adolescence. The failure to maintain the distinction between sexual offenders against children and actual paedophiles raises various issues. Contrary to social justice, it places paedophiles who refrain from sexual contacts with children in the same category as men who actually commit crimes against children. It also serves to heighten public anxiety, while drawing attention from the reality of risk, and obscuring the significant fact that paedophilic and non-paedophilic sex offenders differ in their propensity to reoffend. The literature is unambiguous in the sense that recidivism is significantly higher for sexual offenders who are paedophile, psychopathic, or both (Dorren, 2004; Hanson, 1998; Seto, 2008).

The original moral panic framework by Cohen (1972) remains a useful tool for initial understanding of how the media, politicians, and research have debated and influenced the child protection agenda in Denmark. According to Cohen there are five stages in the creation and disappearance of moral panic. First the phenomenon is characterised as a threat to society; thereafter the threat is identified in the media; as a result of this media coverage, a public concern builds, and the authorities take action; and in the Danish case, this took the form of a full government commission of inquiry. Finally, the panic either disappears over time, or policy changes are introduced.

## Paedophilia and the threat to sport and society

By the start of the twentieth century, sport had become an increasingly important social arena, believed to foster desirable masculine traits such as courage, gameness, and integrity. In Denmark, the fear of physical and moral decay played a prominent role in decisions about initial sports funding and legislation relating to school sport (Jørgensen, 1997; Mortensen, 2004). In the early decades of the century, doctors, physiologists, and other intellectuals argued that sport, and particularly gymnastics, was a formidable tool which could promote hygiene and suppress masturbation among young people (Jørgensen, 1997). In public debate it was asserted that a healthy mind needs to reside in a healthy body, and in this line of thinking physical and mental health went hand in hand with bodily discipline and hygienic regimes (ibid.). Sport became identified as a morally pure activity and over time sports clubs became the guarantor of morality (Mortensen, 2004). Like sport, the scout movement was also associated with morality and considered as an ideal social arena for the formation of children, enhancing values important to society and family such as obedience and self-discipline. Subsequently, sport and scouting were also valued as activities because of the high degree of integral voluntary work, and their alleged contribution to the formation of young people and democratic values. Within a historical perspective, because of this high public regard, both institutions have been able to maintain a high level of autonomy from the state, experiencing little interference or intrusive demands.

However, during the decades around the millennium, the continuous national and international disclosures of sexual abuse in different social domains and institutions, including day care, schools, sports, the scout movement, and the Roman Catholic Church, have prompted disbelief, anger, and subsequently a demand for better child protection measures. Although the incidence of sexual abuse of children and young people in those social arenas is not a new phenomenon, the magnitude of the media driven publicity and political attention has been an important factor in the creation of perceptions of risk, and in eroding the basic trust in traditional authorities and institutions. This can be illustrated by considering the discourses surrounding abuse and paedophilia.

Since the early 1990s, the news media in Denmark has played an important role in lifting the social taboo on discussing child abuse, by documenting the consequences for abused children and the negligence or lack of corporate responsibility at voluntary, local, and state level. In particular, the written media has featured a range of powerful headlines about child molestation, rape, and paedophilia, evoking an emotional reader response including anger, hatred, disgust, disbelief, and surprise, and thus helping sell newspapers. The media use of the essentially pathological terms, paedophilia and paedophile, has proven to be extremely effective in achieving this purpose. A search in *Infomedia*, a Danish online database holding media documents since 1990, illustrates the rapid inflation in the media use of paedophilia and paedophile. Between 1990 and 1994 there were 279 articles containing one or both words. However, a large number of these did not relate to specific cases of sexual abuse; they often related to debates about the acceptability of claims made by representatives of the Danish Paedophiles' Association to the effect that children and adults can interact sexually without causing harm to the child. In three succeeding five-year periods, the number of articles including one or both words increased rapidly: to 2,214 (1995–1999), 7,780 (2000–2004), reaching 16,729 (2005–2009). There is no reason to believe that this sixty-fold increase over only twenty years in the use of the terms paedophilia and paedophile in the Danish media reflected similarly changed rates in the actual incidence of paedophile acts; for it to have done so would have required an epidemic. There may be several contributing reasons for this notable increase, but the case of the Belgian serial killer and child abuser Marc Dutroux played an important role in making the pathological term paedophile such a commonly used term by the media and the wider population in Denmark. Although Dutroux was arrested in 1996 for having kidnapped, tortured, and sexually abused six girls during 1995 to 1996, he was not tried and convicted until 2004. Shortly after his arrest, two girls were rescued from an underground dungeon in his house, and four girls were later found buried in his garden. A slow-moving investigation, during which Dutroux claimed that he was part of an international sex ring that included high-ranking members of the Belgian police force and government, and a sensational prison escape in 1998, led to a massive critique of the Belgian police and the entire justice system. Organized by victim support organizations, this included a petition of almost three million signatures (out of a population of ten million) asking for abolition of conditional release for very serious crimes, and a protest march through Brussels by 300,000 people (Snacken, 2007). The Danish media coverage of the Dutroux case accounts for 1,961 references and in most of the articles he was labelled as a paedophile, and generally described as an extremely deviant, violent, and dangerous person.

In 1995, when sexual abuse involving a sports coach was documented for the first time on national TV in Denmark, the offenders were referred to merely as violators and perpetrators (Melin, 1995). The paedophile-labelling of sexual abuse in sport started in late 1998, when Danish TV, radio, and newspapers started reporting an ongoing criminal investigation against an HIV-positive self-taught martial arts instructor; he was tried in 2000 and sentenced to six years in prison for sexual abuse of ten boys aged between eleven and fourteen. It became clear that he had set up his own private club and disguised it as regular sports club by formally assigning board positions with parents' names, and thereby making it eligible for municipal funding. In the beginning there was also an assistant coach, but he ended involvement having witnessed, and refused to take part in, post-training intimate oil massages of the athletes. The abuse took place on camping trips, in the perpetrator's apartment, and at the club's facilities. The police investigation went on for several months because of multiple inquiries and questioning of victims, and also the medical complexity resulting from the perpetrator's HIV status, and TV, radio, and print media reported on the case from the initial arrest in December 1998 through to the court verdict in April 2000 (J. T. Nielsen, 2004). Although this case involved an unqualified and unaffiliated perpetrator, operating outside the parameters of organised sport, it effectively established the discourse about paedophilia in sport, through the frequency with which it was reported over a substantial period.

In 1999, not long after the arrest of the martial arts instructor, six middle-aged serious-looking men were pictured on the cover of a special edition of the US magazine *Sports Illustrated,* under the headline: 'WHO'S COACHING YOUR KID?', and a subtitle: 'The frightening truth about child molestation in youth sports'. The magazine, commonly read in Danish sport circles, suggested that the men pictured were coaches and paedophiles who had sexually molested children in sport and, based on the details in the article, each coach would probably fit the pathology of paedophilia. The lead article started with the headline and subtitle: 'Every parent's nightmare – the child molester has found a home in the world of youth sports, where as a coach he can gain the trust and loyalty of kids – and then prey on them' (Nack & Yaeger, 1999). Thus the phenomenon of sexual abuse in US sport was dramatically publicised around the same time that it became a big issue in Denmark. Although neither the American cases or the *Sports Illustrated* feature were directly quoted or referred to by the Danish sports organisations, or mentioned in their member magazines, this powerful article, with its focus on paedophilia and the effective demonization of coaches, can only have boosted awareness within and beyond the sporting community, and facilitated panic. Prior to the actual court case with the martial arts instructor, in March 2000 representatives from the Danish Sports Confederation and National Olympic Committee (DIF) and the Danish Sports and Gymnastics Association (DGI) were interviewed for a newspaper article about paedophilia in sport. A DIF special consultant (and former police officer), Jan Darfeldt, stated: 'People are not willing to speak about it [abuse in sport]. So it easily becomes diffuse, and it's hard to have a debate on that basis. There is nothing we can do about it'. The article reported that: 'Jan Darfeldt believes it is impossible for a confederation such as DIF to take up this issue in a campaign without something concrete to hang the debate on. It would not make any impact. So people say that they don't have this problem [in their club], and therefore it doesn't have their interest. People push it away. It must be concrete before it's relevant to them'. According to the article, Leif Mikkelsen, the president of the DGI, did not consider the problem to be extensive, but admitted that there was a risk, because coaches often have a hero status among the young. Further, 'To require clean criminal records is not the way forward, because there is not an employment relationship, but an association based on voluntarism.' (Brahm, 2000).

In April 2000, only weeks after this newspaper interview, a Danish TV documentary, titled *The dangerous volunteers* (Harkamp & Klit, 2000), disclosed at length how easy it was for adult coaches to get close to and abuse children in sport. The programme focussed both on a number of heterosexual abuse cases (between male coaches and post-pubertal female athletes), and a number of homosexual paedophile cases (between male coaches and pre-pubertal athletes). Part of the programme was dedicated to an investigation of how the president of the Danish Paedophile Association was active in two sports club without the board members knowing about his background. It also illustrated how a number of previously convicted paedophiles were active in sports after serving their sentences.

A TV debate with representatives from the sports organisations and politicians voiced a serious concern about the protection of children and young people against coaches with the wrong intentions. In June 2000 the Minister of Justice proposed a compulsory criminal record check by the national police of all persons who, by virtue of the employment relationship, had a direct contact with children and young people (Thrane, 2000). This documentary marked a shift in sports organisations' responses to the issue of abuse, from complete denial to a state of minimal admission; shortly after the transmission, DGI followed DIF's example and started recommending their member clubs to obtain criminal record checks when hiring new coaches or leaders.

## The authorities take action: The government commission of enquiry

In 2002 the Danish Minister of Cultural Affairs, whose responsibility included organised sport, called for an investigation of the prevalence of sexual abuse in sport. During the interview he urged that the commission of inquiry should also propose directions for prevention work for this highly complex problem and added: 'Paedophilia is a gigantic problem for society' and 'we [members of parliament] consider it [paedophilia in sport] to be a problem of such dimensions that we need to solve it together [sports organisations, researchers, and politicians]. We must do everything we can to save young people from being destroyed for the rest of their lives' (Jensen, 2002). He added that he would like all sports clubs to obtain information from the central criminal register when employing new coaches or leaders. According to a study among sports clubs at the time, in 2002 fewer than 5 per cent of sports clubs were making use of this option (Toftegaard-Støckel, 2008). I was invited by the ministry to take part in the commission of inquiry and was informed that this was a very important issue for the minister, who allegedly had received many letters and emails from people who knew of this problem (personal meeting with Hanne Refslund Petersen, head of department in the Ministry of Cultural Affairs, 10 October 2001).

In the early stages, being engaged in doctoral work in a cognate area, I contributed to the work of the commission in exploring the prevalence of sexual abuse in sport. Having taken a six month leave from my PhD, three months into the work I had not received a formal contract, and was aware of some criticism from senior police sources of a colleague's methodological approach and alleged superficial attention during visits to police districts. Accordingly I sought clarity about my role and a clear division of tasks from the ministry and, in order to permit cross-referencing between alleged abuse cases, I requested access to the relevant emails and letters that the minister had apparently received. These requests led to friction, and my involvement with the commission ended (incidentally, without payment). Being neither party to its later deliberations nor invited to the final conference, I cannot comment in detail on the overall conduct of the research or the key finding of a 1 per cent incidence rate for the abuse of children in Danish sport. This noteworthy research outcome may be an underestimate, and is certainly out of line with a number of international findings referred to by Brackenridge (2001). However, different studies employ distinct criteria and methods, which can skew the figures in either direction and provide the basis of very different headlines.

The commission report was presented in 2003 at a conference held by the Ministry of Cultural Affairs; the participants included invited representatives from national governing sports bodies, police, social work, and research. The report presented an estimate of coach-athlete sexual abuse of 1 per cent (Helweg-Larsen, 2003b), based on two sets of data. The first was a survey conducted by Hellweg-Larsen among adolescents in ninth grade [pupils aged fourteen–fifteen] regarding their sexual experiences with adults, and the second a crime study of coach-athlete abuse cases from 1998–2001. The report summarised the main initiatives taken by DIF and DGI, which in brief provided information on homepages, the stimulation of debate in local sports clubs, and gave advice to sports clubs dealing with concerns relating to, or actual handling of cases of sexual abuse. The conference recommendations (Helweg-Larsen, 2003a) were to strengthen positive behavioural norms in sports clubs, to let the issue of sexual abuse be a theme in all coach/leader courses, and to establish a joint helpline and homepage to facilitate better access to correct information about procedures and case handling. In addition a number of recommendations were aimed at the operational level, calling for better support and cooperation between schools, the police and the municipal level. Finally it was recommended that organized sport should seek to comply with Council of Europe (CoE) resolutions on the prevention of sexual harassment and abuse, which Denmark signed in 2000. Unlike the EU, the CoE cannot make binding laws and its resolutions can therefore be construed as advisory. It resolved that:

> Governments . . . shall take the steps necessary . . . to ensure that everyone should have the opportunity to take part in sport . . . in a safe and healthy environment . . . [and] to protect . . . the moral and ethical bases of sport and the human dignity and safety of those involved . . . by safeguarding sports, sportsmen and sportswomen . . . from practices that are abusive or debasing.

Additionally the resolution underlines the need to:

> prepare a national policy which would make a clear statement about the absolute need to safeguard and promote the welfare of children, young people and women in sport; . . . agree that the implementation of the policy within the context of an overall framework of support and protection for children, young people and women in sport, could include such actions as drawing up a basic code of conduct for coaches, trainers and leaders, encouraging national sports organisations to draw up codes of conduct based on the same principles; developing and disseminating information materials for families, athletes and coaches, trainers and leaders; setting up of independent telephone help lines; introducing specific courses on child protection in the education of coaches

and trainers; . . . [and] to draw up a timetable for the rapid implementation of these measures.

(CoE, 2000)

The inclusion in the conference recommendations of reference to the CoE resolution text relates to the fact that Professor Kari Fasting, who contributed to the preparation of the CoE resolution, took part in and presented at the conference. Through drawing attention to international resolutions and existing research, Fasting's contribution could have paved the way for a national prevention strategy, and more detailed policy work within the sport organisations. However, from the conference report it is unclear how the ministry and the commission panel responded to such a possibility. Beyond the general endorsement of the CoE document, the lack of clear objectives, deadlines for implementation, and specified consequences of non-compliance in the commission of inquiry report left Danish sports organisations with effective autonomy with regard to safeguarding measures. Having accepted an incidence rate of 1 per cent, the commission appeared undecided about any definitive subsequent action, and in effect left responsibility with the sport organisations. As a result, the children's certificate [a criminal record check for sexual offences] became the main instrument for child protection within sport.

## The children's certificate and ethical codex

In 2005 the Danish parliament passed a law that made it compulsory for all types of organisations to obtain a specific children's certificate when employing paid or voluntary staff working with children under fifteen years of age (Kulturministeriet, 2005). In short the certificate involves a criminal record search, in which the applicant's background is checked for sexual crimes committed against children under fifteen years of age (and thus excluding offences committed against anyone older). Referring to the compulsory law revision, the Minister of Culture Brian Mikkelsen stated in a TV interview:

> The children's certificate is effective because there have been fewer cases of sexual abuse of children than in the past. Since 2005, 446,576 background checks have been carried out among coaches and managers, of whom 59 persons were previously convicted for paedophilia. Think of the 59 that have been ruled out even though they knew they were being checked. How many have stayed away? In that way, we have saved a lot of children and young people.
>
> (Rasmussen & Dam, 2008)

In 2012 the law was additionally tightened so that not only those working directly with children would need a background check, but also personnel who through their employment have regular access to children. The amendment followed two separate cases which prompted a degree of moral panic. The first was revealed by the tabloid newspaper *Ekstra Bladet* (J. Nielsen, 2010), which used its access to previous crime cases to investigate the whereabouts of perpetrators with past

convictions for child sexual abuse. One of the perpetrators was found to be working as a cleaning assistant at a film school for children. Apparently, this man had
not committed any crimes against any of the children at the film school, but he
was fired when he admitted his past convictions to the management. Shortly after
this newspaper report the Minister of Culture was interviewed about the loop-
hole, and he recommended an update of the existing law to include anyone with
access to children in any of the cultural settings funded by the ministry (Strøyer,
2010). The second case related to a private day-care worker operating from her
own house. The local newspaper received a tip from an upset parent who felt that
the municipality supervisor had not taken her earlier complaint about abuse seriously. As the newspaper *Fyens Stiftstidende* investigated the case, they detected
that the day-care worker's boyfriend, a previously convicted child abuser, might
have had access to up to nine children under her care during their relationship
(Bjørn, Ammitsbøll, & Toft-Nielsen, 2011). The written media covered the case
and repeatedly labelled the day-care worker's boyfriend as a paedophile because
they found out he had been convicted for abusing his own 5-year-old son and
two girls (Bundgaard, 2011). The day-care worker was forced to resign and a
supervisor working for the council was fired for not responding to the formal
complaint made by the parent who had suspected some sort of abuse was taking
place at the day-care centre. In summary, neither cases related to sports, but the
law amendment has now become compulsory and applicable to all personnel who
have access to children.

In 2006 DIF and the elite sports organisation Team Denmark agreed on a set
of ethical principles that apply to all competitive sport, targeting the subgroups of
athletes, coaches, staff and leaders, officials, parents, and spectators (DIF-Team
Denmark, 2006). None of the parties has to officially endorse the ethical principles as each is meant to know about and accept the guidelines. In the behavioural
norms for youth coaches, the code of conduct says: 'Always be aware of the power
you have as a coach and avoid any sexual advance to and intimate contact with athletes'. Likewise, athletes are encouraged to avoid intimate contact with coaches.

DIF and Team Denmark were represented at the landmark 2003 commission
conference and so it appears surprising that there were no references to it, or to
the international resolutions obliging Denmark to establish such ethical standards.
This again suggests a lack of strategic coherence between the national policy level
and the autonomy of national governing sports bodies. In summary, in spite of
high-level political and sporting concern and engagement, beyond the compulsory
reference to criminal records the approach adopted to child protection in Danish
sport has been essentially light-touch, and there has been little or no coherence
or consistency with international resolutions and more interventionist approaches
adopted elsewhere.

## The panic disappears?

A decade after the commission of inquiry conference, there are still no policies,
action plans, or safeguarding strategies within organised sports. Being responsible

for the overall funding and governmental relations with sports organisations, the Ministry of Cultural Affairs has the authority to ensure that above-mentioned recommendations and resolutions are put into practise, but surprisingly little has happened in terms of prevention work. The lack of implementation efforts could stem from one or more reasons, including:

- Inadequate project management, forgetfulness, or neglect of duty by the Ministry of Cultural Affairs
- The ministry trusted that the national sports organisations were capable of developing adequate safeguarding measures according to recommendations and the Council of Europe resolution
- The moral panic relating to paedophilia in sports has disappeared because the problem has been solved, minimised, or forgotten about because of shifting media agendas
- The need for safeguarding policies has been diluted or rendered less urgent by the law requiring sport (and other) organisations to require scrutiny of the children's certificate.

As the previous sections demonstrated, media attention, public debate, and criminal law in Denmark have focused on paedophilia and restricting the access of convicted perpetrators into organised sports. Having achieved this change, the first tide of moral panic about sexual abuse in sport receded. However, new waves are sporadically generated by a particular ongoing case, or new research results. In most cases the media will seek to link a personal story to the sexual abuse issue, often employing powerful tip-of-the-iceberg metaphors (Hallberg & Rigné, 1994). Within this context the media has used expert statements to strengthen the general credibility of the issue and generate public and political attention. As a consequence politicians and sports politicians, managers and administrators have been forced to engage in the debate – often with different rationales and arguments. Sports politicians and senior managers often claim that they have developed good prevention measures, while politicians call for zero tolerance against paedophiles (but at the same time arguing that the children's certificate is a strong tool for deterring perpetrators from entering sport) (Rasmussen & Dam, 2008; Strøyer, 2010). Since 1998 I have been invited to offer expert comments in this type of news story on numerous occasions. While high level sports organisations originally argued from the position of complete denial in the late 1990s, as previously outlined, they have progressed to a state of minimal admission, and the adoption of some prevention measures. Thus, from around 2005 sports organisations crossed an important threshold of engagement, where they no longer can be accused of being passive.

This has particular relevance for the particular template which journalists, in my experience, often follow when they seek to deal with the issue of sexual abuse in sport, involving an interesting relationship between media, research, and sports organisations. Journalists often begin their stories with information from courtrooms or an ongoing police investigation about a specific case to which – for the sake of added credibility – they seek to attach an expert statement. Occasionally an interview with an abused athlete or parents is used to create the personal and emotional story with which the general public can be expected sympathise. In most of the written articles, journalists use this type of material to confront sports managers or sports politicians about particular cases, the issue in general, and sports organisations' procedures for child protection and case handling.

While using terms like paedophile and paedophilia, through drawing attention to the mandatory implementation of children's certificates from 2005, sports organisations and politicians have been able to deflect criticism about perceived inadequate fulfilment of previous recommendations and resolutions in relation to athlete safeguarding. As pointed out by Parent & Demers (2011, p. 128), 'Athlete protection inevitably depends on better prevention in sports organizations. In taking action to deal with sexual abuse, it is essential that sports authorities focus on the factors which influence organizations to act or not to act on sexual abuse as well as on the measures involved.' Danish sports organisations currently appear unwilling to develop more interventionist or higher profile child protection strategies, or to engage in further policy work, unless there is convincing evidence to substantiate a claim that the current level of prevention work is inadequate. Arguably, from the point of view of their status as responsible social institutions wishing to protect their interests and positive public image, in relation to sexual abuse in sport it would be easier for sports organisations to develop child safeguarding policies and practices on a much larger scale. This would permit them to show that general well-being, quality, and sports participation issues are being fully addressed in a demonstrable bureaucratic and managerial way, making it easier to deal with issues and cases as they arise, rather than being drawn into recurring discussions of paedophilia. However, this is not the course of action being chosen, and it seems very likely that Danish sports clubs at a local level believe that there are no paedophiles in their clubs and therefore that no further protection schemes are needed. If this approach and assumption is present at the higher levels in the organisational hierarchy (relating back to the notion of sport as essentially good and moral) then, from the viewpoint of advocates of intrusive safeguarding, this could have serious implications for the safety of young athletes. Child protection knowledge and procedures risk being only randomly accessed, a weaker response to the problem than if accorded a higher profile and mandated as part of a must-do policy for all concerned.

This significantly contrary policy approach has not been challenged by the Danish authorities. While sports organisations in many other Western countries have implemented comprehensive child protection policies, Danish politicians and sports politicians, managers, and administrators have been reluctant to enter the pathway of control, rules, and regulations. This approach has met little public criticism, and several factors may help to explain this. Historically, Danish sports organisations have maintained a strong autonomy from the state and municipal interference, the commonly held belief being that trust is better than control.[2] Since the conclusion of the commission of inquiry in 2003 there have been comments from sporting representatives which can be summarised as 'it couldn't happen here' and 'the debate has been blown out of proportion'. They indicate the belief that the debate about paedophilia and sexual abuse in sport is being blown-up out of proportion in the media (Helweg-Larsen, 2003b; Toftegaard-Støckel, 2008). Parent and Demers (2011) found similar organisational responses from a Canadian sample of national and regional sports organisations to be rooted in a fear of stirring up the problem and insecurity about tackling the issue of abuse in sport, and also concerns about encouraging false allegations.

Rather than assessing whether Danish sports organisations are acting improperly or defensively about an alleged neglect of duty, it may seem more obvious to claim that the Danish system is a better alternative to the situation in the UK, where parents need a criminal record check before they can enter a play area or drive other parents' children to away competitions. An online news article in *Radiovice* fuels the Danish belief that trust is better than control:

> Child protection gone too far – parents unable to play with kids in UK . . . Nanny State to the extreme. Only authorized play rangers are allowed to mingle with the children between the ages of 5 and 15 in two Watford playgrounds. Mayor Dorothy Thornhill argued the council was merely enforcing government policy at the play areas. 'Sadly, in today's climate, you can't have adults walking around unchecked in a children's playground and the adventure playground is not a meeting place for adults,' she said.
>
> (McGough, 2009)

Critics of increased defensive rules and regulations scrutinize such approaches as feel-good measures designed to ban child predators from being around kids, but actually treating all adults in the same way, as if they are all dangerous; hence they regard such approaches as harmful and of little worth. Within the Danish debate these British measures have been used as arguments to illustrate how child protection can get out of hand, damaging life experience for the majority, and turn into modern-day witch hunts. Bureaucratic responses to the risk of abuse are promoted as providing safety but, on the contrary, may create a false sense of security, and cause a problematic demonization of all adult (men) as potential child molesters. The discourse of paedophilia has been an important factor in the decreasing number of men going in to the day-care area and for increasing the fear of false allegations (nabr, 2010). It could be argued that the extreme and emotive discourse of paedophilia in Danish sport has made it more difficult to recognise and deal with the issue, because key stakeholders (clubs and associations) do not believe that they house perpetrators in their own organisation. It may be argued that this response has been in part created by a discourse and matching approach to child protection and the prevention of abuse based on the idea that extremely deviant and recidivistic paedophiles are the sole or primary source of danger. Such a view is clearly inadequate, and overshoots its goal in both theory and practice. It might be remembered that research has indicated that a substantial proportion of sexual harm to children in sport is in fact perpetrated by their peers (Alexander, Stafford, & Lewis, 2011).

The question arises: Danish sport having bypassed the adoption of paternalistic child protection approaches involving increased surveillance and control, what is the alternative in principle and practice? Currently sports clubs are obliged to obtain children's certificates from all new employees, and encouraged to discuss the issue of sexual abuse and appropriate behavioural norms within their organisations. As pointed out in the commission enquiry report through an input from a sports organisation official (Helweg-Larsen, 2003b:44), individual sports clubs do not have the knowledge and insight to develop overarching policies on their own – they would need higher level support. No national sporting organisation or the Ministry of Cultural Affairs have put their weight behind an authoritative intervention, apparently seeing the risk of sexual abuse as being about 'a few rotten apples' rather than more analytically, as an interpersonal and cultural problem nested within organisations with poor leadership. Blocking convicted perpetrators from entering sport has been presented by sports organisations and policymakers as an effective tool, which has increased the protection of children and young people in sport. However, there is little empirical evidence to support this claim. It is an obvious paradox that too much control and regulation may undermine the voluntary culture in sport, and conversely too little control may jeopardise the public's trust in its moral basis and its status as an appropriately safe environment for children.

Trust is significant in Danish culture, matching the account of the theologian and philosopher K. E. Løgstrup:

> In advance, we believe each other's words, in advance, we trust each other. It may be strange enough, but it is part of being human. It would be hostile to life to carry on differently. We simply could not live, our lives would wither, life would be crippled if we met each other with distrust.

> (1958 p. 19)

According to Løgstrup, philosophical specifications of basic moral principles fail when they aim for a 'meta-norm', which is problematic because it leads to an infinite regress, creating an objectifying relation to other people and diminishing the role of ethical intuition. Instead he proposed an ethic 'from below', from what he calls the sovereign or spontaneous expressions of life, which are universal to all humans, and also intrinsically positive. Trust is *per se* a good thing, socially positive, and thus worth protecting. Although there are no doubt a range of factors involved, as stated in a British Medical Journal article (Christensen, Herskind, & Vaupel, 2006), and some may query the research methodology, this national characteristic appears likely to contribute to the repeated finding that the Danish population reports the highest sense of well-being and contentment in the world (Helliwell, Layard, and Sachs, 2012). The 2013 survey confirmed this result, Denmark ranking No. 1 with the UK, while advancing, at No. 41 (Easton, 2013).

The Danish assumption and practice of trust, conceived as a central element to being human, has of course been challenged by the advent of risk society generally, and the phenomenon of sexual abuse in sport in particular. So far, trust, organisational autonomy, and resistance to crossing the threshold of intervention-ist engagement has shielded Danish sport and voluntary work against the rules and regulations that have been implemented in many Western countries. The ideal of sport as a morally pure institution has possibly saved sports in Denmark from the changes which have been proposed on the basis of well-intentioned international resolutions and children's rights declarations, and the question of whether such initiatives in reality contribute to child protection in sport remains unresolved.

The bureaucratic performance of protection is not the same thing as eliminat-ing risk, which in itself appears a problematic and isolated goal. These argu-ments and distinctions need to be very clearly made before a particular strategy is adopted. Denmark has in effect chosen not to follow the mainstream approach implemented in many international contexts. This more intrusive and managerial response of policies and procedures has tended to be promoted by organisations which suggest much (even disconcertingly) higher incidence rates for child abuse in sport than the 1 per cent figure established by the research and commission of inquiry conducted under the direct auspices of the Danish government. Not all research is equally credible, and responses to research outcomes can be signifi-cant. The retention of a relatively light-touch system and the assumption of trust need not mean that Danish sport is unsafe for children and young people. There are legitimate alternatives to the dominant approach, and choosing between them is an issue of costs and benefits. This calculation is appropriately weighted differ-ently in different social and cultural contexts. For this reason, Denmark appears to be an important case study, with a contribution to make to decision making and practice in other jurisdictions.

## Notes

1 My acknowledgements go to Tine Vertommen and Heather Piper for their insightful comments and support.
2 According to Mortensen (2004), voluntary work has been shielded against state and municipal rules and regulations because of the moral values obtained through comrade-ship, genuine commitment, and getting young people away from street corners.

## References

Alexander, K., Stafford, A., & Lewis, R. (2011) The experiences of children participating in organised sport in the UK. London: NSPCC.

American Psychiatric Association. (2013) Diagnostic and statistical manual of mental dis-orders (5th ed.). Washington, DC: American Psychiatric Publishing.

Beck, U. (1986) Risk society: Towards a new modernity. London: Sage.

Bjørn, L., Ammitsbøll, P., & Toft-Nielsen, V. (2011, 17 May) Politi ind i sag om pædofil hos dagplejer (trans.: Police enter case about pedophile resident with daycare worker), Fyens Stiftstidende.

Brackenridge, C. (2001) Spoilsport: Understanding and preventing sexual exploitation in sport. London: Routledge.

Brahm, K. (2000, March 8) Idræt: Pædofili foregår i idrætten, Flere tilfælde i idrættens ver-
den, hvor trænere eller ledere misbruger børn seksuelt (trans.: Sports: Pedophilia takes
place in sports, more cases in sport where coaches or managers sexually abuse children),
Jyllands-Posten (online media), Artikel-id: Z5625593, http://jyllands-posten.dk/sport/
ECE3283134/paedofili-foregar-i-idraetten/

Bundgaard, M. (2011, 16 May) Pædofil boede hos dagplejer (trans.: Paedophile lived with
daycare worker). TV2 Nyheederne (online media) http://nyhederne.tv2.dk/artikel.php/
id-39914566:paedofil-boede-hos-dagplejer.html

Christensen, K., Herskind, A.M., & Vaupel, J. W. (2006) Why Danes are smug: Comparative study of life satisfaction in the European Union. British Medical Journal, 333
(7582):1289–91.

Cohen, S. (1972) Folk devils and moral panics. London: MacGibbon and Kee.

Council of Europe. (2000, March) Resolution on the prevention of sexual harassment and
abuse of women, young people and children in sport. http://www.coe.int/t/dg4/sport/
resources/texts/spres00.3en.asp

DIF-Team Denmark. (2006) Etisk kodeks for dansk konkurrenceidræt (Ethical codex for
competitive sport in Denmark). 1–15. Retrieved from http://www.vark.dk/pdf/diverse/
etisk_kodeks.pdf

Dorren, D. M. (2004) Toward a multidimensional model for sexual recidivism risk. Journal
of Interpersonal Violence, 19(8) 21.

Easton, M. (2013) Why wellbeing is not a silly season filler. BBC News UK. Retrieved
from http://www.bbc.co.uk/news/uk-23509171 website:

Forney, J. C., Lombardo, S., & Toro, P. A. (2007) Diagnostic and other correlates of HIV
risk behaviors in a probability sample of homeless adults. Psychiatric Services, 58(1)
92–99. doi: 10.1176/appi.ps.58.1.92-a

Hallberg, M., & Rigné, E. M. (1994) Child sexual abuse – a study of controversy and construction. Acta Sociologica, 37(2) 22.

Hanson, R., Bussière, K., & Monique T. (1998) Predicting relapse: A meta-analysis of
sexual offender recidivism studies. Journal of Consulting and Clinical Psychology,
66(2) 13.

Harkamp, J., & Klit, L. (writers) (2000 April 18) De farlige Frivillige (trans: The dangerous
volunteers). J. Rosendal (producer). Danmarks Radio kanal 1 (trans: Denmark's Radio
channel 1).

Helliwell, J., Layard, R. and Sachs, J. (2012) The world happiness report, The Earth Institute, Columbia University, http://www.earth.columbia.edu/articles/view/2960

Helweg-Larsen, K. (2003a) Seksuelle krænkelser af børn og unge indenfor idræt, den
aktuelle forekomst og forebyggelse (trans.: Sexual abuse of children and young people,
the current prevalence and prevention). Copenhagen: Institut for Folkesundhed.

Helweg-Larsen, K. (2003b) Seksuelle krænkelser af børn og unge indenfor idræt. Den
aktuelle forekomst og forebyggelse, Resultater af en landsomfattende undersøgelse og
rapport fra konferencen i januar 2003 (trans.: Sexual abuse of children and young people
in sport, prevalence and prevention, results of a national inquiry and report from the
January 2003 conference.)

Jenkins, P. (1998) Moral panic: Changing concepts of the child molester in modern America. New Haven, CT: Yale University Press.

Jensen, J. B. (2002, 30 January) Minister: Omfang af pædofile overgreb skal under-
søges (trans.: The prevalence of paedophiles' sexual abuse needs to be investigated),

Jyllandsposten. (online media) http://jyllands-posten.dk/sport/ECE3440551/minister-omfang-af-paedofile-overgreb-skal-undersoeges/, last retrieved 13 May 2014.

Jørgensen, P. (1997) Ro, Renlighed og Regelmæssighed Dansk Idræts-Forbund og sportens gennembrud ca. 1896–1918 (Tranquillity, cleanliness and regularity – the Danish Sports Confederation and the breakthrough of sport 1896–1918). Odense: Syddansk Universitetsforlag.

Kulturministeriet (2005) Lov om indhentelse af børneattest i forbindelse med ansættelse af personale m.v. (trans.: Law about requiring a children's certificate when hiring personnel), 520 C.F.R. (2005).

Løgstrup, K. (1958) Den etiske Fordring (trans. The ethical demand). Copenhagen: Gyldendal.

McGough, S. (2009) Child protection gone too far – parents unable to play with kids in UK. Accessed 30 October 2009 at http://radioviceonline.com/child-protection-gone-too-far-parents-unableto-play-with-kids-in-uk/

Melin, C. (1995). Illustreret Sort, In: Lige pa og sport, TV2 Sporten.

Mortensen, M. (2004) Idræt som kommunal velfærd – Mentalitet, velfærd og idrætspolitik i København, Ballerup og Skive 1870–1970 (trans.: Sport as a municipal welfare – mentality, welfare and sport policies in Copenhagen, Ballerup and Skive 1870–1970). (PhD), University of Copenhagen, DHL´s Forlag.

nabr. (2010, 20 April) Mænd rammes af pædofiliregler (trans.: Men hit by paedophilia rules), online news article, TV2 Nyheder online. http://nyhederne.tv2.dk/article.php/id-30013568:maend-rammes-afpaedofiliregler.html

Nack, W., & Yaeger, D. (1999, September 13) Who's coaching your kid? Every parent's nightmare – the child molester has found a home in the world of youth sports, where as a coach he can gain the trust and loyalty of kids – and then prey on them, Sports Illustrated special report, 117.

Nielsen, J. (2010, 3 October) Seriedømt pædofil arbejder blandt børn (trans.: Serial paedophile work among children), Ekstra Bladet online. http://ekstrabladet.dk/122/article1423585.ece

Nielsen, J. T. (2004) The illusion of sport intimacy. (PhD), University of Copenhagen.

Parent, S., & Demers, G. (2011) Sexual abuse in sport: A model to prevent and protect athletes. Child Abuse Review, 20(2) 120–133.

Piper, H., Taylor, B., & Garratt, D. (2011) Sports coaching in risk society: No touch! No trust! Sport, Education and Society, 17(3) 331–345.

Rasmussen, H., & Dam, C. (2008) Pædofili-lov har bestået sin prøve (Paedophile-law has stood the test). DR sporten (Denmarks Radio's online news).

Seto, M. C. (2008) Paedophilia and sexual offending against children: Theory, assessment, and intervention. Washington, DC: American Psychological Association.

Seto, M. C. (2009) Paedophilia. The Annual Review of Clinical Psychology, 5, 391–408.

Snacken, S. (2007) Penal policy and practice in Belgium. Crime and Justice, 36(1) 127–215.

Strøyer, R. (2010, 12 October) Kulturminister skærper kampen mod pædofile (trans.: Minister of culture increases the fight against paedophiles). Culture Section, online media, http://www.dr.dk/Nyheder/Kultur/2010/10/12/123728.htm

Thompson, K. A. (1998) Moral panics. London: Sage.

Thrane, M. (2000, 9 June) Flere skal vise ren attest, Pædofile: For at gøre det lettere for kommuner og amter at undgå at ansætte folk, der er dømt for overgreb mod børn, vil justitsministeren nu give mulighed for at udvide brugen af straffeattester (trans.: More must show clean certificate, paedophiles: To make it easier for local governments to avoid hiring people who have been convicted of offenses against children, the minister of justice now make it possible to extend the use of criminal records), Berlingske Tidende, p. 1.

Toftegaard-Støckel, J. (2008). Risks and possibilities for sexual exploitation in the Danish sport club system. In C. Brackenridge, T. Kay, & D. Rhind (eds.), Sport, children's rights and violence prevention: A sourcebook on global issues and local programmes. (pp. 129–135) London: Brunel University.

# 9 She'll be right? An Australian perspective on caring for young people in physical education and sport

*Keith Lyons*

## Introduction

This chapter explores issues surrounding practice, pedagogy, and policy relating to touch in physical education teaching and sport coaching in Australia. It is a contribution to the open discussion of touch inspired by the work of Heather Piper and her colleagues in general and the publication of a special edition of the journal *Sport, Education and Society* (Piper *et al.* 2013a) in particular. It reflects the view that discussions about touch must acknowledge contextual complexity and nuance, at a time when 'common sense is itself a problematic and disputed idea' (Piper *et al.* 2013b: p. 578). Given Australia's cultural diversity, it is important that any discussion of touch in teaching and coaching is sensitive to this reality (Santoro *et al.* 2011).

An immediate example of this contextual complexity is the existence of touch football as an organized sport in Australia, a less physically challenging variant of the relatively robust and confrontational sport of rugby league. There are 400,000 registered members, and 500,000 children participate in school programs (Touch Football Australia, 2014). Any digital search for "touch" in Australia suggests links to the national sporting organization, Touch Football Australia. The rules (Touch Football Australia, 2000 np.) state that 'touch is contact on any part of the body between a player in possession of the ball and a defending player'. A touch includes 'contact on the ball, hair or clothing and may be made by a defending player or by the player in possession' (Definition 1.25). Rule 10.1 stipulates that 'Players of both defending and attacking teams are to use the minimum force necessary to effect touches'. This is an important issue to initiate discussion in this chapter: there is a game that codifies touch. There are other examples of modified games that encourage touch rather than tackling or full-body contact. When we consider some of the taken-for-grantedness in Australian sporting culture, there is a need to address "normal" and normalised behaviours. Scott (2013) indicates that 'sport's role as a locally organized popular pastime and a key focus of community life have protected it thus far from the effects of widely disseminated discourses of the harm and risk residing in unmediated adult-child interactions' (p. 613).

Four decades ago, Cohen (1972) observed that 'Societies appear to be subject, every now and then, to periods of moral panic' (p. 1). He presented a definitive account of how the media's 'reporting of certain "facts" can be sufficient to generate concern, anxiety, indignation or panic'. Cohen added that 'When such feelings coincide with a perception that particular values need to be protected, the preconditions for new rule creation or social problem definition are present'. Since that time the concept of a 'moral panic' has been a powerful heuristic through which to explore social convention and practice.

This chapter is an optimistic account of the possibilities for a sensitive pedagogy. In Australian idiom, "she'll be right" is the expression of hope that whatever is wrong will right itself with time. This is not a complacent argument, but one that seeks to contribute to the transformation of practice and provide support for responsible arguments about relational touch (Stronach & Piper, 2008), communicative touch (Miller *et al.* 2007), comforting tactile communication (Power, 2009), and victimless schools (McWilliam & Sachs, 2004). This is a significant endeavour at a time when 'we have seen an expansion of the parameters of a properly enacted ethic of pedagogical care, so that it now includes an unprecedented array of issues for which teachers can and do hold themselves responsible' (McWilliam, 2003 p. 36). On the basis of her study of primary school teaching in New Zealand, Power (2009 p. 2) cautions that 'touch has become subject to stringent social regulation'.

There is limited research about touch in physical education teaching and sport coaching in Australia (Scott, 2013). However, it could be argued that given a history of institutionalised child abuse it is essential for Australians to be wary of and vigilant about intergenerational relationships and the power wielded by those with ascribed status. In 2008, the prime minister, Kevin Rudd, made a formal apology to indigenous Australians for the forceful removal of Aboriginal and Torres Strait Islander children from their families, their communities and their country. In 2009, he apologised formally to 500,000 Australians who grew up in orphanages and foster care. The establishment in 2013 of the Royal Commission into Institutional Responses to Child Sexual Abuse amplified memories of these stolen and forgotten generations. Its terms of reference include authorisation to inquire into: what institutions and governments should do to better protect children against child sexual abuse and related matters in institutional contexts in the future; and what institutions and governments should do to achieve best practice in encouraging the reporting of, and responding to reports or information about, allegations, incidents or risks of child sexual abuse and related matters in institutional contexts. An "institution" is defined as any 'public or private body, agency, association, club, institution, organization or other entity or group of entities of any kind' (Royal Commission into Institutional Responses to Child Sexual Abuse, 2013 np.).

Australia thus has very substantive reasons to address moral panics about touch. As Cohen (1972) indicated, we can understand these panics through consideration of Gusfield's (1967) concept of moral passage. In the classification of deviant behaviour, Gusfield points out that the public definition of behaviour as deviant is itself changeable, open to reversals of political power, to twists of public opinion, and also to the development of social movements and moral crusades. McWilliam and her colleagues (McWilliam & Sachs, 2004; McWilliam & Jones, 2005) have explored how these panics play out in Australian classrooms and schools. For present purposes however, initially in this chapter, we consider Australians' participation in sport and physical recreation, and the importance attached to sport in Australian culture and society.

## Participation in sport

There has been considerable discussion of the importance of sport in Australian culture (Vamplew & Stoddard, 1994; Cashman, 1995; Adair & Vamplew, 1997; Bloomfield, 2003; Ferguson, 2006). Tonts (2005), amongst others, has explored the social capital value of sport in rural communities. Notwithstanding some of the barriers to social inclusion, he observes that sport fosters 'social interaction, a sense of place and community, and the range of physical and mental health benefits [that] contribute significantly to the well-being of rural citizens' (p.148). More recently the Australian Bureau of Statistics (ABS) (2012) has considered these social capital issues for the whole of Australia.

The ABS (2012) defines "social capital" as being 'a resource available to individuals and communities founded on networks of mutual support, reciprocity and trust' (np.), and suggests that the 'associational nature of sport and sporting clubs is sometimes seen as a forum for the creation of social capital by providing opportunities and settings for social interaction, sharing, common interests and enhancing a sense of community' (np). In New South Wales, for example, the state government has a vision for 'a community that uses sport and recreation to improve its well-being' (New South Wales Government, 2011, np). In Queensland, the state government proposes that 'Queenslanders are increasingly recognizing the benefits to their quality of life from participating in recreation and sport' (Queensland Government, Department of Communities, Sport and Recreation Services, 2011, np).

In 2011, the ABS reported its findings on trust from data derived from the General Household Survey of 2010. With regard to the level of generalized trust, the ABS noted that 'participants in sport and physical recreation reported greater levels of trust in people than did non-participants' (np.). The ABS suggests that 'the participation rate in sport and physical recreation decreased slightly as feelings of trust diminished'. It noted that 'the participation rate amongst those who strongly agreed that most people could be trusted was 74%, compared with 66% for those who strongly disagreed' (np). The ABS reported that 'over half of participants in sport and physical recreation (56%) reported that they either strongly or somewhat agreed that most people could be trusted compared with just under half (48%) of non-participants' (np.).

The ABS's most recent data on participation in sport (2012) indicate that: 65% of Australians aged 15 years and over participated in physical activities for recreation, exercise or sport at some time during the twelve months prior in 2010. Of children aged 5–14 years, 60% participated in organised sport outside of school hours during the twelve months ending April 2012. The Bureau reports that the most popular organised sport for boys was outdoor Australian Rules Football with 22% participating. For girls swimming/diving was the most popular, with 19% participating. In 2013, the ABS reported data on adult female participation in sport: approximately 64% of females (5.8 million) aged 15 years and over responded that they had participated in sport and physical recreation at least once during the twelve months prior to interview in 2011–12. In the same years, the number of females participating in non-organized activities (those activities not organized by a club or recreation association) was 51% (4.7 million); this was almost double that for participation in organized activities (2.4 million or 27%).

## Documenting a duty of care

Australia has a federal government under the Commonwealth of Australia Constitution Act of 1900 (Parliament of Australia, 2014). Section 109 of the constitution provides that 'When a law of a State is inconsistent with a law of the Commonwealth, the latter shall prevail, and the former shall, to the extent of the inconsistency, be invalid'. State (New South Wales, Queensland, South Australia, Tasmania, Western Australia, Victoria) and territory (Australian Capital Territory, Northern Territory) governments are responsible for the administration and operation of child protection services. Legislative acts in each state and territory determine the way these services are delivered (Bromfield & Holzer, 2008). On this basis, working with children checks are implemented in all states and territories in Australia, but each jurisdiction has separate legislation, and checks are not transferrable between them. Work to harmonize these checks and develop a national approach has been identified as a priority under the National Framework for Protecting Australia's Children 2009–2020 (Department of Social Services, 2014), which also states that 'protecting children is everyone's business' (np.). All states and territories have enacted offender registration legislation, and everywhere teachers are required to be screened for criminal offences as part of the professional registration process.

The Australian Sports Commission (ASC) is the peak Australian government body, responsible for the delivery of funding and development of Australian sport through the implementation of the government's national sport policy, with roles and responsibilities as set out in the Australian Sports Commission Act of 1989 (ComLaw, 2014). The ASC made two important governance decisions in the early 2000s. Play by the Rules was launched in 2001 (Play by the Rules, 2014), the product of partnership between the ASC, the Australian Human Rights Commission, all state and territory sport and recreation departments and anti-discrimination agencies, and the Queensland and New South Wales Commissioners for Children and Young People.

The Sports Ethics Unit of the ASC was established a year later, and played a lead role in supporting sports organisations and the sport industry to formulate policies, practices, programs and resources to address ethical issues and enhance ethical conduct in Australian sport. Its approach included: a harassment-free sport strategy; member protection funding criteria; and definition of 'The Essence of

Australian Sport'. The Unit worked with decision makers at every level of sport who 'should ensure that all policies, programs and services are based on the principles of fairness, respect, responsibility and safety' (Ethics in Sport, 2003 np.). It consulted and worked closely with national sporting organisations, state departments of sport and recreation and other agencies, to develop strategies to deal with sport-specific issues related to harassment, discrimination, sexual assault, child protection, inappropriate parent, coach, spectator and athlete behaviour. As a result of the Unit's work, and inputs from other groups within the ASC, all national sporting organisations established Member Protection Policies. Version 7 of the Member Protection Template was published in January 2013. The ASC requires national sporting organizations to develop, implement and update their Member Protection Policy so 'they comply with the law and provide a safe and positive environment for all those involved in their sport and activities' (Australian Sports Commission, 2014). The Unit itself ceased its work after a decade of activity, with some of its responsibilities passing to an Integrity Unit within the ASC. In 2014, much of the work generated by the Unit was included in the ideas and text of Play by the Rules, which has a memorandum of understanding between eighteen contributing partners to continue work through to June 2016.

One of the key figures in the development of child protection guidelines and practice in sport in Australia, Debbie Simms, has observed that:

> Over the past decade child protection has emerged as a key ethical issue for the sport industry in Australia. Factors driving this have included the introduction of new child protection legislation in several states as well as regular media coverage of court cases involving abuse of children in sport. As a result, awareness of child protection has grown throughout society, as have expectations for those working with children. Government authorities have responded by introducing funding criteria that require sporting organizations to meet specific child protection obligations.
>
> (2012 p. 77)

Given these circumstances, it is significant that in Australia, as in other national contexts discussed in this book, there is compelling evidence that teaching and coaching are regarded as moral and social encounters, in which the imperative of care is paramount. This recognition need not entail either disproportionate risk aversion or self-protective practice. In the heterogeneous Australian culture, there will need to be very careful thought given to pedagogic practice and policy, to ensure that the risk of bad things happening to children in physical education and sports contexts will be countered by approaches and interventions that do not at the same time make good things less likely, too. In relevant principles and guidance there are plentiful examples of how this duty of care in practice should be negotiated, both in theory and in specific settings.

In South Australia (Government of South Australia, 2011), for example, the duty of care is defined as a common law concept that 'refers to the responsibility of staff to provide children and young people with an adequate level of protection against harm'. Guidance is offered about how this duty of care occurs in teaching in relation to 'appropriate physical contact by a staff member to assist or encourage a child or young person' (np.). When staff are required to give practical assistance to a child or young person who is hurt, or needs particular support, examples are suggested of appropriate physical contact such as: administration of first aid; supporting children and young people who have hurt themselves; non-intrusive gestures to comfort a child or young person who is experiencing grief and loss or distress, such as a hand on the upper arm or upper back; non-intrusive touch (congratulating a child or young person by shaking hands or a pat on the upper arm or back, accompanied by positive and encouraging words). South Australia (Government of South Australia, 2011) proposes that good practice with school-age children and young people includes: seeking children and young people's permission to touch; avoiding being with a child or young person in a one-to-one, out of sight situation; not presuming that physical contact is acceptable to a particular child or young person; respecting and responding to signs that a child or young person is uncomfortable with touch. This approach requires care and reflexivity, but does not entail 'no touching' or unfocused anxiety.

The focused concern around these issues is demonstrated in other jurisdictions. In Western Australia (WA), the Safe Clubs 4 Kids (SC4K) education project is a partnership between the WA Sports Federation, Department of Sport and Recreation, Working with Children Screening Unit, Surf Life Saving WA, and the WA Child Abuse Squad. It is a proactive initiative that provides information, resources and training to the sport and active recreation industry about how to create child-safe environments (Government of Western Australia Department of Sport and Recreation, 2014).

Unsurprisingly, the high profile of safety and the duty of care have affected the assumptions and practice of Australian adults working with other peoples' children. McWilliam and Sachs (2004) were clear that 'all teachers in our study understood that their duty of care for children was of paramount importance in terms of their claim to be professional teachers' (p.21). They observed that many teachers 'worried about the implications of an expanded duty of care for their own self-conduct, and *particularly in relation to touching children*' (p.21, original emphasis). They reported that young teachers in general seem to regard 'no touch' as both normal and professional. Thus it is becoming apparent just how important clearly articulated policy about 'safe touching' is, for both teachers and sports coaches. As McWilliam and Sachs (2004) indicate, any touching of children may be rendered an 'unacceptable' risk. Their data indicate that many teachers have adapted their pedagogy to incorporate the needs and desires of the child more fully into their daily physical engagement with children. Overall, their research strongly suggested that "no touch' is becoming, either intentionally or unintentionally, the most practical way of minimizing risk to the individual teacher, regardless of whether is it pedagogically appropriate or desirable' (p.21).

The risks and challenges associated with these circumstances are widely recognized. In New South Wales, the Department of Education and Communities acknowledges that having their behaviour under increased scrutiny 'is a professional challenge for teachers' (New South Wales Department of Education and Communities, 2014). The department asserts that 'it is important to remember that the privilege and many benefits associated with employment in a role that involves work with children also carries with it expectations of the highest standards of care and protection for them' (np.). The department is clear that processes are in place to ensure that the rights of staff are protected.

One of the most significant interfaces between school and community sport in Australia is the Active After-school Communities program. This major initiative, and the interplay of the various concerns and tensions referred to above, is the focus of the next part of the chapter.

## Active After-school Communities

The Australian Government's Active After-school Communities program (AASC; Active After-school Communities, 2014) was introduced in 2005. It provides primary school children with access to free sport and other structured physical activity in the after-school time of 3.00pm to 5.30pm, and 900 primary schools and Out of School Hours Care Services (OSHCS; National Outside School Hours Services Association, 2014) from sites across Australia took part in the first year of the program. Nine years later there are 3,270 sites involved in its delivery. The program aims to engage primary school children in structured physical activity and to provide opportunities for ongoing participation in organised sport. It is based on a Playing for Life philosophy that emphasizes fun in an inclusive environment for the introduction of sport and other structured physical activities to primary-school aged children.

The AASC program is managed nationally by the ASC, through a network of locally based regional coordinators spread across four state and territory zones. The coordinators assist schools and after-school care centres in program delivery, recruit and train community coaches, and work with local sporting clubs and organisations to increase junior membership. The cornerstone of this national program is the involvement of local communities in its delivery, which offers opportunities to support and strengthen community cohesion and development.

Anyone may apply to become a community coach in the AASC program. These include, but are not exclusive to: OSHCS staff, teachers, senior and tertiary students, development officers from national and state sporting organizations, local sporting club members, private providers, parents, guardians, athletes and beginner to professional coaches. All such candidates must complete a free community coach training program, submit a probationary registration form and be cleared through working with children checks. The ASC has undertaken National Criminal History Record Checks for community coaches in jurisdictions where there are no relevant legislated requirements, and comprehensive documentation is provided about working with "vulnerable" people. The AASC central database for community coach registration is nationally managed in Canberra, and no coach may take part in any local delivery program until all checks are complete and recorded.

The responsibility and duty of care for the program rests with participating schools and OSHCS sites. Each venue at which AASC is delivered has an identified supervisor who assumes the duty of care for the children participating in the program. The supervisor's responsibilities include the duty to provide appropriate active supervision until the completion of each session, and to ensure that risk management policies and child protection policies are adhered to. Supervisors are encouraged to share any concerns they have about a community coach or a program and to share feedback from parents, family or children, and there are procedures in place to report harassment or abuse. Schools and OSHCS sites delivering AASC are continually required to meet a set of program parameters and requirements in order to maintain their involvement in the program. Regional coordinators monitor program quality throughout the duration of programs at every site to ensure that both sites and community coaches are working towards achieving outcomes established in the Engaging Children and Pathways action plans (Active After-school Communities, 2014).

Despite the scope and careful orientation of the AASC program, there is very little evidence that panics about touch have impacted on the delivery of the program. There is a comprehensive monitoring process in place that assures the quality of local delivery, and the presence of more than one adult in all sessions, as well as the involvement of local and regional coordinators and the national sharing of better practice, offer a level of reassurance about child welfare. Well publicized issues and experiences in other institutions that deal with children *in loco parentis* have heightened the ASC's careful monitoring of the program and, whilst this does not totally eradicate the risk of inappropriate touching within any session, it does go a long way to provide community reassurance.

The most recent evaluation of the AASC program (Australian Sports Commission, 2011) noted

> The majority of participating sites, especially OSHCS, believed that their involvement in the AASC program was improving their capacity to deliver sport and other structured physical activity to children. Two-fifths of schools said that new school teams were being formed as a result of the program. Most stakeholders were also generally satisfied that the program was stimulating community involvement in sport and structured physical activity, and had had an impact on the local community's ability to support the participation of children in sport.

> (p.4)

However, there was one note of caution in the discussion of areas for improvement:

> Satisfaction with the performance of community coaches was mixed. In particular, stakeholders felt that community coach skills in terms of child behaviour management and communication needed development. Although generally well rated, the Community Coach Training Program (CCTP) was least well assessed in terms of helping coaches acquire child management and communication skills (p.4).

In mitigation, the report noted that

> The vast majority of OSHCS and the majority of schools said they always help the community coach supervise the children when the program is being delivered at their site, and community coaches' and program staff assessment of supervision was also generally positive.
>
> (p.4)

However, community coaches and program staff rated assistance from the site in terms of delivery and participation considerably lower than in OSHCS and schools' responses.

Those responsible for the AASC program are confident that clear policy guidelines, diligent working with children checks, supervised instruction of community coaches, and careful monitoring of each site, minimize any concerns about touch. The program has provided evidence about its practice to the Royal Commission into Institutional Responses to Child Sexual Abuse (2013). While a flagship of good practice, it is not unique, and the pedagogical and supervisory practices evident in AASC can be found throughout Australian physical education and sport. In the next section, an example from a specific sport context, canoe slalom, is shared in order to exemplify how a coach can respond to the formal requirements for a protected environment for athletes and other persons.

## In touch with the wilderness

What follows is an autobiographical account shared by the author, presented as a report on a reflective practitioner's coaching behaviours (Lyons, 2011). It predates Australian Canoeing's (AC) Member Protection Policy (Australian Canoeing, 2012) and the revised policy published in January 2014 (Australian Canoeing, 2014). The current policy is introduced in principled terms:

> This Member Protection Policy Bylaw (Policy) aims to assist AC to uphold its core values and create a safe, fair and inclusive environment for everyone associated with our sport. It sets out our commitment to ensure that every person involved in our sport is treated with respect and dignity and protected from discrimination, harassment and abuse. It also ensures that everyone involved in our sport is aware of their legal and ethical rights and responsibilities, as well as the standards of behaviour expected of them.

Long before this, I qualified as a teacher of physical education in 1975 at the then Loughborough College of Education (UK), with the award of a postgraduate certificate in education (PGCE). This was some time before concerns about child and adult protection were addressed in teacher education or received a high public profile, which is not to suggest that issues around safety were not considered during the course. Subsequently, since 1975 I have taught physical education and coached many sports in a variety of settings. My teaching career and coaching experiences were grounded in my own experiences as an athlete. My socialisation into the occupational culture of the physical education teacher and coach took place in England and Wales, and from the outset I believe I was guided (in the words of the AC policy above), by 'legal and ethical rights and responsibilities, as well as the standards of behaviour expected' (np.) from my PGCE course training. I saw myself as an educator with a very open, holistic, and inclusive commitment to the flourishing of those I taught and coached.

Ever since my qualification, I have been involved in the systematic observation of performance as a teacher and a coach. My PhD thesis reported on the teaching of physical education in two schools (Lyons, 1989), the research for this project being conducted at a time when Stenhouse (1975), Eisner (1985), Berliner (1986) and Schön (1987), amongst others, were exploring expert pedagogy. My account of one lesson (Lyons, 1992) makes for interesting reading now in terms of 'an inclusive environment'. When I moved to Australia in 2002 I was very aware that in order to understand a new country and culture I would need to adopt Agar's (1996) practices of being a "professional stranger". I had been a club coach and a national canoe slalom coach in Wales in the 1990s, and continued as a personal coach when I arrived in Australia. After five years of 'being around' (Burgess, 1984), it struck me that there was a group of young canoe slalom athletes who were not being supported in their transition from home to university. Thus, in 2007 I decided to form a coaching group which I named "The Wilderness". I invited five athletes to be the first members of the group, and all accepted. Once news of the group spread, another five athletes asked to join. I was delighted, as my aim was to offer an inclusive, caring coaching environment, and also pleased that a remarkable outdoor education teacher, Steve Etheridge, had offered to support me in this initiative.

I was aware of the work of the ASC's Sport Ethics Unit from 2002 onwards, and was mindful too of the resources emerging from the Play by the Rules unit (Play by the Rules, 2014). Overall my hope was that I would set the highest standards of "reasonable precautions" for a group of potentially vulnerable young athletes, some of whom were living away from home for the first time, so that they could have a daily training environment at the Penrith Whitewater Course in the west of Sydney. There was no particular formal ability requirement for participation in "The Wilderness". By definition there was no organisational support for these athletes and in their transition years they were invisible to the system. Steve and I planned the training programs for the athletes; adherence to the program was voluntary but "The Wilderness' " motto was 'Anybody can be ordinary', which proved to be a very powerful motivational message. In the first year of the program, Steve and I ran coaching sessions on weekend mornings after all the formal groups had completed their training on the Whitewater Course. We were co-present throughout the sessions and at the Course's coffee bar afterwards when we talked about what had happened, and the coming week. Steve and I saw this as 'normal' practice for teachers and coaches. After the athletes left the coffee bar, the two of us stayed on to discuss the session and our future plans. In these sessions I think we applied our own practice refined by years of professional development opportunities. The added bonus for me was that Steve was a parent of two athletes in the group, and he was thus likely to hear of any athletes' concerns, and able to raise them immediately.

We had male and female members of the group and all canoe slalom disciplines (kayak and canoe) were offered. Members' ages ranged from 17 to 24 years and occasionally siblings joined in, with the youngest participant 14 years of age. Although I had been a club and national coach previously, I have never canoed or competed in canoe slalom. This meant that all my coaching was from the bank of the course and all my conversations about technique were air demonstrations. There was no possibility of touch with athletes on the water. Occasionally we used video if an athlete had a persistent behaviour that limited their progress.

"The Wilderness" group became consummate peer coaches. Steve and I tried to encourage the athletes to be sensitive to each other since all shared the same predicament. They were all trying to improve, and if the opportunity arose they might contest selection for the Australian Under 23 team in a couple of years' time. We did make explicit ethical statements in our sessions. Some of these were about personal space, and the help each might offer, appropriately, to any athlete who had capsized in the fast flowing water. My sense is that the group, ignored by the national sporting organisation, developed a profound sense of 'relational touch' (Stronach & Piper, 2008), 'communicative touch' (Miller *et al.* 2007) and 'comforting tactile communication' (Power, 2009). They were a happy group and very articulate about their needs.

Both Steve and I had been screened by New South Wales Police to work with athletes. I think we were very clear about our roles: I coached, Steve organized, and we both reflected on practice. For my part, I drew on my experience of taking part as a volunteer teacher in a Summerhill-like school in Devon in the late 1980s (Lyons, 2008). I had learned at first-hand how a respectful relationship with young learners could thrive when children are included and valued, and I have tried to bring this inclusivity to all my work. "The Wilderness" group was an important exemplification of this inclusivity.

Steve and I understood our work would be monitored. Rather than being concerned about a "moral panic", we trusted that our transparent practice was available for scrutiny and questioning. The program continued in 2008 and, with good fortune and as a reward for a great deal of hard work, some of the athletes were selected for the national Under 23 team, but others missed out. Steve and I had discussed "what if" scenarios for the end of the selection process with its inevitable joys and disappointments. One was 'what if the athletes would like to hug us?' Another was 'how might we console those who were not selected but had ambitions to be so?' Our knowledge of the work of Play by the Rules and the Sports Ethics Unit helped us frame our responses. We were alert to cues from the athletes about how comfortable they were in our proximity and at all times respected individual needs for personal space. We shook hands with all of them, but two elated paddlers asked if they could give me a hug. Steve and I agreed if this occurred it would be in a very public place. I confirmed with them that it was acceptable to hug them on one of their very special days in sport, concluding that this was a time for relational touch. I am delighted that at this very time Stronach and Piper (2008) were exploring these same issues.

After a wonderful summer, participants in "The Wilderness" went their own ways. A number of them have started coaching young athletes. I trust that all of them can share practice that gives them confidence to deal with Power's (2009) four dilemmas about contemporary teaching and coaching: being cautious, careful and visible; worrying about misinterpretation; feeling sad; and battling with boundaries.

## Conclusion

This chapter has been written to share experiences about some aspects of touch in Australian physical education and sport contexts, as a means of contributing to a significant international debate around touch, abuse and risk in physical education and sports coaching. The two examples, the national AASC program and the more specific and informal coaching initiative in canoe slalom, have been presented to illustrate cases of, and possibilities for, "reasonable precautions" at a time when other cultures are experiencing moral panics about personal space.

The optimistic account offered here, of practice and pedagogy empowered through clear policy, has been written to support teaching and coaching as they will be. The reality for today's teachers and coaches is that touch and personal connections will be framed by legislation and the requirements of professional registration. There is a strong sense that newly qualified teachers and coaches understand these requirements. For many, the constraints offer opportunities for a distinctive pedagogy of respect and support. This makes it possible to work as activist professionals rather than 'hunkering down against the chill winds of panic and negative publicity' (McWilliam & Sachs, 2004 p. 26).

Well-judged professional activism offers possibilities for victimless schools and sport communities. As McWilliam and Sachs (2004) argue 'it is an ideal that seeks to re-claim and develop teacher professionalism' (p.28). It also offers scope to explore how this professionalism will facilitate discussions about "relational touch" and how teaching and coaching might be considered as an individual activity framed by biography, professional development, insight and empathy. In this unfolding story of a new pedagogy, attention should be paid to how colleagues concerned with child welfare will deal with pressures on their professional integrity. Steckley (2012), amongst others, has signalled a fundamental dilemma for those who work in close proximity to children in care contexts. She proposes that providing therapeutic containment requires levels of investment: staff must be supported to manage the difficult emotions triggered by the work, they must have clarity of purpose, policy and procedure, and they must have forums for making sense of the uncertain, contentious and complex features of their practice. They, in turn, will be more enabled to absorb the unbearable pain and confusion young people bring to their placements, responding in ways that promote development and healing. She argues that this cannot be achieved by an overreliance on technical-rational approaches to understanding and managing practice. This distinction is fundamental to the argument presented here, the preference for carefully judged professional practice and caring human interaction over rule-bound approaches which diminish the experience of all concerned.

Gusfield (1967) observed that 'the threat to the legitimacy of the norm is a spur to the need for symbolic restatement in legal terms' (p.187). To date, this symbolic restatement has not prevented the emergence of a new pedagogy guided by explicit legislation and codification of professional behaviours, but there is evidence that constraints on teachers and coaches in Australia offer new forms of reflexivity, as has also been noted by Fletcher (2013) in the United Kingdom. I share the enthusiasm of those who find the prospects of this reflexivity very exciting and characteristic of a new and challengingly conceived vocational calling. It is very different from merely hunkering down from the chill wind of suspicion, in pursuit of a quiet life.

At a time of successive new moral panics, now including childhood obesity and early onset of type 2 diabetes, the availability and adoption of a pedagogy that welcomes high level scrutiny of contexts and practices of teacher/pupil or coach/athlete interaction can be socially persuasive. There is a sense in Australia that a new advocacy is possible. This advocacy can move physical education and sport coaching into a pedagogical space that views scrutiny, and the consequent need to have reflected on and to be able to explain professional decision making and practices, as positive and supportive. As McWilliam and Sachs (2004) have argued, these circumstances, and an activist response, have the potential to mitigate 'the likelihood of panic-driven practice while emphasising other ways of caring aside from physical contact' (p.28). This outcome goes beyond being self-protective while claiming to be protecting children, and would be highly beneficial. The approach will become very persuasive if teachers and sports coaches, freed from the imperative to treat themselves and their colleagues as if they are a risk to children in their care, accept it as a profoundly positive outcome. It will position both professions to aspire to a 'she'll be right' outcome, through their own reflexivity and willingness to change.

# References

Active After-school Communities (2014) https://www.ausport.gov.au/participating/aasc accessed 6 February 2014.

Adair, D. and Vamplew, W. (1997) *Sport in Australian history*, Melbourne: Oxford University Press.

Agar, M. (1996) *The Professional Stranger*, San Diego, CA: Academic Press.

Australian Bureau of Statistics (2013) *Women in Sport: The State of Play 2013* www.abs.gov.au/ausstats/abs@.nsf/Products/4156.0.55.001~June+2013~Main+Features~Women+in+Sport+The+State+of+Play+2013?OpenDocument accessed 6 February 2014.

Australian Bureau of Statistics (2012) *Sports and Physical Recreation: A Statistical Overview*, Canberra: Australian Bureau of Statistics www.abs.gov.au/ausstats/abs@.nsf/Products/DAEADFCEF094933DCA257AD9000E28EC?opendocument accessed 6 February 2014.

Australian Bureau of Statistics (2011) *Sports and Physical Recreation: A Statistical Overview, Australia, 2011*, Canberra: Australian Bureau of Statistics www.abs.gov.au/ausstats/

abs@.nsf/Products/CBF9BB8EC6D067B0CA25796B0015197E?opendocument accessed 6 February 2014.

Australian Canoeing (2014) *Member Protection Policy Bylaw* www.canoe.org.au/site/ canoeing/ac/downloads/Bylaws/bl-04%20Member%20Protection%20Policy%20 140122.pdf accessed 6 February 2014.Australian Canoeing (2012) *Member Protection Policy Bylaw* www.canoe.org.au/site/canoeing/ac/downloads/Bylaws/bl-04%20 Member%20Protection%20Policy%20140122.pdf accessed 6 February 2014.

Australian Sports Commission (2014) National *Member Protection Policy Template* www. ausport.gov.au/supporting/integrity_in_sport/resources/national_member_protection_ policy_template accessed 6 February 2014.

Australian Sports Commission (2011) *Evaluation of the Active After-school Communities Program 2011: Summary of Findings* www.ausport.gov.au/__data/assets/word_ doc/0009/526176/Summary_of_evaluation_findings_-_AASC_program_2011.docx accessed 6 February 2014.

Berliner, D. (1986) In pursuit of the expert pedagogue, *Educational Researcher,* 15(7) 5–13.

Bloomfield, J. (2003) *Australia's sporting success: The inside story*, Sydney: University of New South Wales Press.

Bromfield, L. and Holzer, P. (2008) *A national approach for child protection: Project report* www.aifs.gov.au/nch/pubs/reports/cdsmac/cdsmac.pdf accessed 6 February 2014.

Burgess, R. (1984) *The research process in educational settings: Ten case studies,* Abingdon: Routledge.

Cashman, R. (1995) *Paradise of sport: The rise of organised sport in Australia*, Melbourne: Oxford University Press.

Cohen, S. (1972) *Folk devils and moral panics*, London: MacGibbon and Kee.

ComLaw (2014) *Australian Sports Commission Act 1989*, Australian Government www. comlaw.gov.au/Series/C2004A03760 accessed 6 February 2014.

Department of Social Services (2014) *National Framework for Protecting Australia's Children 2009 2020*, Australian Government www.dss.gov.au/our-responsibilities/families-and-children/publications-articles/protecting-children-is-everyones-business accessed 6 February 2014.

Eisner, E. (1985) *The art of educational evaluation: A personal view*, London: Falmer Press.

Ethics in Sport (2003) *Newsletter* https://secure.ausport.gov.au/__data/assets/pdf_file/ 0006/188088/Issue12003.pdf accessed 6 February 2014.

Ferguson, J. (2006) *More than sunshine and Vegemite – Success the Australian way*, Sydney: Halstead Press.

Fletcher, S. (2013) Touching practice and physical education: Deconstruction of a contemporary moral panic, *Sport, Education and Society*, 18(5) 694–709.

Government of South Australia (2011) *Protective Practices for Staff in Their Interactions with Children and Young People* www.decd.sa.gov.au/docs/documents/1/Protec tivePracticesforSta.pdf accessed 6 February 2014.

Government of Western Australia Department of Sport and Recreation (2014) *Safe Clubs 4 Kids* www.dsr.wa.gov.au/safe-clubs-4-kids accessed 6 February 2014.

Gusfield, J. (1967) Moral passage: The symbolic process in public designation of deviance, *Social Problems,* 15(2), 175–188.

Lyons, K. (2011) *Insights for coaches from learning design* [blog post] http://keithlyons. me/insights-for-coaches-from-learning-design/ accessed 6 February 2014.

Lyons, K. (2008) *CCK08: Week 10 utopia amplified* [blog post] http://keithlyons.me/ cck08-week-10-utopia-amplified/ accessed 6 February 2014.

Lyons, K. (1992) Telling stories from the field? A discussion of an ethnographic approach to researching the teaching of physical education, in A. Sparkes (ed) *Research in physical education and sport: Exploring alternative visions*, London: Falmer Press, pp. 248–270.

Lyons, K. (1989) *Sociological analysis of the teaching of boy's physical education in the secondary school.* Unpublished PhD thesis, University of Surrey.

McWilliam, E. (2003) The vulnerable child as a pedagogical subject, *Journal of Curriculum Theorising*, 19(2), 35–45.

McWilliam, E. and Jones, A. (2005) An unprotected species? On teachers as risky subjects, *British Educational Research Journal*, 31(1) 109–120.

McWilliam, E. and Sachs, J. (2004) Towards the victimless school: Power, professionalism and probity in teaching, *Journal of Educational Research for Policy and Practice*, 3(1) 17–30.

Miller, M., Franken, N. and Kiefer, K. (2007) Exploring touch communication between coaches and athletes, *The Indo-Pacific Journal of Phenomenology*, 7(2) 1–13.

National Outside School Hours Services Association (2014) www.netoosh.org.au/noshsa/ accessed 6 February 2014.

New South Wales Department of Education and Communities (2014) *Professional Responsibilities* www.dec.nsw.gov.au/about-us/careers-centre/school-careers/teaching/ your-teaching-career/approved-teachers/casual-teacher-induction/professional-respon sibilities accessed 6 February 2014.

New South Wales Government (2011) *Department of Education and Communities' Annual Report 2011*, Sydney: New South Wales Government.

Parliament of Australia (2014) *The Australian Constitution* www.aph.gov.au/About_Par liament/Senate/Powers_practice_n_procedures/Constitution accessed 6 February 2014.

Piper, H., Garratt, D. and Taylor, B. (2013a) Hands off! The practice and politics of touch in physical education and sports coaching [Special issue], *Sport, Education and Society*, 18(5).

Piper, H., Garratt, D. and Taylor, B. (2013b) Hands off! The practice and politics of touch in physical education and sports coaching, *Sport, Education and Society*, 18(5) 575–582.

Play by the Rules (2014) www.playbytherules.net.au/ accessed 6 February 2014.

Power, N. (2009) *To touch or not to touch. Male primary school teachers' experiences of touch: A hermeneutic phenomenological study.* Unpublished Master of Health Science thesis, Auckland University of Technology.

Queensland Government (2011) *Department of Communities, Sport and Recreation Services Annual Report 2011*, Brisbane: Queensland Government.

Royal Commission into Institutional Responses to Child Sexual Abuse (2013) *Terms of Reference* www.childabuseroyalcommission.gov.au/our-work/terms-of-reference/ accessed 6 February 2014.

Santoro, N., Reid, J., Crawford, L. and Simpson, L. (2011) Teaching indigenous children: Listening to and learning from indigenous teachers, *Australian Journal of Teacher Education*, 36(10). http://ro.ecu.edu.au/ajte/vol36/iss10/5/

Schön, D. (1987) *Educating the reflective practitioner*, San Francisco: Jossey-Bass.

Scott, C. (2013) The Australian situation: Not so touchy? *Sport, Education and Society*, 18(5) 599–614.

Simms, D. (2012) The Australian approach to child protection in sport, in C. Brackenridge, T. Kay and D. Rhind (eds) *Sport, children's rights and violence prevention*, London: Brunel University, pp. 77–82.

Steckley. L. (2012) Touch, Physical restraint and therapeutic containment in residential child care, *British Journal of Social* Work, 42(3), pp. 537–555.

Stenhouse, L. (1975) *An introduction to curriculum research and development*, London: Heinemann.

Stronach, I. and Piper, H. (2008) Can liberal education make a comeback? The case of "relational touch" at Summerhill School, *American Educational Research Journal*, 45(1) 6–37.

Tonts, M. (2005) Competitive sport and social capital in rural Australia, *Journal of Rural Studies*, 21(2) 137–149.

Touch Football Australia (2014) *About Touch Football* www.austouch.com.au/index.php?id=1224 accessed 6 February 2014.

Touch Football Australia (2000) *Playing Rules and Referees Signals* www.austouch.com.au/fileadmin/user_upload/Download_Documents/7th_Edtn_Rule_Book.pdf accessed 6 February 2014.

Vamplew, W. and Stoddard, B. (1994) *Sport in Australia: A social history*, Cambridge: Cambridge University Press.

# 10 Care and touch in trampoline gymnastics

## Reflections and analysis from the UK

*Alun Hardman, Jake Bailey and Rhiannon Lord*

## Introduction

Interest in the phenomenon of child abuse in sport has gained significant prominence in the last twenty years, primarily due to a number of media driven high profile cases (Brackenridge, 2010; Donegan, 1995). This concern and attention, though borne out of good intentions, and because it triggers people's sensibilities and emotions unequivocally, has also propagated a normative discourse remarkable for its narrow focus and degree of universal agreement. As a result, sports organisations, operating within a quasi-public social and political context, have become preoccupied with 'defining the "correct" response to the problem and in cultivating a succession of practices as a means to govern the response of others' (Piper, Garratt, & Taylor, 2013: 595). Sport coaches, who are on the policy-to-practice front line, are enveloped by an institutionalised orthodoxy towards the phenomenon that leaves little space for a more enlightened discourse on the role of the coach conceived as 'one-caring' (Noddings, 2003: 8), and what this might mean in terms of best practice behaviours in caring for the children, young people and adults they coach.

The testimony suggests that the first wave of child abuse sport policy initiatives do not reflect a proportionate, targeted and enlightened understanding of relationship between sports coaching and child well-being. Instead, they have cultivated an atmosphere of anxiety, fear, mistrust, confusion and demoralization amongst coaches (Piper, Taylor, & Garratt, 2011). It is unsurprising therefore, that when faced with matters relating child protection, the primary strategy for coaches, as it is for their employers, is to ensure compliance and avoid litigation. What disappears from the debate is any genuine and relevant discussion as to how coaches can best embrace principles of autonomy and responsibility, promote virtues of trust and consent, and cultivate the practical wisdom required for the kinds of decisions needed to balance the risk and rewards involved in fully engaging in the coaching of young people in sport.

There is a body of evidence to suggest that the 'moral panic' over child abuse in sport has transformed coaching practice into 'a prescriptive and proscriptive environment where coaches and PE teachers are required to exercise great caution in avoiding any behaviour, touching or otherwise, which could be considered suspect' (Piper *et al.* 2013: 584). Furthermore, such changes in coaching behaviour – because they sterilise and depersonalize the entire nurturing and educative process, and in more serious cases, may be felt as a threat to the moral and legal standing of the coach – lead to the unintended consequence of being seen by some as leading to greater overall harm to young people in sport. While this does not mean that the spectre of child abuse in sport should be taken lightly, nor that greater scrutiny and regulation of the coaching workforce is unnecessary, it does mean that such tensions in sport require considered examination, with the care of the child as the foremost consideration.

This backstory is particularly relevant for understanding the coach-athlete relationship that emerges within the sport of trampoline gymnastics. This is particularly evident in the way that actual and perceived changes in the childcare environment and corresponding attitudes towards touch and child athletes influence the coach-athlete relationship in general and coaching behaviour specifically. In this chapter, following some initial conceptual and philosophical ground clearing, we examine the nature and role of touch in the context of trampoline gymnastics in light of Noddings' (2003) relational ethic of care. We then present a fictional narrative vignette, Danny's story, about a head trampoline coach who presents his account of coaching and issues of touch – a construction of coaching experience that provides a conduit for moral discourse among the three authors: a moral philosopher, and active and experienced male and female trampoline coaches. Following a themed analysis, and with Noddings' care framework in mind, we discuss how touch dilemmas are best ameliorated.

## Touch, trampolining and the ethic of care

Touch is a basic human need, a sensory process, and a form of communication – but how touch is interpreted is a complex matter. Complicating the issue in trampoline gymnastics is that touch in the form of physical support plays an important role in the progressive and safe development of skills. The role of touch in trampoline gymnastics therefore retains a broad range of possibilities, is highly contextual and nuanced, and fundamentally provides a testatory moment as to the condition of the coach-athlete relationship. The foundation for effective coach-athlete relationships requires sports coaching to be understood as *praxis*, an ancient Greek term derived from the philosophy of Aristotle, which generally refers to the process of that which entails the interweaving of theoretical knowledge with practice (Hemmestad, Jones, & Standal, 2010). Good coaching, therefore, necessarily involves engaging in a cycle of learning from experience where a constant process of reflection, evaluation, deliberation and action needs to be done well to ensure that there is 'theory in action'. *Praxis* frames coaching as a social, humanistic and moral encounter rather than one directed by a logical, analytical and performative approach (Jones, Bailey, & Santos, 2013).

The coach-athlete relationship becomes central in coaching *praxis*, where virtue, and more precisely the virtue of care, particularly when coaching young athletes, arguably emerges as a foundational ethic rather than one of a number of (potentially competing) coaching values. It is a view that not only sees relations rather than individuals as ontologically basic, but also emphasises that above all else the moral dimension of care underpins such relationships (Noddings, 2003). On this account, and in contrast to other virtue ethicists such as MacIntyre (1984), who provides a more catholic account of the virtues, the caring-self is necessary for sustaining morality and virtue (both in general and in coaching more specifically), rather than vice versa. The caring-self is constituted ahead of, and towards which, all other moral and ethical concerns are directed. This contrast is articulated by Noddings (2003) as the difference between 'natural' and 'ethical' caring, and while she does not necessarily see one as superior to the other, where natural caring occurs, it is associated with the sentiment of wanting to perform the caring act without disruption. In the case of ethical caring, desires may conflict such that 'I want to care' becomes 'I must care – but I don't want to'. The difference is that of a felt compulsion for caring versus a rationalised duty to undertake care responsibilities.

It is quite clear, following Noddings' view, that 'touch' in trampoline gymnastics masks a more fundamental issue of the nature of the caring relationship between the coach and trampolinist. Where an impoverished view of the coach-athlete relationship exists, the 'natural' care ethic that we advocate is unlikely to be paramount and the likely prevailing perspectives, policy directives and coaching practices will come to the fore. In such situations, in order to satisfy the demands of 'ethical' care, coaches may first look to principles, rules and the authority of others, such as the sport's governing body, to solve the 'problem'. In this context, the coach is more likely to develop an understanding of 'touch' in terms of a duty of care – to themselves, to the trampolinist, the trampolinist's parents, to the sporting organisation in which they coach. 'Touch' within such an 'ethical' care perspective is apt to be experienced as a site of confusion and conflict as the coach has to weigh the cost and benefits according to the various individuals to whom a duty is owed. A more unhindered approach to the coach-athlete relationship is one that originates as 'natural' care, and does not see touch as a problem at all, rather something that is always framed by the ethic of care. It is a view that resists and rejects attempts to compartmentalise touch through a premature switch to a rational objective mode that can strip touch of its full meaning. An effective understanding of the role of touch in trampoline gymnastics then, requires a deep appreciation of the care that exists between coach and gymnasts, where the relational nature of care, as forwarded by Noddings (2003), insists that both parties be considered.

## The dilemma of care and touch in trampoline gymnastics: A narrative vignette

To examine the interrelationship between the ethic of care, touch, and the role of the coach in trampoline gymnastics, we present Danny's story, a narrative vignette whose meaning portrays the perspectives taken by trampoline gymnastics coaches in actual events. The vignette, whilst constructed, is an amalgam of two of the authors' personal experiences and values related to issues of touch in trampoline gymnastics coaching. It is also informed by their perceptions and understanding of the views and feelings of others in their sport community, with the intent that it is the combination of richness and perspective that makes the account valid (Denison, 2010).

For any vignette to be successful it needs to resonate effectively with those for whom it is written. This is dependent on two factors – the legitimacy of those authoring the vignette and the degree to which the story told engages the intended reader. In terms of author legitimacy, Rhiannon (RL) is head coach of a trampoline club, and is currently undertaking a PhD focusing on a sociological analysis of the embodied narratives of gymnasts (and coaches) in trampoline gymnastics. Jake (JB) currently coaches a small number of national level trampolinists, has previously been the Welsh National coach, and his PhD study involves the examination of coaching knowledge and practice in trampoline gymnastics. Alun (AH) is a moral philosopher and ethicist, a qualified and practicing cricket coach, whose daughter is involved in trampoline gymnastics at national level. From these brief coaching biographies, it is evident that their experience as practicing male and female coaches in large clubs, in their positions as mentors, tutors and assessors of other coaches, their engagement in coaching, and in particular the complexities of their *praxis,* provide constructive reservoirs that can lead to deep, layered, multi-dimensional understanding of the issues involved. In terms of reader engagement, we have problematised and analysed the morality of touch in trampoline gymnastics through presenting the contrasting perspectives of the different authors. The aim is that greater understanding will emerge through production of divergent views. The discussion offers particular deconstructions of the case study and highlights similarities and tensions related to our different understandings and experiences of touch. We purport it provides insights about 'touch', both particular to coaching trampoline gymnastics and also to the wider coaching community.

Danny is the head coach of his trampoline club, who sees his job principally as a skills teacher. Through hard methodical work and effective problem solving, he consistently produces successful and technically accurate gymnasts. He takes his role seriously, following the mantras of the governing body (British Gymnastics), and attends coaching courses and forums that inform his practice. Danny works mainly with teenage girls and young women, who are more prominent in the sport than boys and men. Working in close proximity to teenage girls, often wearing tight-fitting, revealing clothes, makes him aware of the issues surrounding touch. Danny is a middle-aged, beard-wearing and somewhat rotund bachelor and his friends regularly mock him for spending so much time with attractive young ladies; some openly tell of their envy of his position. Consequently, he is aware of how others perceive his involvement in such activities. Danny is also aware this perception is not entirely unfounded – he knows a number of other male coaches who have been banned from the sport – prosecuted for 'grooming' or having sexual contact with the girls, and sometimes boys, they have coached. He has had conversations with female gymnasts about their concerns regarding other male coaches. Some of these seem more valid than others: for example, when Danny hears concerns that a coach has held a manual support for too long or stood too close, he can't help but think that things have gotten silly. Still, such conversations make him anxious that he should be fully sensitive to all the coaching actions that might cause offence.

Despite all this, in some areas Danny feels on 'safe ground'. He regularly and routinely manually supports gymnasts' somersaults, seeing this simply as a necessary part of safe skill development. He feels comfortable and confident touching all gymnasts of any age or gender this way. Despite feeling able to justify his support methods, he finds himself in conflict with others within the trampoline community. For example, he strongly advocates that the widely accepted hand-to-hand support techniques presented on coaching courses are not fit for purpose. Though he recognises that somersault supports require a more neutral, less intimate way of touching gymnasts, Danny believes that, in terms of biomechanical effectiveness, they cannot compare to 'sandwich' techniques (that necessitate contact towards the mid-body). The hand-to-hand support means that a somersault turns in more of a swing action than a somersault, whereas the 'sandwich' technique allows natural rotation around the centre of mass *and* permits the gymnast free use of both arms. Danny attributes much of his coaching success to the use of this sandwich technique, although he feels the need to toe the line and use hand-to-hand supports in his coaching exams.

Off the trampoline, Danny is less confident about issues of touch, so he found a way to manage these situations by 'routinising' many touching actions. He is a 'hand-shaker', a 'shoulder-to-shoulder squeezer'. For example, when somebody performs an outstanding routine in a big competition (often under the gaze of hundreds of audience members), he offers his hand to help them down from the trampoline, places an arm around their shoulder on the walk back to the holding area, and gives what he hopes is a meaningful squeeze. Most days, he sees these routine actions as good practice and ones that maintain appropriate boundaries between himself and the gymnasts. He is aware this approach protects him from being a target of disparaging stories told of coaches 'too familiar' with their gymnasts. Danny could not bear the thought of being talked about in that way.

As a head coach, Danny questions the awareness that other, younger, coaches have in relation to issues of touch. In many ways it's harder for them; they're closer in age to their gymnasts and may have more informal friendship relationships than purely a coach-athlete relationship. When teaching children, Danny has noticed that junior coaches are playful and have fun when they interact with the gymnasts. On one hand Danny enjoys watching the naturalness of these moments, but on the other, he is aware of how these actions and friendships might be misinterpreted either by an 'outsider' looking in or even by a gymnast at a later point in time. Danny does not want his coaches and, by association, his club, to get labelled as 'dodgy' and so he generally finds it better to have less, rather than more 'touch' in his gym, but doesn't always know how to go about broaching this issue with the coaches involved. He has one coach in the club, Harriet, who he can talk to about such things, but it never feels right discussing touch more widely. He doesn't want to stir up trouble and make people more sensitive than they are already.

In what follows, we present five themed 'framings' as a way of understanding the dialectical relation between Noddings' theoretical account of care in relation to touch in trampoline gymnastics from the coach's perspective. These framings are presented by way of a series of position statements representative of the authors' interpretive lenses.

### Public display and private discourse

**AH**: Danny's story indicates coaches and trampoline gymnasts are aware of 'touch boundaries', and that these are continually reappraised and reconstituted, but there is very little public discourse on such matters. Ought there to be greater openness and discourse with regard to the issue? Would it be possible to raise issues of touch in a way that is tethered to broader virtues of care?

   **RL**: It is true, conversations about touch and care have been somewhat absent from our coaching culture. From my experience, when discourse emerges, it tends to focus on performative touch rather than non-performative touch or care, and tends to be restricted between coaches and gymnasts. Parents very rarely question or engage in conversation about the ways in which I care for and touch the gymnasts I work with. Perhaps the reason for this absence is because there is not really a platform from which these conversations can be initiated; this is something that needs to change. I think having some discussion between practitioners in the sport would be useful and help shape policies or procedures that would better educate coaches about this topic. To involve gymnasts and parents in these discussions would, I fear, lead to some form of 'moral panic' or oversensitivity to touch and care in our sporting context and so this would have to be very delicately and intricately developed.

   **JB**: I have empathy with RL here. There is a strange situation where touch is obviously explicit in terms of its physical manifestation, but strangely absent in terms of dialogue. I'm sure all are aware of the touching that goes on, as is evidenced in Danny's vignette. I can see the appeal of keeping touch out of the discourse – touch should be both natural and is, in many ways, tangential to the important facets of the job. I can imagine it as a distraction not needed on 'centre stage'. I'm not sure if I entirely agree with RL that the reason not to engage gymnasts and parents in the dialogue is for fear of creating moral panic; rather, there is embarrassment about how to begin, and then sustain the conversation in an enlightening way. Danny, for example, is already self-conscious about issues of touch. Is it then likely that he would feel comfortable openly talking, with the subtlety and gravitas required, about such issues? Would doing so more likely place him in a vulnerable position, risking a loss of the authority and competence he has worked hard to create? So, whilst it may be healthy to engage in open dialogue, who is likely to begin this, and what form might it usefully take?

### The synopticon?

**AH**: The synopticon – where the many see the few (the many being National Governing Bodies [NGBs], parents, athletes, other coaches) – may be a useful metaphor to describe the surveillance mechanism that trampoline gymnastic coaches experience, as the private act of coaching is made public for all to witness. Do coaches such as Danny develop a genuine sense of anxiety based on the belief that there is someone out there waiting to point an accusing finger? To what extent do coaches then develop a psychological mindset focused on 'the conduct of one's conduct', which may ultimately erode the natural disposition to exhibit care? How do coaches 'rationalise' their 'touch' actions – as being grounded in the care ethic, or emerging from a process of self-regulation that stems from the feeling of being watched and judged?

**RL**: The synopticon effect certainly presents itself quite clearly in my coaching, as I am very aware of those around me, particularly those who are not coaches, gymnasts or parents. I fear that someone from outside our sporting culture will make an unjustified accusation, because they are not aware of the shared understandings of touch and care within this sporting context. This stems from my awareness and experiences of coaches being accused of improper conduct, which Danny also describes. Although often these 'outsiders' do not physically exist, I self-survey my behaviour based on my interpretation of how others might see a particular act. I do not think this is detrimental; in fact I feel comfortable that I, among other coaches, make these considerations. However, I think this does impact on the more natural ethic of care that I might afford if I were not self-surveying. More interestingly for me, as a sociologist, is the consideration of the locations from which the synoptican is manifest. In particular, I believe I have been influenced by experiences in other sport settings. Originally as a lifeguard I was always taught to be aware of how I was touching people or how I could make it clear that I was not touching someone inappropriately, because of the prevalence of the 'suing culture'. For example, when placing somebody in the recovery position I would always touch the outside of someone's leg, rather than the inside, as a product of my training. It might be interesting to explore whether the synoptican effect, if felt by other coaches, is entirely a result of their trampoline experiences.

**JB**: To me, the synopticon raises questions of normative standards. The determination of who defines what the norms are, as both AH and RL describe above, is a complicated dialectic between individuals and the broader culture within which they operate. Given the relative acceptance of Danny's coaching by others, it seems that he has embodied a set of behaviours and practices which are within normalised boundaries. Although, as a head coach and someone seemingly respected, it is likely that Danny has some agency in shaping how others might perceive and accept given norms. In this regard, it is likely that other coaches in Danny's club may engage in self-surveillance based on their perceptions of what he deems good (or at least accepted) practice. Despite Danny's relative position of power, his behaviour is obviously influenced by his awareness of others' perceptions; for example, his competition behaviour is self-consciously styled 'under the gaze of hundreds of watching audience members'. Whether Danny is content with his own behaviour, influenced through perceptions of surveillance, and less directly by what is best for him and those he coaches, is questionable. There is an argument that negotiating the coaching landscape in this way is simply a normal part of the job (Potrac & Jones, 2009), but even if we accept this, which norms should we work with, which should we work against, and how can we use our agency to make things better? (Jones *et al.* 2011). Perhaps this level of thought should be encouraged amongst the broader coaching community, and in this instance could inform the need to engage in public discourse to negotiate the normative values used to guide practice.

### Performative and non-performative touch

**AH**: To what extent can Danny and other coaches be confident that clear demarcation lines are to be had between touch operating functionally and other forms of touch? Danny largely rejects his sport's code of practice which, advises coaches they ought to avoid the possibility that functional touch might be misinterpreted for something else. Is he right to do so, and how might he justify such a decision based on the ethic of care?

   **RL**: Similarly to JB, I view Danny's move away from the functional touch outlined by the governing body as admirable. It has biomechanical justification and is progressive in nature, moving toward developing more effective trampoline performances in his gymnasts, which in itself is an act of caring. However, in my experience these types of adaptations within the trampoline community are relatively rare, and left to high level coaches with advanced knowledge of the biomechanical principles involved in somersaulting. Discussion and acceptance of such adaptation is often left to inter-club and coach-coach relationships that are willing to engage in knowledge exchange, leading to a fragmented 'filtering down' of this knowledge to lower qualified coaches and less nationally recognised clubs. Contemporary coaching courses which still produce the traditional rhetoric of hand-to-hand physical support do not help the problem. Aside from these issues, Danny's move away from traditional supporting techniques brings to the forefront the need for coaches to ask themselves questions about the potential for misinterpretation of their touch in its performative, functional capacity. Specifically, can I justify what I am doing in this act of touch? Could this justification be explained to a wide range of potential audiences (e.g. the gymnast, other gymnasts, other coaches, parents, facility staff, the police etc.)? Is it supported by the governing body, or does it differ but have solid biomechanical benefits? Does this act of touch lend itself to an act of care (either ethical or natural)? It is in acts of performative touch justification that coaches feel comfortable in not being misinterpreted or misconstrued. For this reason I think many trampoline coaches feel comfortable with greater openness towards performative touch, because often we can justify it in terms of the inherent nature of developing safe somersault skills.

   Discussions surrounding non-performative touch receive much less attention within the sport, leading to ambiguity and discomfort about the nature of care and touch we, as coaches, engage in when off the trampoline. Often discussion about non-performative touch tends to be raised in compulsory child protection workshops, but is limited to questioning the actions of 'others' rather than developing meaningful discussions about our own actions and how these might be interpreted and justified in similar ways to performative touch within the sport. In their current form, these conversations about the 'other' and what is right and wrong, reproduces the synoptican effect which some coaches experience in the trampoline community (see earlier in this chapter). Instead, I feel platforms for discussion surrounding non-performative care and touch, as defined by Noddings (2003), are needed in clubs and the wider trampoline community to create greater openness and comfort among coaches.

**JB**: Danny's rejection of orthodox techniques to make an informed decision about what is in the gymnasts' best interests is commendable. It is also illustrative of issues of power; power afforded Danny through his knowledge of biomechanics provides him a solid means to justify his decision rather than needing any recourse to an ethic of care. Would other, less informed, coaches feel empowered to make such decisions? Perhaps not. The capacity to challenge the accepted and engage in innovative and creative practice is crucial in developing better and more ethical coaching practices (Denison, 2010; Denison & Avner, 2011). Perhaps this example is illustrative of the decontextualised nature of much of the policy and the reluctance (or inability, caused by their assumptions) of policymakers and moral entrepreneurs to listen to the voices of practitioners. We would argue that greater engagement between practitioners and policymakers would be welcome and should be actively sought.

It is clear in the vignette that Danny lacks a similarly robust justificatory framework regarding how to proceed with non-performative touch. Here, Danny is obviously conflicted. He wants to show care for those he coaches, for other coaches to show care, and for the members of his club to feel cared for in the ways Noddings (2003) recommends, but lacks the confidence to openly do so. This creates ambiguity that Danny simply cannot effectively negotiate. Questions that highlight how this dilemma might be experienced by Danny might include: Can I ever really know if and how another wants me to touch them? Is it better I avoid touch than risk making somebody recoil? Do the risks associated with touch outweigh the benefits? As a consequence of this defensive mode of being, I think many coaches, like Danny, have failed to act and touch in care-full ways, even in moments when it might be wholly appropriate. Times when throwing their arms around a gymnast with abandon, to viscerally and obviously share their joy, might be the exactly the right thing to do. It is sad that the somewhat detached responses that Danny has developed would be viewed by many as more acceptable, and even necessary.

### Gendered care and touch

**AH**: To what extent should Danny understand touch in trampoline gymnastics as gendered? To what extent does conceiving care as gendered mediate the role of touch between coach and trampolinists? Ought Danny take such things in to consideration when hiring coaches and allocating coaching responsibilities?

**RL**: As a female coach I feel that I am in a somewhat privileged position in comparison to Danny. Gendered power relations highlight that the sensitive nature of ethical touch in the sport is not as explicit or problematic for female coaches (although not completely eradicated). We can perhaps extend a greater level of care and touch to our gymnasts, because it is less likely that we will be viewed as threatening or inappropriate, even in off-trampoline situations and with male gymnasts. On rare occasions, I have engaged in full frontal hugs with gymnasts in times of competition success or serious distress, where I have thought it would be appropriate and caring to do so. These behaviours have never been questioned. On reflection I wonder if by not extending this level of care and touch, my behaviour might have been questioned as cold or abrasive. I have certainly not experienced the type of sarcastic innuendos that Danny has experienced when I have disclosed my profession in conversation or in discussions with friends.

**JB**: I know of male coaches who have been accused of improper conduct, but can't recall any cases involving women. So, perhaps, touch is inevitably understood differently in some ways for male and female coaches. An example of the differences can be seen in the Vignette, where it is suggested that stories about male coaches can be started by sometimes trivial, or even unconscious and unintentional acts. Would the same be said if it were a woman coach in the Vignette? I very much doubt it. Such considerations raise real issues for how male coaches might proceed. Some seem more aware of this than others, and male coaches I know (including myself) engage in the sort of defensive and self-aware behaviours Danny used, to ensure no untoward gossip is generated. Conversely, I know of other coaches who continue to engage in physical, touching behaviours that make others uncomfortable, regardless of what is being said about them (although whether they know if anything is being said is another issue). These kinds of situations are a real and inescapable part of the coaching landscape in trampoline gymnastics, and, I suspect, other sports. That is why I think sensitising coaches to the subtle relational aspects of their job, using the work of Noddings (2003), amongst others, can be useful in helping coaches navigate this part of the job. It also relates to the work of Jones, Bailey and Thompson (2012) who discussed the importance of noticing not just the technical but the social. Perhaps this aspect of self-awareness is more important for men with regards to touching because they are under greater scrutiny and, according to Noddings (2003), because such acts of caring may come less naturally.

### The innocence of youth?

**AH**: Danny is unsure as to how to respond to the apparent uninhibited role that touch has in the coaching practice of younger coaches. Ought Danny to provide specific guidance to young coaches with regards to how they might deal with the issue in their own coaching, particularly with regards to younger (male) coaches working with older girls?

**RL**: Similar to Danny, I question younger coaches' awareness of issues of care and touch. I have seen junior coaches with young children clinging to their legs, sometimes in groups. These coaches have picked children up and swung them about in playful response, as they would do with a young child in their family. It is this type of behaviour that creates a nice, open, working environment within clubs. Often these small interactions arise in the presence of the children's parents, who laugh and make jokes at this behaviour. However, from an outsider's perspective, such behaviour may be misinterpreted and misconstrued. In the interest of safety and well-being of these young coaches, who are often my gymnasts as well, I have, in the past, confronted them about engaging in these types of interactions. In these conversations I have presented the coach with the general question of 'how might someone else, not another coach, parent or gymnast, perceive that type of behaviour?' to stimulate their thinking and awareness of these issues. Despite feeling comfortable about engaging in these conversations I have not, as the head coach, formulated any written document giving guidance on the subject, although I have presented some younger coaches with selected pages from child protection resources. I think my reluctance to probe what coaches really think is based on the lack of clarity from the governing body on what constitutes good practice in relation to non-performative touch.

**JB**: Reading RL's response reminded me of times when I felt less inhibited about the way I interacted with those I coached. When gymnasts from the club at which I first worked reached national level, I remember going on a 'road-trip' to a competition with two teenage boys. We had a fantastic time; it was something that cemented our relationships, from silly sing-a-longs in the car, to shared restaurant meals. These were moments to which we returned for many years. Whilst this is, perhaps, not directly related to touch, it is the cultural fears associated with touch which now prevents me from engaging similarly. What is more, part of the role of head coach is to ensure that such situations do not arise for other younger coaches – my conscious actions explicitly prevent the development of the type of intense and intimate engagement that was so powerful for both me and the gymnasts with whom I worked during my early career. I'm not sure that I have answered any of AH's questions, but I suppose it is incumbent upon head coaches, like Danny, to act both cautiously and sensitively. Here, club policy can serve as a guide (though of course how it is enacted is another matter), but should, perhaps, be balanced through the organisation of social events where high quality natural interactions can occur, and in ways which minimise the associated risks (perceived and real) for both coaches and gymnasts.

## Discussion

The discourse prompted by the narrative vignette suggests that for our author-coaches, their feelings about their own trampoline coaching experiences with respect to the relation between care and touch are unclear and confusing. Their evidence suggests they inhabit a coaching world pockmarked by ambiguity, inconsistency and contradiction, though at the same time they continue to profess a strong resolve towards coaching practice where a general ethic of care is paramount. They both endure as victims of, but are also complicit in, the propagation of child 'protection' policies and practices that usurp the more foundational and sustaining care ethic we have identified in this chapter.

The blurry landscape they present is evident in multiple ways. Take, for example, what the coaches say about the different moral connotations of performative and non-performative touch. The comments from both RL and JB support Danny's nonconformist support techniques because they have, according to JB, 'biomechanical justification . . . are progressive in nature . . . develop more effective trampoline performances, and are in themselves acts of caring'. RL seems equally forthright and unequivocal that Danny's approach is a preferable alternative despite it being contrary to the technical model advocated by the sport's governing body. She points out however, that this 'best practice' discourse is one hidden, marginalised and disseminated in a fragmented, partial and inchoate way amongst coaches, behind, and in contrast to, the orthodox discourse favoured by the governing body. JB's observations suggest Danny's nonconformist approach to teaching somersaults is primarily a result of the 'power' afforded to him by his knowledge of biomechanics and his own sense of status. But it also seems that to fully understand these two divergent discourses, there is a need to look beyond disparities, inequities and relative levels of enfranchisement felt by different coaches. As RL later suggests, and despite her own convictions, other coaches are not just concerned as to whether or not their techniques do or don't 'toe the party line', but worry and are confused about misinterpretation of touch when used in a performative, functional capacity. JB and RL both agree that there is a fundamental need for a more open discourse on such matters, as they feel coaches would feel more comfortable engaging with this debate, and it could be a catalyst for a more explicit discussion about non-performative touch.

Their comments in response to the vignette and the prompts also highlight the prevailing ambiguity and longing for greater openness surrounding non-performative touch. In Danny's anxiety and uncertainty, they see what is common for many coaches. What neither JB or RL explicitly consider, however, is that the pursuit of a 'robust justificatory framework' might be misdirected, particularly if it takes the form of an instrumentally driven technical means to meet a care pledge or promise. In this regard, Noddings' distinction between an ethic of care and ethical caring is particularly relevant. Caring coaches neither necessarily need a predetermined care framework, nor are all their acts of care likely to reside satisfactorily within such a structure. The nature of care, and therefore the role of non-performative touch in trampoline gymnastics, is highly contextual such that were a formal scaffold to be constructed, it would be constantly challenged as to how useful and relevant it is for coaching *praxis*. By its nature, discourse on care, if aimed broadly and collectively, leads to abstract and general principles that often pass by the dialectical nature of discourse particular to specific cases.

At the same time, both RL and JB seem to acknowledge that solutions will be unclear, as they involve complex ingredients, yet at the same time they also endorse the need to redevelop an orthodoxy designed to reassure coaches (such as Danny) as to what they should do. As JB intimates, it may just be that the uncertainty coaches feel is in part due to having doubts as to whether any procedure can be established for what is in fact undeterminable. In such a climate, it is no wonder coaches are confused, for they see a range of practices from different coaches, and what becomes normalised will depend upon that to which they have become accustomed. Approaches which are different from theirs will be seen as unusual, and, therefore, a problem. Coaches are left to wonder, in the absence of any explicit dialogue on such matters, whether one or the other approach is good or bad.

Further ambiguities emerge in RL's and JB's discussion on self-surveillance. RL acknowledges that though 'often these "outsiders" do not physically exist' she feels comfortable in coaching as if they did. At the same time she admits self-surveillance does 'impact on the more natural ethic of care that I might afford'. Logically, the conclusions we draw from these premises is that she is comfortable with a coaching style where self-surveillance impacts her more natural ethic of care! It is unlikely that this is her intention. JB's discussion sees Danny, because of his head coach position, as both susceptible to, but also an instigator of, the synoptic effect. He suggests this may be normal for all coaching, and focuses on asking the question as to what norms coaches should work with that will be accepted by the coaching community. JB's comments hint that what is important is the pressure coaches feel with regard to their displays of behaviour in the competitive environment. Here, more specific concerns regarding care and touch of athletes tend to fade in terms of their significance within a more general concern for impression management driven by the need for approval from peer coaches.

The paradox that leads to the situation where female coaches can engage in non-performative acts of touch practices which are out of bounds for male coaches is highlighted by RL. Rather than seeing this as providing female coaches relatively greater freedom, she suggests the general 'don't-touch' culture pervasive in the sport actually presents her with a double bind. Whereas her male counterparts primarily face the dilemma of establishing boundaries with regards to excessive and inappropriate touch, RL and other female coaches are also conscious of potential criticism for being inappropriately standoffish and reserved. It means that the blanket defensive 'no touch' response adopted by some male coaches, which in itself is highly problematic, is not really available to her or her female counterparts. The situation calls for an insupportable capacity to know exactly when one's inhibitions are to be switched off and on.

Further difficulties are evident with regard to interactions with younger coaches. Despite acknowledging that younger coaches inhabit a less self-conscious and more spontaneous touch terrain, it is with some regret that RL feels she also must raise their awareness as to how such behaviours are to be perceived by others. We get a glimpse of the kinds of experience that are deserving of such regret from JB, who now sees his 'conscious actions explicitly prevent the development of the type of intense and intimate engagement that was so powerful for both me and the gymnasts with whom I worked during my early career'. What is unclear about both their processes of deliberation that have led to 'consciousness-raising' with other coaches is whether, in balancing the reasons involved, considerations of caring for young trampolinists play a large part.

In trampolining, an enduring barrier to an imperfect or unrealised ethic of care is that it requires the development of an effective three-way relationship between the coach, the gymnast and parent/guardian. Jowett and Timson-Katchis (2005) suggest that parent-coach communication and quality of coach-athlete relationship are positively correlated because

> parents may be more influential if they have the capacity to share more information, provide more opportunities to their child and coach, and become aware of the various struggles in the parent-child relational transitions.
>
> (p. 283)

Yet, in the vignette, and also in the responses from RL and JB, it is evident that parents are, and are to remain, largely absent from any emergent discourse on touch. For RL, 'to involve gymnasts and parents in these discussions would . . . lead to some form of "moral panic" or oversensitivity to touch and care in our sporting context and so this would have to be very delicately and intricately developed'. For JB, his concern is the ability 'to sustain the conversation in an enlightening way' such that there is no 'loss of the authority and competence'.

The coaches' reluctance to be more open on such matters is partly because they find themselves potentially susceptible to criticism from two sides – from parents whose sensibilities are heightened by the 'moral panic' about child protection in sport, and by politically minded observers wanting to show that quasi-political organisations such as sports governing bodies cannot be trusted to monitor and control their organisational behaviour effectively. Danny and our author-coaches reveal a crisis of confidence endemic within sports institutions such as trampoline gymnastics as they attempt to develop greater organisational autonomy and responsibility. The defective discourse on touch in trampolining therefore needs be understood as having origins and causes that cohere with the new political landscape for sport, a landscape which invites us to see how recent public sector policy initiatives lead to arms-length, but greater state control and influence over sport. This non-interventionist approach, designed, or so politicians claim, to empower sports governing bodies, creates the very conditions by which political control and influence can be simultaneously maintained and extended without direct responsibility (Piper *et al.* 2013). Sport organisations have been cut adrift from direct political control, but as their revenue streams remain primarily in the form of public-sector grant funding, their viability remains heavily dependent upon compliance with politically driven regulatory frameworks. The conditions produce a form of indentured servitude. Those who administer and manage sporting organisations, mindful of their financial dependency on political incumbents, play the double role of both administering sport to an increasingly demanding public, and ensuring that those working for the sport do so in approved ways. When trampoline coaches such as JB and RL are faced with matters that are of great concern to the general public such as safeguarding children in sport, they find themselves buffeted by the confluence of anxious parents and critical administrators. It is unsurprising that their focus of care may become redirected towards the self.

## Conclusion

We have suggested that, in relation to adult coaches, 'touch' in trampoline gymnastics has become a matter of concern as a result of a moral panic about child protection in sport. At the same time, touch remains a catalyst for affirming care. That both these narrative possibilities are manifest at the same time suggests that addressing issues of 'touch' is inescapable for those involved in crafting morally wholesome sporting environments. We have argued that a revised, expanded and politicised account of the relational structure of care in trampoline gymnastics – one that involves gymnasts, coaches and parents – provides a better outlook for initiating the kind of dialogue in which an ethic of care might be more fully understood.

## References

Brackenridge, C. H. (2010) Myth and evidence – learning from our journey. Keynote *How safe is your sport conference,* Excel Sports Centre Coventry and NSPCC Child Protection in Sport Unit 25.04.10. Available online at: http://bura.brunel.ac.uk/bitstream/2438/4177/3/Myths%20about%20abuse%20in%20sport%20%281%203%2010%29.pdf (accessed 30 August 2013).

Denison, J. (2010) 'Messy texts', or the unexplainable performance: Reading bodies' evidence. *International Review of Qualitative Research,* 3(1), 149–160.

Denison, J., & Avner, Z. (2011) Positive coaching: Ethical practices for athlete development. *Quest,* 63(2) 209–227.

Donegan, L. (1995) Olympic coach jailed for rapes, *The Guardian,* 28th September, p. 11.

Erickson, F. (1986) Voices, genres, writers, and audiences for the Anthropology & Education Quarterly. *Anthropology & Education Quarterly,* 17(1) 3–5.

Hemmestad, L. B., Jones, R. L., & Standal, Ø. F. (2010) Phronetic social science: A means of better researching and analysing coaching? *Sport, Education and Society,* 15(4) 447–459.

Jones, R. L., Bailey, J., & Santos, S. (2013) Coaching, caring and the politics of touch: A visual exploration. *Sport, Education and Society,* 18(5), 648–662.

Jones, R. L., Bailey, J., & Thompson, I. (2012) Ambiguity, noticing, and orchestration: Further thoughts on managing the complex coaching context. In P. Potrac, W. Gilbert, & J. Denison (eds.) *The Routledge handbook of sports coaching.* London: Routledge, 271–283.

Jones, R. L., Potrac, P., Cushion, C., & Ronglan, L. T. (2011) *The sociology of sports coaching.* London: Routledge.

Jowett, S., & Timson-Katchis, M. (2005) Social networks in sport: Parental influence on the coach-athlete relationship. *Sport Psychologist,* 19(3) 267–287.

MacIntyre, A. (1984) *After virtue: A study in moral theory* (2nd edn). South Bend, IN: University of Notre Dame Press.

Noddings, N. (2003) Why care about caring. In N. Noddings (ed.) *Caring: A feminine approach to ethics & moral education.* Berkeley: University of California Press, 7–29.

Piper, H. Taylor, W., & Garratt, D. (2011) Sports coaching in risk society: No touch! No Trust! *Sport, Education and Society*, 17(3) 331–345.

Piper, H. Garratt, D., & Taylor, B. (2013) Child abuse, child protection, and defensive 'touch' in PE teaching and sports coaching, *Sport, Education and Society*, 18(5) 583–598.

Potrac, P., & Jones, R. L. (2009) Power, conflict, and cooperation: Toward micropolitics of coaching. *Quest*, 61(2), 223–236.

# 11 Fear, risk, and child protection in sport

## Critique and resistance

*Heather Piper*

## Where are we and how did we get here?

Having learned from the data and insights presented in the earlier chapters, and through deploying ideas generated while working with colleagues in recent years[1], I conclude the book with an argumentative overview of the current situation and its genesis. I also offer some thoughts about what is involved in mounting a more effective resistance to the dominant regulatory discourse and fear-based practice than has been managed so far.

As demonstrated in earlier chapters, there are obvious variations between the situations described in distinct national contexts, but there remains a fundamental consistency. Although there is no well-founded reason to think that children and young people are any more at risk of abuse in sport contexts than in other activities and spaces, in many societies there is powerful pressure to act as if they were. Thus we have a prime exemplar of the dictum that 'if men (sic) define situations as real, they are real in their consequences' (Thomas & Thomas, 1929: 572), and it is necessary for anyone who cares about sport, and believes that social science can and should be useful, to explore the situation further. I seek to do so by applying appropriate yet eclectic ideas and frameworks, to support reflection and critical analysis.

### Sport, extreme anxiety, and policy – a special case?

There is no shortage of theoretical or critical models to help understand the current situation and how it was arrived at. Some of those frequently invoked and deployed are predicated on notions of risk society, the culture of fear, and moral panic. Their broad applicability may suggest that the effects described are evenly distributed and consistently experienced by individuals and organisations, but in reality these effects are contingent on specific contextual factors. In the case discussed here, the constrained experience of many sports coaches and PE teachers suggests that sport has felt the manifold impacts of these processes (and arguably embraced them) in a particularly intense way. This may be inevitable, as anxiety around the possibility and avoidance of sexual abuse is likely to impact powerfully on a site of activity where the bodies of children and young people, sometimes hot and wet, are the prime focus of attention; conspicuous nudity is intrinsic to the derivation from Greek of 'gymnastics' and 'gymnasium'. In contemporary circumstances of generalised and rampant sexualisation, sport provides a context where intervention by non-parental adults, including positively motivated touch, can be easily perceived as abusive. However, beyond this, additional factors appear significant.

The high profile and sensitivity attached to sexual abuse, particularly in relation to children, makes it an issue onto which diverse interest groups are able to map their own concerns (Jenkins, 1998). In relation to sport, in the UK this process began with feminist critiques of sexual harassment and inequality (e.g. Brackenridge, 2001). These positively motivated interventions, in combination with negative media coverage, contributed to sports organisations' determination to improve, and be seen to improve, relevant practice (Lyons, 2005). While the intentions were no doubt laudable, the outcome has been the development of a prescriptive and proscriptive environment where coaches and PE teachers are required to exercise caution, to avoid any behaviour which could conceivably be considered suspect. For those with long experience of working with children and young people to improve their sporting opportunities and performance, the change has been profound and (for many) on balance unwelcome. Its relative severity may in part be explained by the organisational and regulatory arrangements which characterise modern sport, and support a process of 'ratcheting-up' (Piper & Stronach, 2008). The multilayered context of regulation and organisation in which sports coaches in particular operate – including quasi-governmental overarching funding bodies, training and accreditation bodies, national governing bodies (NGBs), local government, employers, clubs – provides a fertile environment for the ratcheting effect; at each level, regulations, guidelines, and practices are developed or imported, to demonstrate how seriously the issue of abuse and its prevention is being taken. As a result the professional practice of coaches acting *in loco parentis* becomes ever more tightly constrained and, at least in the dreams of those responsible for determining policy, risk is eradicated from all provision for which they are responsible. At each level there is a determination to avoid reputational damage and the 'bad press' that attends cases of abuse, and developing an auditable set of avoidance-oriented procedures is one way of doing so, even when these are more attuned to placating external scrutiny than delivering real child protection. In this sense the focus of sports coaching on the body and the perfection of the child, and the high public and media profile of sport in many societies, has placed it in the eye of a perfect storm.

Manifestly, the once common assumption that, since the moral and character-forming quality of sport is self-evident, all those involved must be admirable, and individual sporting experience must always be positive, is problematic and even delusional. The Victorian ideal and laudatory narrative of organised sport begged many questions. However, the pendulum of public perception has swung from seeing no evil in sport to seeing it as inevitable, and there appears to be limited capacity or will to arrest this movement. It is difficult to do so in part because of the unhelpful contemporary elision of ideas and perceived realities which are best kept distinct. Risk of any sort has increasingly been perceived as intolerable and unacceptable; the generalised emphasis on risk in society inevitably militates towards panic around particular issues, and sport has not been immune to this tendency. The situation is further complicated by the conflation of risk with moral failure, so that risk is related to something bad, and with real negative outcomes; potential risk is equated to actual harm (Hunt, 2011). The prevalence of 'worst-case' or 'worst-first' thinking (Furedi, 2010; Schneier, 2010; Skenazy, 2011) compounds the situation; the worst thing that could conceivably happen is treated as ever present, and arrangements are made to minimise the risk of its actual occurrence. Probability is downgraded as a component of judgement, and mere possibility is given disproportionate significance. The avoidance of bad outcomes is prioritised at the expense of seeking good ones. In sports coaching, intergenerational relationships have become understood as a site of intrinsic danger, warranting strict regulation. The person of the coach, and the act of coaching, are conceived as obviously dangerous, with the coach in essence treated as just a particular category of 'stranger', inseparable in rhetoric and practice from the idea of 'danger'. As Young (2011: 251) has noted, 'once a group is deemed a dangerous other . . . it often becomes a dangerous other: the conditions for a moral panic are created by the moral panic, fantasy is translated into reality . . .', and in this way the idea of pervasive abuse, and the sports coach as abuser, is effectively normalised.

Just as, in many societies, it has become common to doubt the motivation of men who choose to work in early years and nursery settings, a default response to hearing of a man wanting to teach children swimming or gymnastics has become one of innuendo and suspicion. Once embraced, a view of the world which excludes trust and assumes the worst is very hard to displace, and the danger of a negative spiral of disproportionate fear and anxiety has been frequently recognised. Five centuries ago, Martin Luther formulated the 'paradox of purity' when he observed that 'the more you cleanse yourself, the dirtier you get' (Webster, 1994). More recently, the Roman Catholic philosopher Thomas Merton noted that 'the more you try to avoid suffering, the more you suffer, because smaller and more insignificant things begin to torture you, in proportion to your fear of being hurt' (1948: 82), and the Buddhist Andrew Watts concurred, noting that 'there is a contradiction in wanting to be perfectly secure . . . the more security I can get, the more I shall want' (1951: 77). At the end of the downward spiralling tunnel of anxiety about child abuse and safeguarding in sport, there may be neither redeeming light nor exit.

## *Moral panic and (im)moral crusades*

In a number of the nation-specific chapters in this book, the concept of moral panic is invoked as a response to the situations and problems under discussion. This is understandable; my own writing on child abuse and safeguarding in sport (Piper *et al.* 2011, 2013b), and elsewhere (Piper & Stronach, 2008; Sikes & Piper, 2010), employed moral panic in a similar way. Its appeal and utility is obvious when discussing a context where the dominant discourse, derived policy, and practice, can all be considered significantly disproportionate. A 'clue to disproportion, and thus the moral panic, is a sharp increase in indicators of public concern, media attention, and political and legislative activity at a time when the condition or behaviour remains stable or is declining' (Goode & Ben-Yehuda, 2011: 29), characteristics clearly applicable to child abuse and safeguarding in sport and wider society over recent decades. While some may criticise such comments as intrinsically normative and judgemental, others (including many contributors here) consider judgement a moral and professional imperative. Beyond its analytic and heuristic value in diverse research settings, 'the notion of moral social panic has become . . . an essential argumentative term, a way of saying "no" to the forces of hyperbole' (Garland, 2007: 4). Certainly, moral panic proved indispensible in the current research context, employed in a 'revisionist' manner (Hier, 2011: 12), treating panic as a rational structural phenomenon, understandable in terms of power struggles and the advancement of particular moral and material interests.

However, there is a problem in applying the conceptual toolkit of moral panic to disproportionate anxiety and prescriptive/proscriptive regulation of intergenerational touch in sport and physical education, and relating it to the overarching panic around child abuse. The child abuse panic is now decades old, well established, and reinvigorated periodically by new scandals and exposures (e.g. online bullying, foster-parent, coach, or celebrity abuse). Pervasive anxiety around child abuse is accepted as a 'genuine moral panic' (Garland, 2008: 17), but how long can a moral panic *per se* last, and can panic actually be permanent? Arguably, in 'morally uncertain times . . . crusading against child abuse has become a means to create some semblance of moral purpose', and society has increasingly been reorganised around child abuse and child protection (Black, 2013). The original conception of moral panic was by definition temporary and spasmodic, and Best cautions that a moral panic can only last 'a few weeks, maybe a year or so' (2011: 39). Further, 'once a claim leads to some sort of institutional apparatus assuming ownership . . . the dynamics of making claims and maintaining concern are sufficiently different that the term moral panic no longer seems useful' (ibid: 45). This is a significant distinction; any moral panic *per se* entails moral rationality, but for it to become long term and normalised requires the application of pragmatic, instrumental, amoral rationality. As has been shown, in many national contexts the consequences of extreme anxiety about child abuse and safeguarding have become permanent features of life for sports coaches and others *in loco parentis*. Something has been happening beyond the reasonable scope of moral panic.

The apparent inability of some exponents of the mainstream approach to safeguarding to recognise either the propriety or utility of research which problematises it (Piper, 2011; Piper *et al.* 2013a ) illustrates Furedi's comment that 'one person's moral panic is for another an example of ethical behaviour' (2011: 98). Before moral panic entered the sociological lexicon, Becker noted that all rules are the product of an enterprise, and identified the role of the moral entrepreneur, engaged in a moral crusade: 'the crusading reformer . . . interested in the content of rules . . . because there is some evil which profoundly disturbs him . . . operates with an absolute ethic; what he sees is truly and totally evil . . . any means is justified . . . fervent and . . . often self-righteous' (1963: 147–8). The crusader is unwilling to recognise the problem as solved or solvable; rather they will 'discover something new to view with alarm, a new evil about which something ought to be done' (ibid: 153), where the 'final outcome of the moral crusade is a police force' (ibid: 156). However, the ascription of solely moral motives in such processes was challenged at an early stage (Dickson, 1968; Musto, 1973) by the identification of bureaucratic processes and organisational interests as prime factors in motivating and sustaining powerful moral crusades. Such insight helps in understanding this well established moral panic as a particular example of social problem construction; 'constructions that endure usually involve ownership . . . responsibility for continuing to press the issue . . . continually calling for action . . . gaining recognition as the authoritative voice for the cause . . . And once the policy is in place, the agent responsible . . . also can assume ownership . . . justify their work as important and call for resources to continue their efforts' (Best, 2011: 44). While the mainstream approach to safeguarding in sport and elsewhere is no doubt advanced with good intention, and underpinned by moral certainty, the significance of individual and organisational interests should not be overlooked. Once large and powerful organisations in effect claim ownership of expertise in a particular area, and of relevant discourse, there is an interest in defending this status as a form of capital, important to the material and psychological well-being of both the organisation and the individuals it employs. This has particular resonance when such emotionally charged issues as child abuse and safeguarding are involved; 'the capital of fear can be turned to any kind of profit, commercial or political' (Bauman, 2007: 12).

This account begs the question of whether such an enterprise can accurately be called moral. The mainstream approach to child protection, relying on the spectre of abuse and the abuser, and indifferent to damaging side effects, has a parallel with security and the 'war on terror'. In a number of societies, although terrorism has not really constituted a major threat to national security, values, and everyday life, it has been used to justify draconian infringements of civil liberties. Normal freedoms have been suspended, and policy has been driven by special interest groups (including defence contractors and consultants) with narrow concerns and much to gain. They manage public opinion by scaring it at appropriate intervals, and ignore the collateral damage caused to society and those they claim to protect (Jenkins, 2013). The willingness in effect to treat citizens as enemy combatants or terrorists directly matches child safeguarding practices which treat all adults *in loco parentis* as sources of risk, with evil motives. In each case, negative consequences of the policy, and less than moral drivers behind it, can be identified, but these realities are masked by the sensitivity of the issues and the moral certainty with which they are promoted.

## Neoliberalism and managerialism

Obviously, diverse national, economic, cultural, and political contexts characterise the previous chapters, making some constituencies more able to retain and defend traditional sporting practices and assumptions in the face of contradictory ideas. However, all have to a varying degree been affected by the neoliberal tsunami of recent decades, some to a considerable extent. The argument that neoliberal governance provides a fertile environment for the concerns and processes in physical education and sports coaching discussed here has been made elsewhere (Piper *et al.* 2013b), the concept of governmentality in the advanced liberal state having been elaborated by Foucault (1991) and explored by others (see Rose, 1996, 1998; Besley, 2010). In the contemporary liberal (shrunken) state, government is presented and practiced as the management of risk. The balance between control and freedom of the individual shifts towards, in Foucault's terms, technologies of the self, increasingly achieved through the work of non-governmental organisations which monitor and control behaviour, through individuals, allowing disciplinary practices to play upon their own habits and behaviours, exercising their best judgement and free will as part of an ethic of caring for the self (Hodgson & Spours, 2006). The state actually extends its influence, harnessing relative freedom through forms of self-governance linking autonomy and responsibility, trust and consent, decision-making and risk. At the same time, the status and significance of a plethora of variably autonomous entities (community organisations, professional groups, private enterprises, third sector experts in policy and practice) is greatly increased. The techniques employed reflect the account of risk society developed by Beck (1992), which noted the replacement of the logic of productivity and effectiveness with the imperatives of risk and management.

The competitive and barely regulated discourse market which operates in this situation favours the policy and organisational interests of those purveying unitary high impact messages, and the halo of protecting children from sexual abuse in sport and elsewhere confers significant power. This Foucauldian account of how organisations promoting a particular conception of child abuse and safeguarding in sport have flourished in the discourse market reflects Naim's discussion of the relative decline in central government (2013). The dispersal of capability and power has democratic benefits but also supports the establishment of narrowly concerned interest groups, which have grown stronger while political parties, more broadly focused coalitions based on shared interests and values, have become too weak to counter simplistic world views promulgated by single-issue pressure groups, certain of their moral duty and opposed to compromise. As a result, 'power devolves to myriad new forces that often exercise their power with narrow obsessions in mind. Who now . . . has the courage to make decisions based on a strategic view of all our interests, not just sectional ones' (Hutton, 2013: 38)? Thus, a particular conception of child protection can be implanted in sports organisations, at some cost to their intrinsic priorities, and the organisations responsible are effectively immune from moderating scrutiny.

Beyond reference to the marketised society characteristic of neoliberalism, the nature and role of managerialism is critical to understanding the processes and problems identified and discussed by contributors here (Piper, Duggan and Walker, 2013). Managerialism has spread beyond its private sector origins and, being 'an assemblage of practices, strategies, techniques and knowledges [with the] capacity to colonise other forms of power, reassembling alternative rationalities within its own logics' (Newman & Clarke, 2009: 109), has fundamentally repositioned professionals and practitioners in all *in loco parentis* contexts, including sport coaching. Flybjerg (2001) describes how managerial thinking fosters a technocratic approach to the management of risk, emphasizing decontextualized and rational knowledge so that performance decisions are based on standardized and regulated procedures rather than experience and judgment. Thus autonomy is lost and the practicing coach or teacher is transformed into a 'ventriloquist' (Smyth, 1998), an automaton performing preordained functions outlined in guidelines and procedures, even though in relatively unstructured environments like coaching, where individual choice and performance is central, such an approach appears dysfunctional. Whatever it lacks in nuanced understanding and application, this approach bestows on government the capacity to blame or scapegoat the individual coach or teacher if anything goes wrong. Having decreased coaches' discretionary scope by providing precise guidance to inform practice, if a child is abused or dies then the blame must rest with them or with the local organisational hierarchy, since they must not have complied with the guidelines and standards for practice.

In exploring the regulatory environment of sports coaching, the distinction made by Dawson (1994) between outside-in and inside-out approaches to regulation is informative. In the former, agencies list principles that define appropriate conduct and the discretionary role of the coach, who merely applies the appropriate principle at the right time. In contrast, the latter originates in Aristotle's discussion of wisdom, focusing on the coach knowing and recognising the right thing to do, and doing it. The ubiquity of outside-in regulation is unfortunate since 'knowing based on rules is a form of knowing *that*, whereas the richer notion is more a case of knowing *how*' (Dawson, 1994: 150; emphasis added); codes of conduct, guidelines, and principles are inflexible when applied in unenvisioned situations, leaving the coach unsure which rule to apply and what to do. Further, some rules conflict with others, challenging individuals to choose priorities. What is missing from outside-in regulation in the present case is an understanding of the coach's motivation to achieve something positive, as discussed later.

This insistence on the importance of motivation, in both prompting and understanding desired behaviours, is echoed by Schwartz and Sharpe (2010) in their 'wisdom-deficit' critique of managerial regulatory regimes. They draw on Aristotelian notions of practical wisdom in discussing practitioners learning to do the 'right' thing. In contrast with mere rule-following, ethical conduct needs to be nuanced and contextualised, and involves 'figuring out the right way to do the right thing in a particular circumstance, with a particular person, at a particular time' (ibid: 5–6); context and motives are key. However, by relying on sets of guidelines and principles purporting to be applicable in all situations, contemporary professional regulatory regimes constrain the development and practice of practical wisdom, with collateral negative effects for sports coaches and the young people they work with (Duggan & Piper, 2013).

## What is to be done?

When the original proposal for this book was sent by the publisher to expert anonymous reviewers, their responses were positive in agreeing that the identified issues and problems deserved serious and wide consideration. However, one reviewer stressed that the book should not merely be 'critical', but should provide *solutions* to the dilemmas around touch, abuse, anxiety, and safeguarding in sport and physical education, which practitioners could apply in order to avoid problems. It would obviously be pleasing to deliver on this hope, but anyone who has read around the issue, or tried to negotiate its reality in an informed and reflexive way, will know that there are no simple or foolproof solutions to complex and profound problems. Thus I feel like the pedestrian on a country lane, asked by a lost motorist how they can get to a distant and remote destination, and whose initial response is, 'Well, I wouldn't start from here!' However, with this disclaimer, the final sections of the chapter attempt to map pathways out of the current situation, albeit arguments and concepts rather than 'useful tips', which would merely trivialise the difficulties faced by policymakers and practitioners.

### *Challenging the rationality and effectiveness of mainstream safeguarding policy*

Commenting on Australian experiences and data, Lumby and Funnell matched the argument made earlier in this chapter, that in moral panic studies it is not enough to take a merely academic interest; the researcher should also consider how the ideas 'might be used to frame strategic interventions into public and policy' (2011: 279). Following this prescription they outline a case and a response which are directly transferrable to parallel contested practices and responses in sport. Reflecting on public furore and protests over a major artist's use of an unclothed 12-year-old girl on a promotional poster for an exhibition, they suggest an intervention strategy which accepts the importance of child protection, but also unpacks questions of how best to protect children, and what they need protection from. To claim that the girl was being sexualised presumes that everyone seeing the poster is aberrant, yet in such an argument an implicit distinction is maintained between right-thinking good folk and the phantom aberrant viewer. 'A useful intervention . . . might . . . point out that, since the great majority of viewers do not find images of naked children sexually arousing, it makes little sense to evaluate this image by looking through the eyes of a paedophile' (284). Thus the debate is reframed by highlighting the fact that most adults do not respond sexually to images of children, thus narrowing attention toward informed strategies for protecting children from the minority of adults' intent on sexual abuse. In contrast, banning the poster could not be shown to prevent child abuse.

   This discussion illuminates practical and conceptual problems at the core of mainstream approaches to child protection and safeguarding in sport coaching, physical education, and beyond. The key point, crudely put, is that we will not prevent bad people doing bad things by stopping good people doing good things.

Further, there are no substantive benefits from requiring them to publicly perform their acceptance of proscriptions which in effect require people with no interest in abusing children to act and think as if they have. Just as most adults are not aroused by images of children, most coaches and teachers are not intent on sexual abuse. Preventing them from touching children and young people as part of the proper task of coaching, or as a normal human response to desolation or joy (whether by explicit regulation or through seeding the environment with such fear that self-restriction and protection becomes inevitable) does not contribute to child protection. Treating all coaches, and all adults who enter coaching spaces, as if they are paedophiles or abusers (e.g. by imposing blanket restrictions on parents making images of their own children enjoying sport) serves a merely performative function; in terms of actual child protection it is essentially unproductive. To think otherwise requires rationalisation through an elaborate fear-based and phantom-rich scenario, held together by hypothetical assumptions and connections. Thus, engagement with moral panics and the crusaders who promote them can serve as a basis for challenging the rationality of what has been presented as child protection and safeguarding in sport.

### Identifying collateral damage (technical, social, cultural)

With fifteen years' professional experience as a social worker, most in child protection work, I wholly accept the imperative to protect children from abuse. However, the pursuit of a desirable and moral end does not guarantee good judgement about the means employed. Further, careful consideration should be given to unintended negative consequences, and careless collateral damage should obviously be avoided by responsible organisations, policymakers, and practitioners. Now, with approaching another twenty years' experience as a researcher with a particular interest in the issues discussed here, the reality of collateral damage arising from mainstream approaches to safeguarding in sport and elsewhere, incorporating the pervasive discouragement of touching and other behaviours once considered normal and positive, appears incontrovertible. Negative effects transcend the 'merely' technical (i.e. the issues which impinge most strongly on the everyday practice of teachers and coaches, subverting their confidence and effectiveness), and impact more broadly on social and cultural well-being.

The disruption of long established coaching practices by outside-in or wisdom-deficit regulation is well documented. In research outcomes there are numerous examples of coaches and PE teachers citing adherence to rules when acting in a manner contrary to the safety, well-being, and learning of the young people they work with – even to the extent of placing them in danger (Piper *et al.* 2011). This matched earlier data from childcare workers (Piper & Stronach, 2008). The purpose, legitimacy, and rationality of practices once treated as appropriate and unexceptional, have been disturbed and rearticulated through particular formulations of rules and guidance, leading to the institutionalisation of 'no touch' policies which have fundamentally changed both what it means to be a coach, and the nature of coach–young person relationships. When negative collateral effects of this behaviour-based managerial approach are identified, the response of agencies responsible for the regulations tends to be that they have been misinterpreted or that training has been inadequate. This was illustrated by a Child Protection in Sport Unit (CPSU) rejoinder to a newspaper report (*Daily Telegraph*, 2012) of UK research, to the effect that touch had never been banned and that guidelines were being misinterpreted. As noted elsewhere (Piper *et al.* 2013a), beyond conveniently evading responsibility, this argument ignores the pervasive climate of anxiety surrounding such issues. If coaches are told often and strongly enough that they are at constant risk of being accused of abuse, telling them that in fact they may touch young people, while still reminding them of seriously unpleasant consequences if they do, amounts to a blanket injunction.

This pressure affects the performance of technical aspects of the coach's role, but also reduces the possibility of pastoral, social, and emotional inputs, as the coach and young person have each been constructed as being dangerous to the other. The damaging consequences for any adult of even unproven or discredited allegations of inappropriate behaviour towards a child in their care make risk-averse and defensive practice an unsurprising response. Acting as if all adults acting *in loco parentis* are potentially toxic to those in their care has rendered children and young people potentially dangerous to coaches' professional and personal well-being; a mutually toxic relationship has been constructed. This reality is far removed from the ethical strictures of Knud Ejler Løgstrup, referred to earlier by Jan Toftegaard Støckel: 'We simply could not live, our lives would wither, life would be crippled if we met each other with distrust' (Løgstrup, 1958: 19). It is also heartbreakingly distant from the positive input to young lives that coaches can make, particularly for those young people most in need of help from outside the family. After rioting and arson in London in August 2011, an 18-year-old black youth, who had previously told reporters that trouble was imminent, was asked why he had stayed away from nearby looting and burning. He responded that, after he was excluded from school at age eleven, coaches at the local boxing club had turned his life around: 'These coaches are like my parents . . . they love me, they give me good advice. If I started going down the wrong path, they would tell me to sort it out' (Topping, 2011, p. 6). This is not the quality of relationship prescribed by typical contemporary guidelines, and society is damaged by it becoming less common than it once was, and by practices and policies which lead volunteer coaches to question their continued commitment.

The routine recourse to blame in mainstream discourse and media coverage around child abuse and protection is significant here, blocking sensible discussion through imposing a particular understanding of risk. Apparently, harm to children not only always should be prevented, but always could be; 'luck' must not come into it. Evans-Pritchard's classic anthropological account of the Asande explained that they had no concept of luck; as a result, anything bad that happened was always someone's fault, and blame could be assigned (Smith, 2013). This did not make for harmonious relationships or a happy society, and those responsible for the current safeguarding discourse might consider the parallels. Abuse apparently can always be prevented by intrusive regimentation and regulation, but a collateral negative effect of this approach is that prioritising the elimination of 'all things bad', makes 'anything good' less accessible. Adults become less willing to be sports coaches, will not act on intuition or with warm spontaneity, and thus children are less likely to encounter inspiring teachers and coaches. Adults with abusive intent are unlikely to be put off, but others may well be. The mission to rule out risk creates an unforgiving, blame-based culture, with damaging consequences. While the recent re-emergence of rickets in the UK obviously has complex causes, even Vitamin D deficiency can in part be blamed on parental unwillingness to let their children play in the sunshine, and their encouragement through high level discourse to view *in loco parentis* adults (including sports coaches) as dangerous sources of risk and abuse. For some young people, health deficits join those of opportunity, experience, and trust, all identifiable as collateral damage from risk-averse discourse presented as child safeguarding.

### Identifying disjunctures between real experience and risk discourses

Having written and spoken on this topic for a number of years, it is clear that changing the status quo presents a considerable challenge. Troubling the mainstream institutionalised discourse of safeguarding in sport, accepted by many as 'common sense', has proved difficult. A lesson may be learned from Apple's (2006) 'interrupting the right' consideration of the rise and dominance of the discourse of conservative modernisation, which noted that the right was not always so powerful. The current hegemony was deliberately articulated and consolidated, but such a process could be imitated by more progressive groups with fewer resources. To replicate the success of the conservative modernisation project it would be necessary to develop a 'very creative articulation of themes that resonate deeply with the experiences, fears, hopes and dreams of people as they go about their daily lives' (ibid: 28). In the present case, the disjuncture between most people's actual experiences of sports coaches and the demonising and risk-averse discourse could be exploited.

Even in the context of sensationalist media coverage, it should be effective to evoke and reinforce a wisdom-and-trust-rich public understanding of coaches (or any group of adults acting *in loco parentis*). This could be achieved through reminding people why coaches do what they do, and asking them to recall and honour their own positive experiences, inserting an interruptive theme of emotion into the discourse. The coach as predator and threat is a common trope in news reporting, populating the narrative around the interaction between adults and minors, but telling contrary positive stories, rich in virtue and meaning for many adults remembering their own childhood, could have a gradual interrupting effect. Displacing the straw-man image of the coach as the embodiment of stranger-danger with a richer image of their personhood and their work in pursuit of positive outcomes would constitute a significant troubling of the mainstream fear-based discourse. Paradoxically, although many US sports coaches are subject to annual finger-printing (Piper *et al.* 2013a), the popular and well populated US film genre featuring sports coaches and their adolescent charges typically portrays a touch and trust rich environment, in uncritically positive terms (Chare, 2013). If such films were far removed from how their audience understands and experiences the world, the genre would perish.

The disjuncture between mainstream discourse and people's experience was illuminated by Nash (2010), who used an online search facility to access all 429 child abuse in sport stories in five major UK newspapers between 1995 and 2008. Of these, 129 featured intensive over-training or verbal bullying from coaches and/or parents. The remaining 333 covered more significant physical or sexual abuse by a coach, but 150 (45%) of these reported background events or research rather than any actual incident of abuse. A further 120 (36%) referred to individual cases while reporting research findings. Only 63 (19%) described a specific case, and over the thirteen years they referred only to 24 individual cases of child abuse in sports coaching and PE. Admittedly these were cases which resulted in public legal proceedings; others will have remained unacknowledged or did not justify prosecution and remained unreported. Obviously too, no case of abuse can be condoned and the experience and its implications for any young person will be damaging and serious. However, these data indicate that most people very seldom encounter abusive coaches and abused children, and begs questions about the disjuncture between the rhetoric behind safeguarding and real life experience.

This disconnect relates in part to variable accounts of the incidence of child abuse in sport and other contexts. Solid data are notoriously hard to achieve, and the emotive nature of the issue renders the imperative of research accuracy and integrity prone to challenge by the siren call of public relations. Currently in Europe, many national organisations are responding to the 'fact' that 'One in Five' children in Europe are subject to sexual abuse (Council of Europe, 2012). Should this eye-catching figure lead concerned parents to think that in their son's junior rugby team there will be three or four victims of abuse? If not, is sport safer than other social contexts, and if so why has it been subject to such pressure on safeguarding? While the Council of Europe promotes the one in five slogan, in the UK the National Society for the Prevention of Cruelty to Children [NSPCC] (2011) refers to one in twenty children having been sexually abused, applying criteria which excludes both 'non-contact' abuse and 'consensual' activity between adolescents. The gap between these figures demonstrates the inadequacy of such data, and of the potential for manipulation to achieve a particular effect. Commenting on NSPCC statistics, Furedi notes that its category of emotional abuse included both parental over- and under- protectiveness, and both high and low expectations. He suggests that the use of broad definitions blurs distinctions between 'troublesome experience, serious victimisation, and . . . physical and sexual violence' and that 'coupling the rape and physical attack of a child with the behaviour of a pushy parent has only one merit – which is the construction of big numbers' (2013: 61). From the international contributions earlier in this book there is clearly no reliable source of data on the incidence of abuse in sporting contexts, and no real basis for judging whether regulation-rich responses are effective in child protection. However, the disconnection between the mainstream discourse (with its attendant high levels of anxiety) and most people's everyday experience remains clear.

## *Stressing the positive nature of coaches* in loco parentis

In essence, the problems and dilemmas discussed throughout this book result from a collision between two discourses, each characterised by distinct assumptions, imperatives, and priorities. The discourse associated with sport, coaching, and physical education is multichannelled, flexible, and inclusive, having to incorporate varied contexts (e.g. team-individual, elite performance–grassroots fun, professional-amateur or volunteer) and multiple goals (e.g. health and fitness, competition and winning, participation and experience, technical and pastoral). In contrast, the discourse associated with safeguarding and the protection of children and young people from abuse is unitary and inflexible; the absolute priority accorded to preventing abuse excludes recognition of, or sensitive response to, contextual variations or the goals and imperatives considered important by others. This difference is particularly significant, given the massive power of proponents of child protection in the contemporary discourse market, and the exclusionary impact of outside-in managerial techniques in all settings, as discussed earlier. The troubled experience of many coaches and teachers (like other adults *in loco parentis*) arises directly from this clash. The concept of the coach applied through the dominant discourse around safeguarding in sport is essentially dehumanised; the coach is conceived as a potential source of danger, to be managed. Questions of identity, motive, and meaning are disregarded; the only issue of significance is whether or not the coach behaves in a manner which is abusive or could be considered so. Thus it is no surprise that a depersonalised and performative notion of touch (something to be avoided as dangerous, risky, or worse) has been imposed. This makes no more sense, and is as inhumane as the next conceivable step of banning *in loco parentis* adults smiling at children, since smiling could (self-evidently!) be a prelude to more serious grooming behaviour. As a corrective to such limited and damaging understandings of human interaction, it seems timely to substantiate an account of the sports coach which stresses motive, virtue, and morality.

Although approaching issues in a different way from Løgstrup or Noddings, each referred to in previous chapters, MacIntyre's writing on ethics and action addresses similar concerns. In his key work, originally published in 1981, and subsequently, MacIntyre (1994) explores the individual's lifelong pursuit of the good life, in the context of pre-existent traditions, informed and defined by a particular *telos* and set of virtues. People should, and most do, do things for good reasons, and the route to conceiving and achieving this is in terms of practices. Individuals engage in a particular practice, which provides the knowledge and context to enable them to develop practical wisdom. Practices have internal goods, achieved and demonstrated through the skilful performance of, say, gymnastics or kayaking (e.g. strength, grace, courage, skill). This entails compliance with standards of excellence embedded in and maintained by the relevant practice community, which reflect the highest levels of understanding and performance achieved in the practice. It behoves any newcomer to show respect and subordination, seeking to emulate such standards and improve their performance through virtuous dedication. Any practice has its base in a collaborative community of members; honouring and passing down skills and ideas between members is intrinsic to continuity and improved standards of achievement. However, practices also have external goods, including money, power, and status. These are distinct from those intrinsic to the practice, and particularly significant to the institutions which govern the practice, which thus risk being diverted from the internal goods and virtues. This is an elaborate way of arguing that people choose to do things for good and virtuous reasons; sports coaches and teachers engage in their chosen practice because they care about the relevant intrinsic virtues, particularly the good of helping others share them. Any intervention which fails to understand and respect this will provoke anxiety and dissent, and is likely to damage the practice (see Duggan & Piper, 2013, and Piper, Duggan and Walker, 2013 for more detail).

This assertion of the virtuous and ethical basis on which the sports coach operates supports revisiting the critique of managerialism, echoing Foucault's discussion of governmentalism and the advanced liberal state. The liberal tradition has proved unable to provide or implement rational grounds for resolving ethical conflicts and difficulties, preferring to reframe ethical questions in technical terms, imposing managerial responses which result in the subjectification of the professional as their own manager. However, the construction and insertion of the 'manager' as the arbiter of supposedly technical judgements in complex and emotion-rich contexts like coaching, teaching, and child protection, disguises a range of unexamined moral positions behind a mask of claimed technical rationality. For MacIntyre, 'the concept of managerial effectiveness is . . . one more contemporary moral fiction and perhaps the most important one' (1994: 106–7). This is because managerial claims rest on illusions: a mechanistic view of human action, the assumption that law-like generalisations and predictions can be made by experts, and the tendentious appeal of such experts and managers to knowledge presented as morally neutral.

In the present case, through the appeal to managerial authority, systematic public ethical discussion of the *telos*, or ends, of sports coaching and physical education are negated in favour of technical specification of means. Seemingly rational interventions such as 'not touching' are presented as morally neutral and objectively appropriate, and the coach is cut off from engagement in their chosen practice in a way which develops their judgement and practical wisdom. This account provides critical substance to the experiences of practitioners in teaching and sports coaching, where managerial interventions around safeguarding have reshaped practice and associated knowledge. The managerial approach is ill-equipped to recognise or value different ways of knowing, or complex and competing goals; core priorities, the goods of established practices like physical education and sports coaching are overridden and treated as secondary or illegitimate. The extent to which sports governing bodies (in MacIntyre's terms, the institutions) have colluded and contributed to this disempowerment appears to confirm his suggestion that, although institutions sustain practices, they are primarily focused on external goods. Consequently there is a risk that self-interest, image management, competitiveness, and acquisitiveness will have a damaging effect on the practice and those essential to its well-being.

### Developing a human and positive approach to protection

For all such argument, there remains an important question: when is it okay for a coach to touch a child they are coaching, and when is it not? No contributor to this book wishes interactions between adults and young people to be unrestrained, for children to be put at risk, for abuse not to be a criminal offence, or for perpetrators to go unpunished. However, mainstream 'outside-in' and 'wisdom-deficit' approaches diminish the internal goods and standards of excellence of coaching, and the challenge is to find better ways to ensure that coaches act correctly. Adults acting *in loco parentis*, including teachers and sports coaches, are expected to treat young people in their care as a parent would, but not in some intimate ways. Touching behaviour is on the normative border, and the problem is to distinguish its appropriate use from something less desirable or even reprehensible. A framework based on MacIntyre's discussion of practice is useful for thinking about how sports coaches may be guided. It involves sensitive understanding of why these adults do what they do, how should they judge what action is appropriate in circumstances that could be contested, and how is such behaviour best regulated in the interests of all concerned. These questions are ultimately about ethics.

Conceiving the coach as a moral agent is directly contradictory to the mainstream approach to child protection in sport, which tends to treat both adult and child in a dehumanised manner. While the child's individual characteristics and needs are ignored (with negative consequences as some children will benefit more than others from nurturing touch) the adult coach *in loco parentis* is in effect conceived as an automaton, devoid of ethical purpose or any motivation beyond an assumed propensity for harm, and thus suitable for control through regulation; subtle understanding of motive, purpose, and morality are rendered irrelevant. In essence, the mainstream approach is focused on 'bad' reasons why coaches acting *in loco parentis* do things. On the contrary, it seems more fruitful to focus on the 'good' ones; we should understand the coach as an agent seeking to live the good life, whose actions can be understood in terms of the narrative unity of their life and career, including membership of a particular practice community in sport. They coach as they were once taught, according to evolving rules, standards of excellence, and technical skills of the practice, seeking to realise the internal goods. This approach helps to frame and answer the question of when it is appropriate for a coach to touch a child, as appropriate relationships and conduct between coach and student are inherent to the historical tradition of the sport, and to judgements about when to touch or not touch. These decisions are grounded in the virtues and the coach's knowledge, experience, and skill in the ongoing search for the good life, and in striving to improve the standards of excellence of their particular practice.

This account has an assumption of the coach acting virtuously, sharing the goods of a practice with the next generation of practitioners. Any approach to practice and safeguarding predicated on the idea that the coach is a self-evident source of risk and danger should be rejected. However, it is important to consider the immoral and abusive coach; we may stress virtues, but vices cannot be wished away. This prompts the question of how best to achieve arrangements and processes which prevent, deter, identify, and report abusive adults. The argument here is that current regulatory approaches give a false sense of confidence, and that promoting the application of wisdom and judgement would be more effective. Empowering young people and coaches to recognise and report abusive touch is likely to be more educational and more effective than fear-based approaches which ban touch altogether. This requires prioritising and valuing the building of a community, the institution that sustains a practice. The virtues of justice, courage, truthfulness, and the awareness of the tradition or practice to which one belongs should therefore be integral to the decision-making process of institutions as they relate to regulations and practices, even when under pressure on issues of child protection.

Certainly, there should be institutions overseeing the relationships between coaches and young people, and those who abuse children should be subject to criminal charges. However, a coaching community in which the members feel confident and trusted and are properly focused on the internal goods of their practice with young people, rather than having to treat themselves and every colleague as a likely abuser and every young person as a threat, is one in which the wisdom and judgement needed to protect children without causing collateral damage is most likely to flourish. Imposing a regulation- and guideline-rich environment may appear to be a quick fix, but it provides the semblance rather than the reality of safeguarding.

## Final words

This book, like the decade of research and writing which preceded it, was not conceived merely as an academic product. Rather, the work was done with the hope that it would make a difference, in part by empowering others to challenge a dominant discourse and derived social practices which are misguided and damaging. The previous chapters demonstrate that this critical concern is evident in diverse national contexts. While the issues are experienced and understood in different ways, which reflect local history and culture, the basic argument is shared. It does not make sense to think that we will really protect children (in sport and elsewhere) from adults with abusive *intent* by focusing on mere *behaviour*, and requiring all adults who work with children to think of, and manage, themselves as if carrying an intrinsic risk. The ineffective and toxic relationships which result from this approach are themselves harmful to the well-being of all concerned, and the claimed benefit of preventing abuse is arguably illusory and unprovable. An obvious lesson from the previous chapters is that alternative and better ways of maximising children's safety in sport must be context-sensitive; in a globalised world, a one-size-fits-all imperial approach will prove counterproductive and ineffective. Different cultures and organisational arrangements will support different approaches that deserve careful evaluation, which cannot be assumed to be generally exportable.

It may be facile to liken patterns of thought which we disagree with to quasi-religious belief systems or even cults, but in this case the emphasis placed on behaviour, performance, *observance*, invites such a suggestion. Those steeped in the mainstream safeguarding discourse appear impervious to critique or the demonstration of collateral damage; the important thing is apparently to ensure that everyone behaves in the prescribed manner and observes their performative obligations. Failure to do so leads to sanctions or exclusion. The resulting *theatre of safeguarding* provides a sense of security for adults and organisations, but little extra protection for children. Meanwhile, those who are able to control the theatre, write the script, sell the tickets, and monitor the performance, have a vested interest in pleasing the audience. Dissenting voices are unwelcome, and critics of how safeguarding is being done are all too easily presented as being indifferent to child abuse, and placed in an uncomfortable and even dangerous position.

Obviously, opinions on this book and the concerns and arguments presented will vary. Some reviews will be penned by individuals with close and beneficial connections with organisations whose health and wealth is predicated on current taken-for-granted assumptions about child abuse and child protection, and no doubt there will be expressions of irritation, puzzlement, and rejection. As editor, I can only hope that such reviewers, and all readers, consider carefully what the authors of the preceding chapters have written. During the United Kingdom's brief experience as a Republic, in a letter to the synod of the Church of Scotland Oliver Cromwell used a phrase which has since been deployed as an exhortation to avoid harm, think critically, and do proper science. Jacob Bronowski (1973) famously used it while arguing that what killed people at Auschwitz, beyond the gas, was arrogance, dogma, and ignorance: 'I beseech you, in the bowels of Christ, think it possible that you may be mistaken' (Carlyle, 1855: 448). If such a possibility occurs to some of those responsible for promoting or colluding with the currently dominant and dehumanising approach to protecting children in sports and other contexts, and if others are empowered to oppose it, then this book will have done its job.

## Note

1   In particular I acknowledge the many ideas and insights gathered while working with Dean Garratt and Bill Taylor on the project referred to in Chapter Two, and on related publications. Understandings generated through subsequent collaboration and writing with James Duggan and Stephen Rogers are also deployed here, and are gratefully acknowledged.

## References

Apple, M. W. (2006) Interrupting the right: On doing critical educational work in conservative times, in G. Ladson-Billings and W. F. Tate (eds.) *Education research in the public interest,* New York: Teacher's College Press, 27–45.

Bauman, Z. (2007) *Liquid times: Living in an age of uncertainty*, Cambridge, UK: Polity Press

Beck, U. (1992) *Risk society: Towards a new modernity*, London: Sage.

Becker, H. S. (1963) *The outsiders*, New York: Free Press

Besley, T. (2010) Governmentality of youth: Managing risky subjects, *Policy Futures in Education,* 8(5) 528–547.

Best, J. (2011) Locating moral panics within the sociology of social problems, in S. P. Hier (ed.) *Moral panic and the politics of anxiety*, London: Routledge, 37–52.

Black, T. (2013) Jimmy Savile: The Satanic panic resurrected, *Spiked online* 2nd July www.spiked-online.com/newsite/article/jimmy_savile_the_satanic_panic_resur rected1/13765 (accessed 21.8.13).

Brackenridge, C. H. (2001) *Spoilsports: Understanding and preventing sexual exploitation in sport,* London: Routledge.

Bronowski, J. (1973) *The ascent of man: A personal view,* London: BBC Books.

Carlyle, T. (1855) *Oliver Cromwell's letters and speeches*, New York: Harper.

Chare, N. (2013) Handling pressures: Analysing touch in American films about youth sport, *Sport, Education and Society,* 18(5) 663–677.

Council of Europe (2012) One in five: The Council of Europe campaign to stop sexual violence against children www.coe.int/t/dg3/children/1in5/default_en.asp (accessed 30.1.14).

*Daily Telegraph* (2012) 'Climate of fear surrounds children's sports coaches' (2012, July 22) www.telegraph.co.uk/news/uknews/9417560/Climate-of-fear-surrounds-childrens-sports-coaches.html (accessed 30.1.14)

Dawson, A. J. (1994) Professional codes of practice and ethical conduct, *Journal of Applied Philosophy*, 11(2) 145–153.

Dickson, D. T. (1968) Bureaucracy and morality: An organisational perspective on a moral crusade, *Social Problems*, 16(2) 143–156.

Duggan, J. and Piper, H. (2013) Interrupting the immoral panic around child abuse and professional touch: Thinking about impact, *International Review of Qualitative Research*, 6(4) 440–459.

Flybjerg, B. (2001) *Making social science matter: Why social inquiry fails and how it can succeed again*, Cambridge and New York: Cambridge University Press.

Foucault, M. (1991) Governmentality, in G. Burchell, C. Gordon and P. Miller (eds.) *The Foucault effect: Studies in governmentality*, Hemel Hempstead: Harvester Wheatsheaf, 87–104.

Furedi, F. (2013) *Moral crusades in an age of mistrust,* Basingstoke: Palgrave Macmillan

Furedi, F. (2011) The objectification of fear and the grammar of morality, in S. P. Hier (ed.) *Moral panic and the politics of anxiety*, London: Routledge, 90–103.

Furedi, F. (2010, April 19) This shut down is about more than volcanic ash, *Spiked online* www.spiked-online.com/index.php/site/article/8607/ (accessed 29.8.11).

Garland, D. (2008) On the concept of moral panic, *Crime, Media, Culture,* 4(9) 9–30.

Garland, D. (2007) Moral panics: Then and now, *British Academy Review,* 10: 4–5

Goode E. and Ben-Yehuda N. (2011) Grounding and defending the sociology of moral panic, in S. P. Hier (ed.) *Moral panic and the politics of anxiety*, London: Routledge, 20–36.

Hier, S. P. (2011) (ed.) *Moral panic and the politics of anxiety*, London: Routledge.

Hunt, A. (2011) Fractious rivals? Moral panics and moral regulation, in S. P. Hier (ed.) *Moral panic and the politics of anxiety*, London: Routledge, 53–70.

Hodgson, A. and Spours, K. (2006) An analytical framework for policy engagement: The contested case of 14–19 reform in England, *Journal of Education Policy*, 21(6) 679–696.

Hutton, W. (2013) Power is fragmenting. But what is the true cost to democracy? *The Observer*, 25.8.13: 38.

Jenkins, P. (1998) *Changing concepts of the child molester in modern America*, New Haven, CT: Yale University Press.

Jenkins, S. (2013) The real threat to our way of life? Not terrorists or faraway dictators, but our own politicians and securocrats, *The Guardian*, 27.8.13. p. 28.

Løgstrup, K. (1958/2007) *The ethical demand*, Notre Dame, Indiana: University of Notre Dame Press.

Lumby, C. and Funnell, N. (2011) Between heat and light: The opportunity in moral panics. *Crime, Media, Culture*, 7(3) 277–291.

Lyons, K. (2005) Performance analysis in applied contexts, *International Journal of Performance Analysis in Sport*, 5(3) 155–162.

MacIntyre, A. (1994) *After virtue: A study in moral theory*, London: Duckworth.

Merton, T. (1948) *The seven storey mountain*, New York: Harcourt Brace.

Musto, D. (1973) *The American disease: Origins of narcotics control*, Boston: Yale University Press.

Naim, M. (2013) *The end of power*, New York: Basic Books.

Nash, D. (2010) The social construction of the issue of child abuse in sport, unpublished Master's thesis, Canterbury: University of Kent.

Newman, J. and Clarke, J. (2009) *Publics, politics and power?: Remaking the public in public services?*, London: Sage.

NSPCC (2011) *Child abuse and neglect in the UK today*, London: National Society for the Prevention of Cruelty to Children.

Piper, H. (2011, August 8) Daring to criticise child protection policies, *Spiked online* www.spiked-online.com/index.php/site/article/10969/ (accessed 28.11.12).

Piper, H., Garratt and D. Taylor, B. (2013a) Hands off! The practice and politics of touch in physical education and sports coaching, *Sport, Education and Society*, 18(5) 575–582.

Piper, H., Garratt, D. and Taylor, B. (2013b) Child abuse, child protection, and defensive 'touch' in PE teaching and sports coaching. *Sport, Education and Society*, 18(5) 583–598.

Piper H., Duggan J. and Walker, S. (2013) Managerial discourse, child safeguarding, and the elimination of virtue from *in loco parentis* relationships: An example from music education, *Power & Education*, 5(3) 209–221.

Piper, H. and Stronach, I. (2008) *Don't touch! The educational story of a panic*, London: Routledge.

Piper, H., Taylor, W. and Garratt, D. (2011) Sports coaching in risk society: No touch! No trust!, *Sport, Education and Society*, 17(3) 331–345.

Rose, N. (1998) *Inventing ourselves: Psychology, power, personhood*, Cambridge: Cambridge University Press.

Rose, N. (1996) Governing 'advanced' liberal democracies, in A. Barry, T. Osborne and N. Rose (eds.) *Foucault and political reason*, Chicago: University of Chicago Press, 37–64.

Schneier, B. (2010) Worst-case thinking, Schneier on Security (blog). www.schneier.com/blog/archives/2010/05/worst-case_thin.html (accessed 29.8.11).

Schwartz, B. and Sharpe, K. (2010) *Practical wisdom: The right way to do the right thing*, New York: Riverhead Books.

Sikes, P. and Piper, H. (2010) *Researching sex and lies in the classroom: Allegations of sexual misconduct in schools*, London: Routledge.

Skenazy, L. (2011) 'Worst first' thinking brings out the worst in all of us www.rrstar.com/x552985524/Lenore-Skenazy-Worst-first-thinking-brings-out-worst-in-us-all (accessed 29.8.11).

Smith, E. (2013) *Luck*, London: Bloomsbury.

Smyth, J. (1998) Finding the 'enunciative space' for teacher leadership and teacher learning in schools, *Asia-Pacific Journal of Teacher Education*, 26(3) 191–202.

Thomas, W. I. and Thomas, D. S. (1929) *The child in America* (2nd ed), New York: Alfred Knopf.

Topping, A. (2011, August 13). Looting fueled by social exclusion. *The Guardian*, p. 6. www.theguardian.com/uk/2011/aug/08/looting-fuelled-by-social-exclusion

Watts, A. (1951) *The wisdom of insecurity*, Arlington, VA: Vintage.

Webster, R. (1994) The body politic and the politics of the body: The religious origins of Western secularism www.richardwebster.net/thepoliticsofthebody.html (accessed 17.3.13).

Young, J. (2011) Moral panics and the transgressive other, *Crime, Media, Culture* 7(3) 245–258.

# Index